Tales *of a* TEAMSTER PREACHER

A Daily Devotional

Timothy A. Mills

ISBN 979-8-89345-192-4 (paperback)
ISBN 979-8-89345-193-1 (digital)

Copyright © 2024 by Timothy A. Mills

All rights reserved. No part of this publication may be reproduced, distributed, or transmitted in any form or by any means, including photocopying, recording, or other electronic or mechanical methods without the prior written permission of the publisher. For permission requests, solicit the publisher via the address below.

Christian Faith Publishing
832 Park Avenue
Meadville, PA 16335
www.christianfaithpublishing.com

Printed in the United States of America

PROLOGUE

Dear Reader,

    From the bottom of my heart, I want to thank you for opening this book. I pray that wherever you are in life, you can use this as a tool to become closer to the Lord as we journey through this year together. In this book, you will find one entry for each day of the year. In 2023, I devoted each day to writing an entry. These stories are my real-life experiences throughout that year that, with God's help, I have turned into a devotional for you. I'm just a regular blue-collar family man that's been saved by grace. I pray that the Lord opens your heart to hear what He says, not just through this book but forever and always.

JANUARY 1

A New Creation!

> Therefore, if anyone is in Christ,
> he is a new creation. The old has passed
> away; behold, the new has come!
>
> —2 Corinthians 5:17

Happy New Year! What a blessing it is to start another year. Some of us may have had many blessings in the past year yet also many challenges. No matter where we are, it's always a great day to start over and become that new creation Christ has called us to be. On New Year's Day of 2023, my family and I went to the mall after church and bought a few new sets in the Lego store. On the box, you can see what the finished product looks like, but inside are several bags of mixed loose pieces and an instruction manual on how to assemble your new set. As Christians, we need to be that new set and have a willingness to let God put us together. The Word of God is our instruction manual on how to slowly assemble those bricks together to build our foundation. "On Christ…the solid rock I stand!"

How can you show the world you are a new creation in Christ?

JANUARY 2

Where to Begin?

> For God so loved the world, that He gave his only Son, that whoever believes in him should not perish, but have eternal life.
>
> —John 3:16

True love! It starts with Jesus! He came to this earth as God in human form to walk in our ways, yet He never sinned. Getting to know Him is where we must begin because nothing matters without Him. Christ's offering of His own life on the cross closed the gap for us. You see, because of our own sin, we needed a Savior. We could not do anything on our own to merit our own salvation. The penalty for sin is death, and the price has been paid for us.

Think of all the parts of an automobile if one is fully assembled but left without an oil plug. The automobile may seem fine, and it may run for a while, but the engine is going to fail without that oil plug. As it is in our own life, we can do this, that, and the other. We can give to this charity, serve in that church, and help a neighbor out. And while those are all great things to do, without putting Jesus as the reason for doing those things, we are only really glorifying ourselves. We must humble ourselves and put Him before us daily. Christ is who we need, every day and always.

How can you get to know Christ better?

JANUARY 3

Righteous Anger

> Be angry and do not sin; do not let the sun go down on your anger, and give no opportunity to the devil.
>
> —Ephesians 4:26–27

Man, am I preaching to myself on this one! As the years go by, the world seems to be more impatient and quick to get angry these days. As Christians, we need to remember that even in our anger, it's important to remember what sets us apart from those of this world.

On this day, my wife was coming home with our younger daughter in our minivan when a fireman directing traffic began screaming obscenities at her after he told her to proceed through the intersection. As a husband and father, my blood was boiling after hearing that someone talked to my wife like that. I was thrown off the whole night and very disheartened over it. It's important in these times to count our blessings and be mindful that nothing serious had happened that day. A few nasty words may hurt our feelings and of the one's we love, but at the end of the day, we were all okay.

Sinning because of anger just lets the devil get his way. As hard as it is, when we want to stand up with our fists in the air, in the eyes of the Lord, it's much better we be on our knees with our hands folded. Anger itself isn't a bad thing. It's what we do with it that matters.

How can you turn your anger into something positive?

JANUARY 4

According to Plan

> For I know the plans I have for you, declares the Lord, plans for welfare and not for evil, to give you a future and a hope.
>
> —Jeremiah 29:11

Plans! That's a word we hear a lot. Everyone has plans. Everyone plans to do something. It's very common that we have goals and ideas in our minds that we would like to accomplish, but it's important to remember that our plans may not coincide with God's plans for our lives. I believe as Christians, we should find opportunities every day to seek God's plan for us. It takes a true willingness to surrender and tune our hearts to hear what God has in store for us.

I think back to years past and some of the things I planned to do that never really came to fruition. I have, however, seen why some things just didn't go as I wanted them to, and I realized that God had a way better plan than I ever could have. It may be a hard thing to come to terms with because if your plans are not of the Spirit and of the world, then what real good could actually come from them?

I remember when my wife was pregnant for the first time. As men, I think in some ways, we want our first child to be a boy to carry on our names and protect his younger siblings if the time comes for more children. I specifically remember praying for a happy and healthy baby boy, and what did we get? A beautiful, happy, healthy baby girl followed by another beautiful, happy, healthy baby girl a year and ten months later. The moment these daughters of ours were born, I knew instantly that this was what God wanted for us. I look back now and see why His plans are so much better than my own!

How can you hear God's plan for your life?

JANUARY 5

Running out of Steam

> Come to me, all who labor and are heavy laden, and I will give you rest. Take my yoke upon you, and learn from me, for I am gentle and lowly in heart, and you will find rest for your souls.
>
> —Matthew 11:28–29

As the new year has only just begun and the holidays are over, some of us may be exhausted. Rest is something that some of us don't get much of, unfortunately, and eventually, it will catch up with us. Most of us go back to work with our regular schedules and normal stresses of the week, and it can become even more tiring as the days of the dead of winter go by. It's crucial in these times that we turn to the Lord for our strength.

As a union commercial driver myself, this time of year can always be a struggle. For those of us who drive for a living, bad weather and icy roads are always concerns for this time of year. Getting delayed and working longer days in the cold can take its toll on anyone. As Christians going through this or any hard time, we must remember to rest easy in the Father, be guided by the Son, and feel the warmth of the Spirit.

Always remember, friends, even in those dire moments regarding weariness, lack of sleep, and unrest in general in our lives, our God is the key to the true rest we all seek.

How can you attain rest through God?

JANUARY 6

The Next Generation

> Train up a child in the way he should go; even
> when he is old he will not depart from it.
>
> —Proverbs 22:6

When someone comes to Christ, there's never a specific age defined of when it should happen. For some of us, we made that commitment very young growing up in a Christian home. For others, we may have had a conversion somewhere along the lines. Whichever way it happens, we must be willing to share the good news with everyone, especially the younger generations. As we all know, we won't be on planet Earth forever, so it's important to keep the fire of the faith burning in the hearts of the youth to carry it on.

On this day, while at work, I had the desire to rock our youngest daughter to sleep later in the evening. I realized with an eighteen-month-old, those days of rocking her to sleep would be very few. She may have originally protested, but as tired as she was, it didn't take long for her to be fast asleep in my arms. As young as both my daughters are, just initiating those acts of kindness and gentleness toward them will hopefully show them how a Christian father should be. Little by little, as they grow, they are already being taught about the gospel even at a young age. One day, I do pray they make their own commitments to Christ and be grounded in their own solid foundations in Him.

For those out there who don't have children and those who never will, there are always opportunities to teach the young and help guide them in the faith. We must always be diligent in passing the message down to those much younger than us, no matter what age. I often think about the legacy I'll leave my family. I pray it's in Christ!

> How can you lead by example
> for the next generation?

JANUARY 7

Working for the Lord

> Whatever you do, work heartily, as for the Lord and not for men, knowing that from the Lord you will receive the inheritance as your reward. You are serving the lord Christ.
>
> —Colossians 3:23–24

Work ain't spelled F-U-N, as my coworkers and friends always joke about. For those of us well into our careers, it may seem monotonous, or we just work because we have to. However, work can also be very rewarding if we change our perspective. Many of us with families and young children, especially, know how necessary it is to have a career that helps us to provide.

When I first got married, I was working a part-time job hoping to eventually get full time. With no time line or any inkling that full time would come, I had to make a move to get a career job. After four months of marriage and a sinking bank account, it was time. It was tough at first getting away from my old schedule and adjusting to a new workplace, but in the long run, it was one of the biggest blessings I could have asked for.

Being a delivery driver is tough sometimes, but it's definitely shown me how God can use me in that workplace to be a light for him, whether it's a coworker or a customer. Even the secular workplace can't hold back our almighty God. Each day, I continue to find my strength in him to stick with my job and get through the days. There have sure been some trying times in my workplace when I wanted to quit and move on, but every time, God was nudging me, saying, "Just hold on and I'll take care of it." I'm sure glad He did, and ultimately, I work for Him!

How can you find ways to rejoice and be a light for Christ in your workplace?

JANUARY 8

Set Apart

> Do not be conformed to this world, but be transformed by the renewal of your mind that by testing you may discern what is the will of God, what is good and acceptable and perfect.
>
> —Romans 12:2

To break down holiness in its most simple form, it means "set apart." When we're living as Christians in a world that continues to tell us that their way is best, it is even more important to stand firm and resist the temptations of what's convenient or easy. We must live in this world for now, but that does not mean we have to be of the world. Greater is the reward in heaven for standing firm on this earth.

We live in a time of cancel culture, where the most persecuted faith on the earth is Christianity. I can recall meeting different people in my life who get particularly vicious at the mention of the Bible and the faith in God in general. They hear the good news and just mock it. We must try to be the best examples we can be for those people but also guard ourselves from being pulled into some of the lifestyles they may live. I personally have lost friends over the years that I tried, at my own expense, to lead them in the right direction, but they ultimately decided to go a different way. I've never been good at losing friends or acquaintances, but in the bigger scheme of things, some of those folks just weren't good for me or my family.

On the brighter side of being set apart, some will notice. The big hope for being holy is that some will see what you have and crave it. Some will hear that good news and run toward it! We never know who we'll come across in life, and we must be ready to show them how we are different. We are saved by grace by an almighty, ever-loving God!

How will the world know that you're set apart?

JANUARY 9

On the Wrong Path

All we like sheep have gone astray; we have turned-every one-to his own way; and the Lord has laid on him the iniquity of us all.

—Isaiah 53:6

No matter where we come from and what kind of background we have, every one of us has gone astray at some point. Some more than others, but nevertheless, we've disobeyed God at different times in our lives. What is so important when we do realize we've strayed is to run as fast as we can back into the arms of the Lord. Repenting for our sins and allowing His grace and mercy to restore us is what we must do to get back on the right path.

There have been many of times in my own life when I have sinned and strayed so bad that I had gotten so low in my thinking and so ashamed that I felt like I wasn't good enough for God. I felt almost as though I was too unclean and that I ruined my life forever. As humans on planet Earth, it almost seems impossible because of the example of the world we live in, for us to be so bad and receive so much mercy. I'm sure at some points, we find it hard to even believe that we could be loved so much along with all the times we've failed.

Truth is, we're not good enough, but as the verse says where the Lord laid our iniquities, that is why we are able to be forgiven. We're able to move on and come back to Him because the price has been paid for us by the death and resurrection of the only one who ever lived a perfect life—Jesus!

How can you come to terms with your own sin and turn back to the Lord?

JANUARY 10

Waiting for the Lord

> Say therefore to the people of Israel, "I am the Lord, and I will bring you out from under the burdens of the Egyptians, and I will deliver you from slavery to them, and I will redeem you with an outstretched arm and with great acts of judgement."
>
> —Exodus 6:6

Like the Israelites many years ago in the clutches of Egypt, we must be patient of God's timing. Are you going through something that you're waiting for an answer to? Fear not. Think of the Israelites enslaved in Egypt. At any point in time, the Lord could have slaughtered all the Egyptians and freed every one of the Israelites. They were, of course, His chosen people, but His timing is always perfect.

Years ago, when I was still in school, my mother remarried, and we moved two hours away from our home. I spent four years of high school in a place where I was a complete stranger, and I wasn't used to a very different lifestyle in that area. It sure made me feel, back then, like I was enslaved in a place that I could do nothing about. There was so much heartache involved in that period that I thought it would never end. Looking back on those years now, they seem so far away, just a tiny speck on the footprint of my life thus far.

We may never know the reasons behind our struggles or suffering, and as hard as it can be in the midst of the battle, we must cling to the Lord even more. I'm sure a lot of the Israelites back in Egypt had their doubts and struggles, but once they got out and the Egyptians were lost to the Red Sea, they really saw the Lord's plan for them.

How can you wait patiently and faithfully for the Lord's timing?

JANUARY 11

Uplifting Fellowship

> Do not be unequally yoked with unbelievers. For
> what partnership has righteousness with lawlessness?
> Or what fellowship has light with darkness?
> —2 Corinthians 6:14

The world is a dangerous place for followers of Christ. The levels of temptation are extremely high because of our sinful nature and our earthly desires alone. That being said, we are already flawed to begin with and must watch who we keep company with. For those of us in secular work, we might hear a lot of vulgar conversations at work about things that the Lord would not want us involved in, and it's a perfect opportunity for us to stand firm and not conform to the crowd.

Looking back on my own life as a nerdy kid who never really fit in anywhere in school, I can think of many times where I let my faith go to the wayside, hoping I'd impress another. It's not an easy life for kids who feel on the outs in school and with their peers. I can say now that I've grown a few years. It was so pointless, and there really wasn't any reward or merit to any of that. Those who don't have much faith or refuse to believe it have the potential to drag you down to their levels if they don't want to make the necessary steps to change their own lives.

The body of believers is a home for every follower of Christ. In a world that tries to shut out the Gospel, we, as Christians, need to stand together and shine bright. As I've heard many pastors say, when a coal is taken out of a fire, it will burn for a little while but eventually go out. If it's placed back in the fire with the rest of the coals, it will once again burn bright! That's how we are. When we go out into the world away from our body of believers, we risk losing our fire in a way. Stand firm in your church and surround yourselves with other believers.

*How can you get deeper involved
with a body of believers?*

JANUARY 12

Hated in the Name

> Blessed are you when others revile you and persecute you and utter all kinds of evil against you falsely on my account. Rejoice and be glad, for your reward is great in Heaven, for so they persecuted the prophets who were before you.
>
> —Matthew 5:11–12

You heard it from the Man himself. It's no coincidence that Christians are persecuted around this world. Rather, it's foretold. When we look at Christ down to his apostles and followers after that, we can see that the world hated them all. It goes to show how much sin has a stronghold in this world for people to viciously reject the greatest news ever!

In my own life, I've been met with great hostility over my faith. This verse does sum it up, but growing up and growing older as Christians, it still baffles me that anyone would reject the truth. People truly do not know anything about Jesus if they reject him and persecute His followers so viciously. It's hard to pray for those kinds of folks, but they are the ones who definitely need it most.

It's so easy to get caught up in hurt and anger over such persecution, but in the end, greater is our reward in heaven. This life is just a speck compared to an eternity with Christ the way God originally planned for us before sin entered the world. So why get too upset about it? Easier said than done, I know, but they can scream or beat you. And in some countries even today, they are killing our brothers and sisters, but they can never take away that peace and salvation we have in our Lord.

How can you be persecuted with peace of mind?

JANUARY 13

Living Joyfully

> When the cares of my heart are many, your
> consolations cheer my soul.
>
> —Psalm 94:19

 A common misconception of the Christian faith is that we must always do what we don't want to do because it's the right thing to do. The world tells us we're just bound to follow religious law and can't have any fun, but that couldn't be further from the truth. The Christian person can still have fun and be truly joyful if we're doing that in the confines of what the Lord would want. Some would call that a restriction, but it's more of a privilege to enjoy things that still fall in line with what God would want.

 One of my lifelong passions has always been model trains, and now my daughters are enjoying it as much as I do. There's a little hobby shop that we go to whose motto has always been "Relax with a hobby." Their message is about slowing down. Taking time out of the daily stresses to enjoy something so simple can really take your mind off those cares of the world. We may find that things like that can sometimes get us through a stressful day or situation, and I think God can use interests like that to sometimes slow us down so we can hear what he has in store for us.

 There's a lot in this world we can be overwhelmed or stressed about, and that is where we must lean on the Lord for our strength. Finding joy in hobbies, extracurricular activities, and even work are all great things, but nothing compares to the joy we have in our Lord.

 How can you slow down and feel God's peace?

JANUARY 14

Sing a Song

Sing to Him, sing praises to Him; tell of all His wondrous works!

—Psalm 105:2

Worship's most common form, I believe, would have to be music. As we stand in church and sing those old hymns and new contemporary songs, we are praising our Lord for what He has done. As the bass guitarist in our church band, it's important to keep in mind that it's not a performance up on stage every week. It's an offering of praise and worship to our king.

On this day, my wife and I were going through the music for our upcoming church retreat. We were asked to lead worship this year. As we sat in the kitchen listening and singing along to songs and searching chords and lyrics on our phones, it was a great reminder that the praises we sing don't just have to be limited to a Sunday morning service. We can praise Him with song anytime.

Music is always good for the soul, and when it's a song of thankfulness and praise, it's so humbling to know what a mighty God we serve. May His name always be praised throughout each day, through song and prayer and all that we say.

How can you praise the Lord daily?

JANUARY 15

To Be Like Him

Therefore be imitators of God, as beloved children.

—Ephesians 5:1

Every day is often filled with things that distract us, things that can hinder our walk with the Lord. It's quite easy to want to be someone other than being an imitator of God. As life can be challenging at times when dealing with marriage, children, tight schedules, and careers, we can often get lost in the business and just drift through the monotonous motions.

From a young age, it's important that we find our identity in Christ and get on that narrow path. It's especially easy for children to get distracted. Going to school and seeing those friends or more the popular crowd and wanting to be like them. I can remember in middle school when it really peaked for some who sought out the approval of those in what you'd call a higher social status. Looking back on some of those kids and even myself at times back then, none of it mattered at all!

May we continue to grow closer to the Lord, knowing what He would want for us and what He would do. Even though we may fall short, it's important to keep in mind and heart His commands for us. We must take up our cross daily and follow Him.

How can you show the world you want to live according to Him?

JANUARY 16

Knowing the Word

> In the beginning was the Word, and the Word
> was with God, and the Word was God.
>
> —John 1:1

When we think about Christ throughout the Bible, most of us instantly think of the four gospels being the only place Jesus was referred to in scripture. When we see the Word capitalized in scripture, we know that is reference to Jesus. He was there in the beginning—was, always, and will be.

Getting to know Jesus is what every Christian must do and dig deep and discern scripture. For around thirty-three years, He walked this earth to go through what we may be going through today. His biggest difference is that he conquered it all and never sinned throughout his life. Whenever we are going through a trial or temptation in life, we can have more peace knowing that Jesus went through some of the same things in his time on earth.

A true leader walks among his people, paving the way for him. He's not high and mighty or vain with power. When it comes to Jesus, as He foretold, we would be hated over His name. The ones who hate Him truly don't know Him. If everyone actually sat down and read scripture and got to know who Jesus is, they would truly find what they've always been looking for! Have peace in Jesus. He gave us the way. He is the way!

How can you have peace in Christ?

JANUARY 17

More Than Physical Healing

Be not wise in your own eyes; fear the Lord, and turn away from evil. It will be healing to your flesh and refreshment to your bones.

—Proverbs 3:7–8

When we think of healing, we often think of just physical ailments being taken away from us. But there's also spiritual healing that can come with that. Those who are sick physically will often pray, even if that's something they wouldn't normally do. I believe God can use those physical healings to show us His glory and also give us a spiritual healing as well.

It always seems that after the holidays are over and we get into January, my family and I start getting sick. Perhaps we're just run down from all the business, or we're run down from the colder weather. Whatever the reason, it's important for us to find our rest, but not just physical rest. As we always pray for healing in these times, it's a reminder to know that we are loved by an almighty God who we can trust in for that healing.

Now on some occasions where those who have lost a loved one to sickness who diligently prayed for them, God may just be trying to heal the one praying spiritually than heal the one being prayed for physically. Most of us in those situations always ask God why it feels like prayer isn't working, but we need to be reminded that even if our loved one is no longer with us, He is enough. God is enough.

How can you trust in the Lord for your healing?

JANUARY 18

Pray without Ceasing

> Rejoice always, pray without ceasing, give thanks in all circumstances, for this is the will of God in Christ Jesus for you.
>
> —1 Thessalonians 5:16–18

Just thinking of our title, it's hard to imagine praying all the time. However, it's a beautiful reminder that even in our simplest cares in life, God still cares about us. Jesus longs to hear from us.

I think of my daily stresses of work and how sometimes I feel like I'm too mad to pray or that I just want to do things myself. I, too, need to be in prayer constantly because I feel much worse about the situation if I'm not in the word or prayer daily. Life is stressful some days, but we serve a mighty God who cares for us and loves us so much that we are free to talk to Him daily.

Never stop praying, whatever the situation may be. Ask for His guidance daily to keep you on the right path. May He continue to guide you in all aspects of life each and every day.

How can you find more reasons to lift in prayer?

JANUARY 19

Desire of Discipline

Discipline your son, and he will give you rest;
he will give delight to your heart.

—Proverbs 29:17

Discipline is something most of us aren't big fans of, but in Christian maturity, it's something we must grasp if we hope to be grounded in our faith. We must eat daily to maintain our physical health, but are we in the word every day, maintaining our spiritual health? Usually, when discipline is brought up, the first thing that comes to mind is children, but adults need discipline too!

On this day, my wife and I attended a parent meeting for our oldest daughter's preschool. The different topics and discussions about encouraging our children and working with them as they learn in school were all very good reminders on instilling that discipline in our children at a young age. If they are put on the right path at a young age, they will need to be taught discipline to stay on it.

Everyone needs discipline, especially when it comes to their spiritual health. We must make it a priority to grow closer to the Lord each and every day through prayer and reading the word. Even on the days we don't necessarily feel like praying, those are the days we probably need it the most.

*How can you strengthen your own discipline
to stay close to the Lord?*

JANUARY 20

One Body, Many Parts

*For just as the body is one and has many members,
and all the members of the body, though many,
are one body, so it is with Christ.*

—1 Corinthians 12:12

When we think of the body, we usually think of the human body at first. Many different parts that work together make up a whole human. The body of Christ, however, is many of us joined together with the common goal of serving Him. Everyone serves a purpose, especially in a church body.

This weekend, we arrived at our annual all church retreat. Occasions like this are a beautiful time for our church to go away for a weekend in a smaller setting and worship more intimately. It takes many of us to plan this weekend and help to operate the schedule of events to come. Everyone plays a part in this body of Christ as we go forth on this weekend together. I look around watching everyone enjoy their time here. It's wonderful to see everyone here for the purpose of growing closer to the Lord.

The body of Christ is very diverse and at sometimes complex, but there is always something for everyone within this body. We must continue to work together to further the goal of the kingdom and grow closer together in Christ.

How do you fit into the body of Christ?

JANUARY 21

Rise up and Lead

> He must hold firm to the trustworthy word as taught, so that he may be able to give instruction in sound doctrine and also to rebuke those who contradict it.
>
> —Titus 1:9

Christian leadership in today's society must be extremely strong to avoid being shattered like the broken world we live in. When we are growing in the word and learning meaning of scriptures, it's absolutely necessary to be able to answer questions or accusations any unbeliever may have about the faith. This also requires not just knowing the word but also actively living it every day.

I can recall in years past when I was a much weaker man in the faith. I knew it, but I rarely presented it right and focused too much on God's law rather than His love. To be frank, I was a royal hypocrite in this part of my life. The most important thing in my life I was a horrible example of, and I'm sure I turned some people off from ever having faith in God. How could I truly show someone else the light when I lived just as much in the dark as they did? As I've grown a little older, I have realized it's less talk and more action. Be the leader as opposed to telling someone that they just have to believe.

We truly have a gift to share with the world, but we need to be all in with the way we show it. When we're living according to scripture, we're setting the example of how a Christian should act in this world. When we're doing it joyfully, that attitude can go a long way with those watching. We can also lovingly combat those who come against us through knowledge of the word. Everyone in this world who doesn't know Christ is searching for something that can meet their needs. Christ can truly do that, even if they don't know it yet. We have a major responsibility and also an opportunity to share the greatest message ever. Let's lead by example and present it right.

> How can you present the truth
> the way God would want?

JANUARY 22

Against the Wind

> Now the word of the Lord came to Jonah the son of Amittai, saying, "Arise, go to Ninevah, that great city, and call out against it, for their evil has come up before me."
>
> —Jonah 1:1–2

We've all had to do things we don't like doing. Sometimes the Lord is calling us out of our comfort zone to do what we think may be impossible. Just like Jonah, we may be scared of what or where God is telling us to do or go. In the end of this book, Jonah really saw what God was doing. Even if he was still angry over it, God used him to do His work.

There are still people in this world, like Jonah, who go way out of their comfort zones to share the good news in some of the darkest corners of the earth. The persecution that some missionaries face even in today's world is horrific. You would think these people would pack up and head home with all the violence and persecution in the world, but a lot stand firm to continue the call of whom they serve. God's calling.

It's so easy to get caught up in our daily routines and normal schedules that anything outside of that can be uncomfortable or foreign to us, but as a follower of Christ, we must be ready and in tune to hear His calling and His plan for us. The Lord equips the called to do His will. We may not think we're ready, but He knows the plans even when we don't.

How can you find peace outside your comfort zone?

JANUARY 23

No Sin Bad Enough

> But Ananias answered, "Lord, I have heard from many about this man, how much evil has done to your saints at Jerusalem."
>
> —Acts 9:13

I'm sure when Paul was converted to the faith, Ananias wasn't the only one who had a reaction like this. For Paul, formerly Saul, was about as far away from God as you could get in those days. Earlier on in the book of Acts, it talks about his treatment of the church. Someone so rotten to the core that God turned around to use for His glory.

If the Lord can take someone like Paul and turn him around, then what's your excuse? Whenever we think we're not good enough or we've committed too many sins to be saved, we need to remember that nothing is too great for God, especially now that the price has been paid on the cross by Jesus. There's a lot of Paul like conversions throughout history that bring many to the Lord. Paul had it very wrong before his conversion, and there's so much we can learn from him, and it's still very relevant to today.

May we not be discouraged if we've made a mistake or we're stuck in an addiction that makes us feel like we'll never see the light. See the light every day through Christ. Rise up, put the past behind you, and march forward for the greater good of the Lord.

How can you give grace to others no matter what they have done?

JANUARY 24

The Right Building Materials

> Therefore encourage one another and build
> one another up, just as you are doing.
> —1 Thessalonians 5:11

It's a wonder what being around the right kind of people can do for morale. When you are surrounded by Bible-believing people who try every day to live better Christian lives, it's easier to want to live that Christian life. Being around people who are always down or negative makes it even easier for you to fall into the same trap they're in. We must be careful of whom we keep company as to not be caught up in the ways of this world.

Years ago, my wife and I were friends with another couple close to our age who weren't really believers. We did just about everything together, other than go to church. We even moved to the area they lived in. We all just had fun together, but when it came to serious things, these two couldn't handle some simple boundaries and ended up cutting our family out of their lives. He was one of my best friends for over a decade, and as it broke my heart to see him walk out of our lives, it was also very eye-opening. These were not the people who were encouraging and holding us spiritually accountable. My wife and I have grown a lot since then, and we love the company of other younger couples at our church. We all have the same foundation, and we build on that together.

We must be careful who we're close with and who we let into our lives. It's very easy to get entangled with people who aren't good for us just because they may give us that "feel good" feeling or tell us what we want to hear. Strong bonds are formed through faith in Christ, not just interests of the world. Build up relationships with those who can help you in your walk with faith just as you may be able to help them.

How can you build strong bonds with other believers?

JANUARY 25

When Blind Men See

How great are his signs, how mighty his wonders! His kingdom, and his dominion endures from generation to generation.

—Daniel 4:3

When old King Nebuchadnezzar had Shadrach, Meshach, and Abednego thrown into the fiery furnace, he never expected where his beliefs would turn to after they were delivered from his cruelty by God. Sometimes in life, we do experience things that are just so powerful that our eyes are opened to what God is telling us.

It's not an everyday thing to see a full-blown miracle, but if you tune your heart to the right channel, you may sure find little miracles everyday proving God's wonders. Every night, when we say our family prayer at bedtime, I always thank God for our blessings, especially those little blessings that we may not see or take for granted. God is revealing Himself to us daily even when we may not be tuned to see it.

Think of all the things you have—health, gifts, even material things that are given to us by Him. God is with us always. I think of my own field of work as a commercial driver and how many times I am convinced He took the wheel when I didn't realize until after a near miss that I needed a little help from above. Believe and listen to what He is showing you. Trust me, He wants your attention!

How can your eyes be opened to what God wants to show you?

JANUARY 26

Biblical Judgment

> Judge not, that you be not judged. For with the
> judgment you pronounce you will be judged, and with
> the measure you use it will be measured to you.
>
> —Matthew 7:1–2

I've always said this is one of the two favorite verses of the unbeliever. It's probably one of the verses that gets taken out of context the most. When we judge people not according to God's word, then we are reflecting behavior that the unbelievers constantly accuse us of. The most common misconception of this verse is that to an unbeliever, if you state a biblical fact, it means you're judging someone. We must present it in love.

I have had many people come and go from my life. More than once, when someone walked away, it was because they felt judged by my faith. I recall an old coworker in high school who befriended me but was living a sinful lifestyle. He knew where I stood on things and eventually cut me out of his life, saying I was judging him for his lifestyle. I never once said an unkind thing to him about it other than what the Bible says.

It's a shame, but sometimes people will walk away from you because our faith doesn't coincide with someone else's lifestyle. We can only pray for those who walk away and let God handle them from there. Some may come back, and others may not. It's important to not be led astray while trying to pull someone up who wants to pull you down with them.

How can you use biblical judgment in a loving way to win others over to Christ?

JANUARY 27

Encouragement in Marriage

> Husbands love your wives, as Christ love the church and gave himself up for her, that he might sanctify her, having cleansed her by the washing of water with the word, so that he might present the church to himself in splendor, without spot or wrinkle or any such thing that she might be holy and without blemish.
>
> —Ephesians 5:25–27

This one's more for the men, but, ladies, encourage your men to do the right thing, and don't be too critical when they fall short. Whether you're married or single, this is a good lesson. Men, your bride is your queen, and with the many distractions in the world, it can be hard to show her the love she deserves. At some points in marriage, we may get so frustrated that we don't want to do the right thing.

My wife and I try to keep things simple. We never need an extravagant vacation or night on the town to make us happy. We just truly need each other's sincerity. One thing we enjoy doing is playing backgammon. Years ago, I got back into the game and taught her how to play, and she was hooked! We can get very competitive though! On this day, after a stressful couple of weeks of sickness and packing up the house to get ready to move, we just needed a simple carefree evening of playing a game, conversing, and just enjoying each other's company to feel a little rejuvenation amid the craziness in our lives.

Fear not if your situation isn't like ours. Men especially, if you feel like giving up, there is a way. Also on this night, I got a text from a coworker of mine who had thoughts of leaving his wife. As a Christian friend, it's my duty to encourage him in a biblical way. I pray for anyone struggling to make that decision as I myself was once there too. Even us men can be a little sensitive and overwhelmed at times. It's time to be men of courage and rise up to do the right thing, but first, we need to be on our knees in surrender to the King!

> Men, how can you love your wives more each day?
> Women, how can you show more grace to
> your man in his shortcomings?

JANUARY 28

Together with the King

And they devoted themselves to the apostles teaching and the fellowship, to the breaking of bread and the prayers.

—Acts 2:42

In America today, we Christian people sometimes don't realize how good we have it. We can gather in worship on Sunday freely. We can pray together, even in public. And legally, in this country, we cannot be arrested for our faith. These simple things may be insignificant, but there are believers in other countries who pray that one day, they might be able to share in the same privileges we do. Let us take advantage of these opportunities.

Throughout my life, I've invited many to church and other related functions. Some people have given me the typical response that they don't need to go to church to believe in God. That may be true, however, but being outside that body of believers and being spiritually fed by someone older and wiser means not much growth. We have every opportunity to be in church on Sunday mornings and find other opportunities to be with believers and in the word all through the week.

When we gather in His name, there is a holy power that brightens within us. Let us continue to encourage others into our body of believers. In a world that can sometimes be against us for following Christ, it's more important that we to stick together and build one another up on the foundation of the Lord.

How can we encourage others to be a part of fellowship?

JANUARY 29

Being Content

> You shall not covet your neighbor's house; you shall not covet your neighbor's wife, or his male servant, or his female servant, or his ox, or his donkey, or anything that is your neighbor's.
>
> —Exodus 20:17

In our world today, it's always about getting what you don't have. What can you attain in life? Getting power or money. Some move from partner to partner, hoping they'll find what they're looking for. These are all ways that one can covet what they don't have. It's common for us to want, but it's how and what we want that determines if we are breaking the tenth commandment.

We talked about this commandment in Sunday school today, and lusting after something or someone was an example given of coveting what you don't have. Some things that we shouldn't have or can't have, we tend to covet. After church, we were at a birthday celebration for my oldest daughter's best friend. The two are a few months apart in age, and while at the get-together, they were arguing over who got to play with a certain toy. There must have been hundreds of toys to play with, but both of them wanted this particular one. They finally calmed down and shared, by the guidance of us parents. Watching this, it was a good reminder to me that we shouldn't always want what someone else has just because they have it.

In the Christian faith, life is about being content. It's a humbleness and a thankfulness to appreciate what we have and not obsess over what we don't have. Some people truly won't understand why we have content attitudes when we share our true blessings, but some may look on and wonder how they can reach that contentment as well. We want the world to covet what we have, the Son of God.

How can you be content in faith throughout your days?

JANUARY 30

Send Me on My Way

And I heard the voice of the Lord saying, "Whom shall I send, and who will go for us?" Then I said, "Here I am! Send me."

—Isaiah 6:8

You never know where you might end up in life, but as our pastor says every Sunday during the benediction, "You go nowhere by accident, wherever you go, God is sending you there." Sometimes we find ourselves in places way out of our comfort zones, and if we tune our hearts to hear the Lord, we can hear His plans for us right where we're at.

Our first house we bought was in an area we were never really planning to live in for very long. We were planning to sell it in five years after buying it and move farther north to get a little more property. When I realized that dream was not going to work for our family, we decided to go back to our home church after the pandemic slowed down, and from then on, I knew we needed to get back to that area. I felt foolish, in a way, moving us to the area we were in, but I knew even in my selfish desires of wanting to move us here that God still used us in our time here. We may not know every reason, but we know He had a plan for us.

We must be willing to listen to Him and where He wants to send us. Think of missionaries that pack up everything and move to third world countries to answer the call of God's ministry. We never know where we might end up, but we can rest assured knowing that God has a greater plan for us even when we feel like we're in the wrong place.

How can you go where God is sending you?

JANUARY 31

Walk Straight the Path

Let your eyes look directly forward, and
your gaze be straight before you.

—Proverbs 4:25

It's very easy in a world surrounded by distraction to lose focus. There's good days and bad days, and sometimes, there's even worse days that leave us feeling so empty. Sometimes we feel like not talking to God because we think we can handle it on our own or we're too mad about something to talk to Him. We must let go and surrender to Him if we truly want to find refuge.

This week, I was having such a bad time at work, and it was only Tuesday. Nothing seemed to go right. I had problems with my boss, recurring problems with a certain customer of mine. And on top of all that, it's another winter of working out in the cold. I had trouble focusing at work, and getting home gave me some peace of mind after being around my family. I was beyond angry and didn't pray enough over this situation though and finally had to just give it to God to calm me down.

When we're so frustrated about things that just don't matter in the greater view of life, all we're doing is letting the devil win. He doesn't want us to cry out to God for help. He wants us to try to do it on our own and fail. Look to the heavens and look in your heart. By our almighty God, may we be set apart.

*How can you trade anger for
comfort in the Lord?*

FEBRUARY 1

All Good Things

> And we know that for those who love God all things work together for good, for those who are called according to his purpose.
>
> —Romans 8:28

What an encouragement for those of us going through hard times. It's often hard to realize sometimes that we don't have to do everything ourselves. Remain faithful, and even when you feel like you're walking through a valley alone, God is still with you. When you're in a situation that you feel isn't going to work the way you want it to, God is still in control.

I've had to take multiple steps back in life to see where I went wrong. Sometimes we want something, but it may not be glorifying to God, or we may not have the right motives for it. Even when it's something we're so sure of that would be great for us and we think that's God's plan for us, sometimes He has something better in store. We may not live long enough to see His plans on earth unfold for us, but if we remain faithful to Him, we will reap the reward of eternal life with Him.

The whole point of faith is believing in something you cannot see and may not have a full understanding of, but understand this, God loves you. Let us show Him love daily by action and reading the word He has given us. May we all seek His purpose for us each and every day.

How can you find your call for His purpose?

FEBRUARY 2

The Unfinished Book

> Blessed is the one who reads aloud the words of the prophecy, and blessed are those who hear, and who keep what is written in it, for the time is near.
>
> —Revelation 1:3

When we think of the Bible as a whole, we're usually focused on it being set thousands of years ago. However, Revelation technically hasn't happened yet. As it was revealed to the apostle John as a foreshadow, it still has yet to come. The final book is a prophecy about the end of times and God restoring His kingdom to it's true form.

Living each day as if the end is near is a hard concept, but if we live for God like the end is tomorrow, then let us continue to stand firm in our faith in a very dark world. In the bigger scheme of things, this life is so short compared to eternity. The daily struggles and trials may be difficult, but why worry about things that really don't matter? If we're not meant to live forever on earth and earth isn't meant to live forever, then what is forever? The Lord Almighty and His plan for us.

When you start to worry about things of this world or have to make a choice on following God or not, consider the end result. We have a gift given to us that will give us that eternal life in the end. Why not spend our days living out and encouraging others to believe?

How can you live better for Him each day knowing that the end of times is coming?

FEBRUARY 3

When a Little Is More Than Enough

But Jesus said, "They need not go away;
you give them something to eat."

—Matthew 14:16

With only five loaves of bread and two fish along with a crowd of five thousand men, not including women and children, Christ fed them all. Wouldn't it have been a sight to be in that crowd watching the food just multiply endlessly to satisfy everyone and even have plenty left over? It doesn't take much sometimes to do great things. Those little things we do that may seem insignificant to us may be a huge deal for another.

Over the course of my time in youth ministry, I had the opportunity to go on several mission trips. On one in Harrisburg in 2009, we were running a vacation Bible school for inner city kids in an area with very high racial tensions. This was my sixth trip. I was on leadership at the time, and all of us had the same mindset in making a positive impact on these kids in direction of Christ. I'll never forget a free period of one of those days. I was sitting on stage and tuning up my bass guitar when one of the kids struck up short conversation with me. To this day, I regret not remembering most of it, but the one thing he said before he walked away was "You guys are gonna change the world someday."

This young man may have admired our group, but there is only one who can truly change the world and His name is Jesus. It's a great honor as a Christian to be a part of His plan for bringing others to Him. So no matter what the circumstance, be willing to serve, and do not be discouraged even if you feel an act is so insignificant. To someone else, it could change their life.

How can you give little acts to make big impacts?

FEBRUARY 4

Make and Maintain

> Therefore a man shall leave his father and mother and hold fast to his wife, and the two shall become one flesh.
>
> —Ephesians 5:31

A pastor friend and mentor to me always told me, "Your marriage is the second most important decision you'll make. The first is your salvation." That being said, marriage is far from easy. In today's society, marriage is somewhat looked down on or looked at like it's insignificant. Some are scared to get married because they look at commitment and want to run in the other direction. Marriage is a covenant between a man and a woman before God and their loved ones, and it truly is for better or for worse.

My own marriage has been no easy street, especially in the beginning. I failed miserably in more ways than one. When my wife and I attended "A Weekend to Remember," which is a Christian-based marriage conference, it definitely helped us make a big step up in our marriage. Making that step isn't enough, though. Each and every day, it takes work and a lot of effort to maintain what we have. It's been very easy to get discouraged, but it's even easier to rely on God for strength. If He orchestrated your marriage, He can help you keep your marriage.

In this world today, staying with one person your entire life seems like it's a prison, but on the contrary, the real prison is to sexually sin for those who choose not to get married and go from partner to partner. There is a massive attack on the husband and wife and family unit as a whole in today's world. It's up to us to do things God's way and keep them His way!

How can you maintain your marriage daily?

FEBRUARY 5

Last-Minute Conversion

But the other rebuked him, saying, "Do you not fear God, since are under the same sentence of condemnation? And we indeed justly, for we are receiving the due reward of our deeds; but this man has done nothing wrong." And he said, "Jesus, remember me when you come into your kingdom." And he said to him, "Truly, I say to you, today you will be with me in paradise."

—Luke 23:40–43

That thief on the cross, for whatever reason, was being punished for the deeds he had done. Knocking on death's door, he still knew who Jesus was and confessed in the end who his Savior was. It doesn't matter if we're raised a Christian from the start or we find Him on our deathbed. We're not getting out of this world alive, and He is our ticket out no matter when in life we find Him.

I've shared the gospel with many people in my life, and a few have believed, but a lot haven't. To those that haven't, I can only pray for them to find Him eventually, even if He just used me to plant the seed. We see it in our own families with other members that may not be on the same page spiritually that we are.

Since some of us know better than this thief on the cross did before he confessed to Jesus, we know that we can be free in Christ while on earth. For others, it may just be a life of sin and then a deathbed confession to Christ. May we be encouraged by this story to witness to others, showing them that it's never too late!

How can you witness to others through this story?

FEBRUARY 6

This Is the Way

> Jesus said to him, "I am the way, the truth, and the life.
> No one comes to the Father, except through me."
>
> —John 14:6

In a world of different beliefs, no one likes to be told theirs is wrong, but the fact of the matter is, if you don't have this verse at the head of your belief structure, then you are lost. All these different religions of the world and different paths of life, but only one road to heaven. Most unbelievers find this to be intolerant and judgmental, but it's neither. Jesus gave us the gift of salvation by dying on the cross and rising from the dead. Why would we not want that?

I've mentioned in an early entry that those who reject Jesus don't truly know Him, and I think it's very important to keep reminding ourselves of that. We need to try and get to know Him better every day and introduce Him to those who don't know Him. If everyone that rejects Him would take time to actually understand what He's about and get to know Him, one would think there would be no unbelievers.

In your witness to those in the dark, this crucial verse must be brought up in sharing the gospel with others. There's definitely a right and wrong way of presenting it, and we must be very loving to those who may be on the fence a little. Christ came here bring us back with Him. One day, we will rise from the dead as he did and take our place in heaven. Wouldn't it be nice to show more and more people that opportunity? This is the way.

> How can you show others the
> only path to salvation?

FEBRUARY 7

God Made Me

> For you formed my inward parts; you knitted me together in my mother's womb. I praise you, for I am fearfully and wonderfully made. Wonderful are your works; my soul knows it very well.
>
> —Psalm 139:13–14

It's pretty awesome to think that with the amount of people throughout history, God knew everyone and made them. He made you! Even as you were in your mother's womb, you were perfectly orchestrated from conception. When we look at how small we are in the bigger scheme of things, we are a big deal to an almighty God who loves us!

I've thought about what my purpose is in life many times. Your salvation is the most important thing, but I feel like our human nature has us still searching. Not that our salvation isn't enough, but where do we fit in this world as a Bible-believing Christian where the odds are against you from the words of Jesus himself? I think just staying grounded in your own faith and getting to know Christ better can give you peace of mind, knowing that getting through life doesn't have to be as hard as we make it.

So when you feel like your life isn't significant enough or you're struggling to find your place in this world, just remember that God made each and every one of us special. We were created for a purpose. Let's make our purpose to serve Him and get to know Him more and more each day.

How can you find your place in this world as a Christian?

FEBRUARY 8

Into the Wild

> Fear not, for I am with you; be not dismayed, for I
> am your God; I will strengthen you, I will help you, I
> will uphold you with my righteous right hand.
>
> —Isaiah 41:10

Day-to-day life in the secular work world can be very tiring for a Christian. We hear lots of foul language, we hear questionable talk, and people can be so nice. It's not uncommon, as a Christian, to feel completely exhausted from the week when you walk into church on a Sunday morning. It's easy to be discouraged throughout the week when it feels like you're the only one going against the grain trying to live a holy life.

In years past, I wasn't a very good Christian. I still made it to church every Sunday, but I didn't live right during the week. I still felt convicted every Sunday knowing that I wasn't living the right lifestyle, but it took years to change that. Even in my darkest days, I knew God was with me. He delivered me from a lot over the years, even occasions that I probably wouldn't have lived through had it not been for Him.

So fear not! Even in the darkness, the light can shine the brightest. When you strike a match in the dark, the darkness doesn't swarm and put it out; the light scares back the darkness. Every time! So we can be that light with God's guidance. In our workplaces, in our homes, in public, and in the wild!

*How can you fear not in those situations
where you may be the only light?*

FEBRUARY 9

Lead Astray in the Name

But false prophets also arose among the people, just as there will be false teachers among you, who will secretly bring in destructive heresies, even denying the Master who bought them, bringing upon themselves swift destruction.

—2 Peter 2:1

It's hard to believe that the Bible, the church, or God would ever lead someone astray, but when humans get involved with the wrong motives and the wrong way of viewing scripture, things can get ugly pretty quick! I've said in earlier entries how people that base their opinions of God on man truly don't know the Father and who Jesus really is. We must be diligent in learning the scriptures and being loving yet firm with unbelievers to win more over in the name of Christ.

Years ago, it hit me that two of the biggest things mentioned in the Bible are God's love and God's law. Imagine an old-fashioned scale where you put both those things on opposite sides and they perfectly balance. That is how we need to be in our actions as Christians. In some cases, those that come down too hard on others with the law and very little love often push them away from the church. On the other hand, too much love and little law leads to no accountability for an individual's sin, and you might as well just hold their hand and walk them to hell. It may sound harsh, but we truly need to balance both these characteristics of God.

Watch out for those that pervert the gospel and trade it for a lie. Be quick with scripture and continue to learn it daily so that you may be ready when the enemy attacks, even if it is from within the body of believers.

How can you discern a false teacher?

FEBRUARY 10

A Companion Fit for You

> Then the Lord God said, "It is not good that the man should be alone; I will make him a helper fit for him."
>
> —Genesis 2:18

Men, this one's for you. Women, pay attention as well because you're not out of this either. God specifically created women for men. The "helper" fit for the man will always be the woman. God knew our needs in that way long before we knew we needed them. Marriage is hard but also very rewarding. We must continue to grow stronger as couples living as God planned for us.

My wife and I have had some rough times over the years, and we've been at some very low points more than once. We have also saved each other through God's grace on separate occasions when one of us wanted out and the other one didn't, and vice versa. Her and I work very hard nowadays to keep our marriage moving forward. Not that everything will ever be perfect, but we work toward bettering ourselves. When I found her, I was so sick of being single, and she will always be the helper for me.

So go forth in your marriage and grow together. It's easier said than done, but let's do our best to try and obey God's commandments for us, especially in our marriage. Adam and Eve may have not had a formal marriage, but they sure were made for each other. Let us continue to live out the roles God designed for us. For you single folk out there, these are all things to think about for when that day comes for you to get married.

How can I fill the right role in my marriage?

FEBRUARY 11

Churched

> The Lord is good, a stronghold in the day of trouble;
> he knows those who take refuge in Him.
>
> —Nahum 1:7

One of the most common things you hear a lot from those who aren't truly grounded in the faith is "I don't need to go to church to believe in God." That much is true, but how do you grow when you are not involved in a body of believers or being spiritually fed on daily basis? You don't! Consider the practice of gardening. Plants don't bear fruit or vegetables without water or sunlight. They must be fed and taken care of just like we do in our faith.

Sunday mornings without church have never felt the same to me. Whether we had to miss because of illness or being out of town, there always feels like a void when I'm not in church on a Sunday morning. For me, personally, it's a rejuvenation from some of the weeks I tend to have being out on the road at work. It's a time for my family to also be spiritually fed and for our own family unity to grow closer together and in Christ.

Taking refuge in the Lord is something we all may struggle with from time to time. Even if you're struggling with sin and the guilt that comes with it, or you feel like you're not good enough to be in church, believe me, the church is waiting for you. If you're not plugged into one, try to find one that suits you best and still gives you the right message. There's a lot of churches out there, and there is definitely a seat at the table for all.

> How can you make church a
> priority every week?

FEBRUARY 12

Straight Up

> It is better for a man to hear the rebuke of the wise than to hear the song of fools.
>
> —Ecclesiastes 6:5

We often don't like being told we're wrong. Okay, lesson over. Just kidding! It's easier to hear what we want to hear instead of being told there is something we're doing that needs to change. I lived the bar life and the church life at the same time at one point of my life, and let me tell you, there's two completely different sources of advice given.

I'm a coffee drinker. I'd rather go without electricity than coffee. I'm a big fan of the strongest, darkest coffee you could find, and I don't put anything in it. Just spring water and coffee grounds is the best way I've found to get coffee in its purest form. Most people who drink coffee have to put something in it like sugar or flavored creamer or something to water it down. The same goes for the truth and the gospel. Too many are watering it down and distorting biblical advice compared to what it really means.

So what do we do when rebuked by the wise? We listen. We make the necessary changes in our lives to become closer to God and try to live holier lives. We may not like hearing we need to change, but if those people giving us the wise advice are solid in scripture, then we should reflect on those scriptures and take them seriously. Let's continue to lift one another up in prayer and in love and take the gospel like I take my coffee—strong, hot, and no additives!

> How can you change after being rebuked by the wise?

FEBRUARY 13

Orders from Headquarters

Go therefore and make disciples of all nations, baptizing them in the name of the Father and of the Son and of the Holy Spirit, teaching them to observe all that I have commanded you. And behold, I am with you always, to the end of the age.

—Matthew 28:19–20

When you're a Bible-believing Christian and you know the scriptures and the truth, you also know that some people don't. Too many people in this world are walking in darkness. Some because they are truly lost and others because they have rejected the truth. It's up to us to be vessels for Christ in sharing the good news so that others may repent and be saved. We're not called to save them; we're called to give them the message. As the gardener waters his seeds, God works in everyone who has heard His message.

Being in a secular job, especially union trucking, you would think it's hard to share the gospel with some. I've found as the years go by that God is truly giving me the words to speak to who needs to hear them. I've prayed for my coworkers by name and shared the good news with those who I earned the right to be heard by. These union brothers of mine are all at different places, but I pray each and every one of them truly finds the message to be what it is—the truth. I'm privileged to be able to share what I know with them.

So are we going to get everyone to instantly repent and want to get baptized? Certainly not, but God has done marvelous things before, and He can do them again. Don't beg people to repent and threaten them with the fires of hell if they don't. Love those folks because they need it most. Preach the message in the right presentation, and you never know, some may be eager to hear more. There may be some new unlikely disciples.

How can you make disciples through God's guidance?

FEBRUARY 14

What Is Love?

> Love is patient and kind; love does not envy or boast; it is not arrogant or rude. It does not insist on its own way; it is not irritable or resentful; it does not rejoice at wrongdoing, but rejoices with the truth. Love bears all things, believes all things, hopes all things, endures all things. Love never ends. As for prophecies, they will pass away; as for tongues, they will cease; as for knowledge, it will pass away.
>
> —1 Corinthians 13:4–8

Love never fails! On this Valentine's Day, when we are celebrating our love for our spouse, let us not forget God's love, the creator of love. For you single folk, don't feel bad about this day, but rejoice in the fact that you are learning God's love even more in preparation for marriage. When we hear so many people use the word *love* so loosely, many of them don't know what true love is. God sent His Son, Jesus, to stand in the gap for us and give us a hope and a future.

If you're married, do yourself a favor and hang this verse on the wall in your home. If a couple continues to dive into this verse daily and trust in the Lord, prepare to have a very solid and prosperous marriage. Complications will inevitably arise, but keeping the right foundation can get you through anything. My wife and I struggled in our marriage in the beginning and almost didn't make it, but by God's grace, we continue to live the vows we made every day.

So enjoy this day! Thank the Lord for your spouse, and if you're single, pray for your future spouse even if you don't know who he or she is yet. Dive deeper into God's love. I guarantee you, it's the greatest love story you've ever heard!

How can you learn more about God's love for us?

FEBRUARY 15

Responsibility of Power

> Then King Darius wrote to all the peoples, nations, and languages that dwell in all the earth: "Peace be multiplied to you. I make a decree, that in all my royal dominion people are to tremble and fear before the God of Daniel, for He is the living God, enduring forever, his kingdom shall never be destroyed, and his dominion shall be to the end. He delivers and rescues; he works signs and wonders in Heaven and on earth, he who has saved Daniel from the power of the lions."
>
> —Daniel 6:25–28

We hear about some of these big shot celebrities influencing others in different ways, good or bad. When you hold a position where people are looking to you for answers, there comes great responsibility. When people follow ungodly celebrities who live lives going against the scriptures, my personal belief is that they will be held accountable to a higher standard for leading more and more away from God.

Every now and then, someone does rise from a filthy Hollywood life and repents. There are more than you would think out there who have openly spoken out against the lives that they lived after they found the Lord and repented of their sins. Sometimes, like King Darius in the book of Daniel, it does take a full-blown God miracle to get folks to believe.

On much smaller scales in our churches, workplaces, and families, we have great responsibilities as Christians to be leaders and be examples for others, especially others who we may have authority over in a workplace or others that just look up to us in other ways. Let us lead by example and not let power or status make us forget where we came from.

How can you use your power or status for the greater good of the Lord?

FEBRUARY 16

Law of the Lord

And the king stood by the pillar and made a covenant before the Lord, to walk after the Lord and keep His commandments and his testimonies and his statutes with all his heart and all his soul, to perform the words of the covenant that were written in this book. And all the people joined in the covenant.

—2 Kings 23:3

Law must be used to keep order. Some countries focus on too much law, and it becomes a way for some to stay in power while other countries are freer with the laws of their land. Nevertheless, of man's law, let us embrace God's laws set up for us. In the Old Testament, King Josiah restored that law. A revival in the kingdom of Judah coming back to the ways of the Lord. We have to have God's laws in place for a society to survive.

Most of the biblical doctrine has influenced our laws in America. Even some of the ten commandments are illegal to break by law. Christianity is truly a life of restraint, not giving into desires that God clearly tells us are sin. It's not an easy path to follow, but this life is so short compared to eternity.

A lot of folks that are unbelievers look at us like we're enslaved to religion and have too many rules and laws to follow. On the contrary, we're the free ones, and they're enslaved to sin. Too much freedom in the world eventually backfires you right into being enslaved to something ungodly. It's a narrow way to walk but an incredible reward in keeping His commands.

How can you be held accountable
to keep God's laws daily?

FEBRUARY 17

The Waiting

> The Lord is good to those who wait for
> him, to the soul who seeks him.
>
> —Lamentations 3:25

Who likes waiting? Not I for sure! Waiting is a part of life. We wait in lines. We wait for things we want. We wait on the right career and spouses to come into our lives. As Christians, there's a lot of waiting involved with our faith; sometimes longer than we expect. The Lord's timing is perfect even when we might not understand why.

In my early to mid-twenties, I went from job to job and had so many failed chances at a relationship that I became very frustrated. Not to mention wanting to be a father so bad. Trying to find a career with no college degree and not much further education became challenging. I really didn't know what I truly wanted to do for work either. Date after date with different women I'd meet and none of them seemed to have the spark for a true relationship. I ended up meeting my wife in late 2016. We were married in 2017, and four months later, I got into the career that I work at today. The years 2019 and 2021 were the years she gave birth to our daughters. I got all I ever wanted, and even though it might not have turned out or worked out like I planned, the Lord showed me His ways are so much greater than my own. I'm so thankful for my family and my career and all the many blessings God has given me.

So don't give up hope. In times when we feel like nothing is going our way, that's all the more reason to wait patiently for God's timing and be reassured that He has everything under control.

How can you wait for God and trust His timing?

FEBRUARY 18

Get the Word Out

> Oh give thanks to the Lord; call upon his name;
> make known his deeds among the peoples!
>
> —Psalm 105:1

Good news! There's good news to share! As Christians who know we've found the truth in our faith in God through Jesus, why wouldn't we want to share that with the world? If we truly believe in the scriptures and the only way to heaven is through Christ, then we know many will refuse to believe no matter what we say. It's sometimes not an easy task, but we must be courageous, by God's grace, to share what we know.

I once heard a quote from an offensive atheist comedian who said, "If these Christians truly know the way to heaven, then how dare they not share that!" If that's coming from someone who refuses to believe in God, then he's right, how dare we not share the gospel with the world.

We live in godless times according to the world, but God is truly alive and well and cannot be stopped by us mere humans. Even in the secular workplaces where, in some cases, bringing up "religion" could cost you your job, there are little glimpses and whispers of His glory if you tune your heart to hear. Let us put our faith and trust in the Lord, take up our cross daily, and be courageous to tell the story. I want to see more people in heaven knowing that so many will perish not knowing Jesus.

> How can you be courageous every
> day to share the gospel?

FEBRUARY 19

So Long, Self

> And when you pray, do not heap up empty phrases as the Gentiles do, for they think that they will be heard for their many words. Do not be like them, for your Father knows what you need before you ask him.
>
> —Matthew 6:7–8

It's our human nature to want recognition for things. It's easy to crave attention for some when they feel like they don't get enough of it. It even happens in the Christian community. Other translations say, "Do not be like the hypocrites." When people act like this, it almost turns into a self thing over a Christ thing. We can't do anything on our own.

While in worship today, up on stage, my bass guitar cut out and only had sound for one of the four songs we were playing. It worked fine through practice, and then I could only play the first song with sound. I kept playing anyway. It wasn't because I was embarrassed I had no sound or because I wanted the attention on me. I kept playing because I wanted to keep on worshipping. It's not a performance up there; it's a service.

In too many churches, worship becomes a self thing, where too many obsess over music or sound or speaking. We need to remember why we're there—to give it all to God and make Him more known instead of ourselves. Greater is He than us. Let's put the focus on Him, not just in worship, but in all we do.

How can you put God first over yourself?

FEBRUARY 20

The Final Days

> He said to them, "It is not for you to know times or seasons that the Father has fixed by His own authority. But you will receive power when the Holy Spirit has come upon you, and you will be my witnesses in Jerusalem and in all Judea and Samaria, and to the end of the earth."
>
> —Acts 1:7–8

You hear a lot about the final days or the last days or the days of our Lord. Truthfully, when Jesus ascended into heaven, from that moment on, it became the last days. We don't know when Jesus is coming back, and that is all the more reason to live out His commands for our lives and be as ready as humanly possible for any moment in time.

Don't wait. Procrastination is something we all deal with for one reason or another. I think back to the years between high school and when I got married. I wasted a lot of time not living a Christian life and talking about plans and things I wanted to do, but never put the effort into accomplishing those goals. Some of those things now, I feel I've missed the time for. However, it is never too late to focus on your faith.

In every day in this crazy world that seems like it's drifting further from the Lord, the time is now to repent and come back to Him. He may not come back while we're still living. I'm sure the disciples expected Him to return in their lifetime. So why wouldn't we, as Christians, want to live like He is coming back in our lifetime if we know it's truly possible? Let's do what we can and encourage one another to stand firm and live in truth.

How can you ready yourself knowing Christ could return at any time?

FEBRUARY 21

Restraint for Reason

So to keep me from becoming conceited because of the surpassing greatness of the revelations, a thorn was given me in the flesh, a messenger of Satan to harass me, to keep me from becoming conceited. Three times I pleaded with the Lord about this, that it should leave me. But he said to me, "My grace is sufficient for you, for my power is made perfect in weakness." Therefore I will boast all the more gladly of my weaknesses, so that the power of Christ may rest upon me.

—2 Corinthians 12:7–9

In our lives, we have some things we struggle with. Physical ailments, addictions, temptations, and things of all sorts that are a lot different from one to another. It's quite possible you may have prayed for a long time for God to take it away and He doesn't. Consider the apostle Paul and this thorn in his side. Whatever it may have been, the Lord showed Paul that He is enough.

I've prayed for different things over the years, and some things I've been left with for whatever reason. Satan's messengers sent to harass Paul are still alive and well today and are sent to harass us. I, too, have a thorn in my side that for years hasn't gone away. Why it's there is probably the same reason as Paul. I also believe that sometimes, when we have these thorns in our lives, for myself, I never quit crying out to God over it. It doesn't matter whether it ever goes away or not. What matters is putting my trust in the Lord.

So fear not, for those things in this life are so insignificant compared to an eternity with Christ. Let us stand firm in the Word daily and be encouraged by the scriptures to understand that these thorns are only small specs in the bigger picture. Whatever you're struggling with, God has a plan for you, whether He removes that thorn or not.

How can you trust God when you have a thorn in your side?

FEBRUARY 22

Faith to Go

I can do all things through Him who strengthens me.

—Philippians 4:13

This one seems so simple. I believe a lot of the things we don't have or the things we don't do can be because we don't ask for them or we don't put enough faith in God to get us through. I think of all the miracles Christ performed with healing and other things. After the ascension, similar miracles were performed by the apostles. Peter heals a paralytic in the book of Acts. Peter was just a man, but through the Holy Spirit, he was able to heal.

We may not feel like some of the things we want to do are that extravagant, but if our motives are toward Christ, then let us have faith and courage, and He will do the rest. This verse has been always near to me because my late grandmother always reminded me of it. When I'm having a bad day, it's a good one to focus on as God is carrying me through those hard times.

If nothing is impossible with God, then what have we to fear? What should we worry about? We can do all those things through Him. Keep the faith and grow closer to Him.

How can you be strengthened by Christ?

FEBRUARY 23

Obedience in Check

Take care lest you forget the Lord your God by not keeping his commandments and his rules and his statutes, which I command you today.

—Deuteronomy 8:11

Do we forget thing sometimes? I know I do. Just ask my wife! It's easy to let things slip your mind or get complacent just coasting by doing the bare minimum. God gave us His commandments to follow to live a holy life, and even when we don't want to, we have to obey and be held accountable.

Throughout the scriptures, it can seem like there are just too many things to follow and that we'll never be able to do everything right. That much is true, and that is why we have a Savior. Jesus paid the price for us to be flawed and still have a relationship with the Father. Grace has been given to us, and in turn, we should have a deep desire to obey the commandments of the Lord.

This life won't last forever, and when we have that peace of mind knowing where we'll be when we die, then let us live each day serving the Lord and obeying His commandments. We're all going to mess up, but having the desire of repentance and bettering ourselves through Christ to make it right is where our hearts need to be.

How can you obey the Lord?

FEBRUARY 24

Mercy > Justice

> You shall do no injustice in court. You shall not be partial to the poor or defer to the great, but in righteousness shall you judge your neighbor.
>
> —Leviticus 19:15

We're living in a world where people scream for justice. There's so much victimhood in today's world that people believe they are owed something. Justice, however, is not what people think it means.

In our Sunday school class, our teacher was talking about this very subject last Sunday. The real justice in this world would be punishment for sin. If only one sin gets us condemned from the beginning, then justice for that sin would be death and an eternity in hell. God loves us so much that He sent Jesus to take that punishment for us on the cross. We're not getting justice; we're getting mercy.

Instead of fighting for justice, let's continue to pray for mercy. How many people today think they're fighting for some kind of justice and they have no peace? They're miserable people who are going about these so-called injustices all wrong. Mostly, there's no forgiveness, and if we are forgiven by the almighty God, then we need to extend the mercy we're given instead of screaming for justice and acting like victims.

How can you turn justice into mercy in your everyday life?

FEBRUARY 25

Sarcastic Scripture

And at noon Elijah mocked them, saying, "Cry aloud, for he is a god. Either he is musing, or he is relieving himself, or he is on a journey, or perhaps he is asleep and must be awakened."

—1 Kings 18:27

The prophet Elijah knew there was no such thing as Baal. He knew who he had on side when going up against the prophets of Baal to show that the Lord is greater than any man-made false god. I love this story, especially this verse, because Elijah had all his faith in the Lord and knew what He is capable of.

In today's world, there are many false gods that people follow. People are convinced that something other than the Lord will help them find what they are looking for, but in the end, it's never enough. However, we shouldn't be sarcastic or condescending toward them for what they put their faith in. We should show them, in love, who they really need to find.

Sometimes we may find ourselves in these situations where it's like we're standing against a legion all alone, but we are most definitely not alone. God is greater than anything man could come up with. Even if it comes down to our own death, God is still prevailing.

How can you have Elijah's confidence when standing up for the truth?

FEBRUARY 26

Breaking Bread Together

> And they devoted themselves to the apostles' teaching and the fellowship, to the breaking of bread and the prayers.
>
> —Acts 2:42

It's amazing what having a simple meal with someone can do. Whether it be with friends, family, church, or even a complete stranger, I believe we can feel on the same level with one another and sometimes open up to one another. I personally love cooking and grilling, and my wife is an excellent cook and baker. God's given us these gifts, and we love to give back with them.

Today was our chili lunch after church. Several folks made chili, and there was a vote on who made the best. It was a splendid time being together in our fellowship hall as a body of believers enjoying a meal together. The conversations, the food, even the children running around and playing together made it a truly joyous occasion. It's moments like these you can appreciate when Monday rolls around and you're back to your normal schedule.

For our new house we're in the process of buying, I've made it my mission that whenever we invite someone over for a meal, they will hear the good news of Christ. No matter who they are or what background they come from, this is a goal I have. Besides, if the food's good, they probably won't walk out during the Gospel talk!

How can you make ministry out of meal?

FEBRUARY 27

Keep Watch

Be sober-minded; be watchful. Your adversary the devil prowls around like a roaring lion, seeking someone to devour.

—1 Peter 5:8

When God tells us to love our enemies, He doesn't mean this one! When someone professes to be a Christian, the more temptation can get thrown at them. It's so important we stand firm and be fully grounded in our foundation. We all have things we're tempted by, and some are different from one person to the next. It's crucial we recognize those things and stay away from them by trusting in the Lord.

There have been many things I've personally struggled with over the years, and I've come to terms with things that I may have overcome by God's grace, but if I toy with other ideas, it will wreck my mind. I've given into temptation for what I thought would have just been a harmless good time, but it's nothing but a pollutant for the mind and the soul. Above all, it takes you away from what is right.

As I grow older, I recognize more and more every day that the further one can fall from God, the further it is to get back to Him. Not saying that He doesn't welcome us back with open arms, but there are definitely consequences to sin. Build your foundation on Him, and do not let the evil one into your mind as he is always whispering deception.

How can you recognize your temptations and avoid them?

FEBRUARY 28

Street Preach

> Until I come, devote yourself to the public reading
> of Scripture, to exhortation, to teaching.
>
> —1 Timothy 4:13

We know as Christians, we are to share the gospel, but how do we do it all the time? If you take this verse literal, then I'm sure you're going to make a lot of people mad in this world of today. I think when we present the message right, we can make a huge difference with God's guidance.

Working in a secular environment, as I've said in past entries, is hard for a Christian. It almost seems like the odds are immediately stacked against you, but it doesn't have to be that hard if we have that heavenly peace of mind. In sharing the Gospel in a secular workplace, presentation is everything. We must earn the right to be heard in our coworkers' lives. Simply doing your job well, as if you were working for the Lord, is something people definitely notice. There is a Holy Spirit living inside of you at work every day, and it's all completely possible to be able to share the good news even in the midst of work.

We must teach, but we also must maintain holy lives as well. Even when we are struggling internally, I'd rather be struggling and know God than be struggling and not know Him. In my walk of faith, those that have had some of the greatest influences on me are those that have screwed up their lives so bad, hit rock bottom, and, through God's grace, overcame it. That's the people I want to learn from. So it doesn't matter what you've done. Repent and go forth into this world preaching the many wonders of our Lord, especially when He sent His Son to take the blame on the cross for our sins.

How can you be more public with your faith?

MARCH 1

Dark before the Dawn

> Why do you make me see iniquity, and why do you idly look at wrong? Destruction and violence are before me; strife and contention arise.
>
> —Habakkuk 1:3

In today's society, it's easy to wonder what God is up to. We know what happens in the end. We know He wins the final battle, but we see all the suffering in today's world, and even standing firm in our faith still can lead us to ask God why? Tragedy surrounds us, but we serve an almighty God, and this life is just a vapor in the wind compared to eternity.

I used to think you should never ask God why and that we just need to trust. However, even as Christ hung on that cross, He asked the Father why. The amount of things that have felt like they've gone wrong in my life are countless, and several of those things I now see why. His plans will always be greater for us than our own, even if we don't see it at first.

So rejoice in the midst of troubles. Nothing in this life lasts forever, and even in sorrow and anger, God is still loving and ever-present in our lives. We must cling even tighter to Him in our times of struggles. Trust in Him always.

How can you still rely on God even when wondering why He's allowing something to happen?

MARCH 2

Paying Your Dues

Jesus said to them, "Render to Caeser the things that are Caesar's, and to God the things that are God's." And they marveled at Him.

—Mark 12:17

Everybody loves paying taxes, right? Probably not! Taxes are a necessary thing, but it's not the end of the world when we have to give the government money. It's important to realize that money ultimately comes from God. The Lord has blessed you with the ability to earn it, so rejoice and be wise with your money.

Tonight, while my mother watched our two daughters, my wife and I had an appointment to get our taxes done. We're always excited to get money back, but we know it's a part of life in the taxes we pay. Financially speaking, God has blessed us immensely. I'm fortunate to have married an accountant. My wife is particularly great at managing our money. We both know that it comes from God and that we must give back to Him also.

Money is an easy thing to become out of control in one's life, and it's the cause of many arguments, especially in marriage. Handle your money right, and may it be pleasing to the Lord. Give back, not only when you have to through taxes but also when you can as a form of giving.

How can your financial decisions glorify God?

MARCH 3

All Are Welcome

> And the Pharisees and their scribes grumbled at his disciples, saying, "Why do you eat and drink with tax collectors and sinners." And Jesus answered them, "Those who are well have no need of a physician, but those who are sick. I have not come to call the righteous but sinners to repentance."
>
> —Luke 5:30–32

Have any of you been judged by church folk? Maybe you've been the judgmental churchgoer unwilling to be welcoming to those new people who may not fit the typical mold of a Christian? I myself have been in both of those roles in my life. Everyone deserves a chance at salvation, and who are we to judge those seeking Christ? Those that may not look the same as we do or live the same lifestyle may be searching. You may be the first example of Christ they see. Don't screw it up!

It was a hectic day for us. I had to work longer than normal for a Friday. I got held up, and after a work appointment, we almost missed the movie we were planning to see tonight. Once all the dust settled and we dropped off our two daughters at my mother's house, we finally made it to the movies. We got our chance to see *Jesus Revolution*. My, what a powerful message. Who would've thought in the late sixties that the hippie community was coming to Christ? They sure faced their fair share of judgmental church folk.

If we're all seeking to follow Jesus, no matter where we come from, then let us encourage one another and not try to micromanage. Let's build one another up for the sake of the kingdom. Come alongside one another and walk together in a world that does enough tearing down of Christians from outsiders. The light always shines brighter the more bulbs there are!

How can you turn judgmental thoughts into positive encouragement?

MARCH 4

Look to the Son

> In the beginning was the Word, and the Word
> was with God, and the Word was God.
>
> —John 1:1

The book of John is a fantastic gospel for those newer to the faith. It doesn't preach the Christmas story but goes right into the ministry of Jesus. The first verse parallels Genesis in a way, but it proves that Jesus was always present with the Father, even in the beginning. Jesus is the living Word.

I had an opportunity that I'd been building up for yesterday to share the gospel with a coworker of mine. We've had conversations in the past, but I really laid down the message for him this time. I don't ever want to go with the guns blazing gospel method of witnessing but build up to it in a way where I've earned the right to be heard. This started with him asking questions, and it led right into the gospel talk and ended with prayer. The main message I was preaching to him was to get to know Jesus.

Those who reject Jesus truly don't know Him. In our own human nature, it's often hard, even for Christians, to comprehend what He did for us on that cross. The Son is the light, and he's been around since the dawn of time. Through Him, may we know the Father. Since Christ is our only way to be raised from the dead and have a place in heaven, then let us get to know Him more and more, day by day.

*How can you truly comprehend
Jesus's love for you?*

MARCH 5

Take It to the Limit

And he said, "Behold, I see the heavens opened, and the Son of Man standing at the right hand of God." But they cried out with a loud voice and stopped their ears and rushed together at him.

—Acts 7:56–57

Our sermon series has been in the book of Acts for a while now, and it's sure been fitting for me. This passage was about Stephen. They say he was the first martyr for our faith. Just like Stephen many years ago who preached the truth and was met with great hostility, believers around the world face persecution today. Some far worse than others.

Here in America, we might not have to worry about physical violence as much as other parts of the world. Mostly, I think, we'll end up getting shunned, excluded, or screamed at by those who refuse to believe. Words definitely hurt sometimes but aren't called to pick and choose who to share the message with. Presentation is everything, but all who listen should definitely hear it.

This life is so short that even if we are martyred for our faith, we know the reward in heaven. It's time we lived out our faith openly in public, presenting it properly. Many folks on this earth are walking around with no idea of what's in store for them when they pass on. May we be the ones courageous enough to take the rejection of the world with a smile and stand firm on our foundation in Christ.

How can you start a conversation with someone
to share the message with them?

MARCH 6

Spirit on Earth

> But you will receive power when the Holy Spirit has come upon you, and you will be my witnesses in Jerusalem and in all Judea and Samaria, and to the end of the earth.
>
> —Acts 1:8

When Christ ascended into heaven, He didn't just leave us alone. The Holy Spirit came down to earth to work in all of us who believe. We often don't think about the third member of the trinity as often as the first two, but the Spirit is alive and well in the hearts of believers all throughout the earth.

I believe the Spirit is where we get our convictions from. As Christians, we want to follow God's commands, and the Spirit encourages us to do right and helps keep us from doing wrong. In my own walk with God, I've really felt the Spirit working lately. I'm more in tune with the spiritual side. I feel as though God has been using the Spirit to remind me daily of whom I serve. Lately, I've been feeling the Spirit speak to me just through music. I've even become emotional listening to some songs because God is so good, and that Spirit continues to move!

We have power in ourselves given to us by the Holy Spirit. I want to use that to spread the Word of God as much as I can. I pray daily for courage to be able to share the message with anyone who needs to hear it. May the Spirit move in all of us to further the kingdom, and may we be in tune to listen to what the Spirit is telling us.

How can you be in tune with Spirit?

MARCH 7

Joy

From Flesh to Faith

Count it all joy, my brothers, when you meet trials of various kinds, for you know that the testing of your faith produces steadfastness.

—James 1:2–3

Joy to the world! Joy isn't necessarily a thing but more so an attitude. With a joyful attitude in our faith, there is a lot we can achieve. As the verse says, even in trials, if we have that joyful attitude, we can count it as a blessing knowing that even in a hard situation, God is still in control. People who haven't found God yet might think they're getting joy in a life of the flesh, but that all goes away when you're in a period of a trial. The faith in the Lord is forever.

I've often found things in this world do bring us great joy. I don't think the Lord has any problems with our interests or hobbies as long as they don't go against scripture. He alone, though, is our real joy. Tonight, my youngest daughter left her stuffed Dumbo downstairs. I noticed it was not in her crib when I put her to bed. For not even two yet, this little girl is crazy about Dumbo! When I found it downstairs, I brought it up to her room, and she was already asleep. After I set it near her in the crib, with her eyes closed, she reached out and pulled Dumbo in closer to her. Just like that stuffed Dumbo just needed to be in the crib to help her to bed, the Lord needs to be in our lives to help us through. Even when we can't see and just know that He's present, He is all we need.

So take some time to work on a joyful attitude. Think of all the Lord has done for you that even in the hard times, you can smile and say, "Okay, Lord, you've got this!"

> How can you maintain a joyful
> attitude through struggles?

MARCH 8

When Things Can't Be Undone

> So when the woman saw that the tree was good for food, and that is was a delight to the eyes, and that the tree was to be desired to make one wise, she took of its fruit and ate, and she also gave some to her, and he ate. Then the eyes of both were opened, and they knew that they were naked. And they sewed fig leaves together and made themselves loinclothes.
>
> —Genesis 5:6–7

You want to know why things are so bad in the world today? This whole chapter is your answer. The fall of man. Most folks don't realize what the "forbidden fruit" actually was. The tree of the knowledge of good and evil. Evil entered the world that day and has been here ever since. When Adam and Eve were kicked out of the garden of Eden, they weren't going to live forever anymore, and they were separated from God. There became a gap between man and God that could never be closed by man's efforts.

It's hard to unknow something. Things that we fill our minds with just don't go away. When we gaze at things of this world that are evil, it only furthers that gap between us and God. We must keep watch and be diligent, knowing there are things of this world that want to get us further from God. Just like the serpent tempting Adam and Eve back then, he is still alive and well in today's world, trying to tempt us every day.

There is hope. Fast-forward to the gospels of the new testament, and there you'll find that Jesus came and paid the price for all that generational sin. Only through Him is the gap closed between us and God. Since Jesus offered up His own life to save us from our sin, let us try our best every day to show gratitude and follow His commands.

How can you follow Jesus's commands with a grateful heart?

MARCH 9

Serving with Humility

He must increase, but I must decrease.

—John 3:30

It's quite easy to get caught up in ourselves, and even in our ministry, we put the focus on ourselves rather than God. We need to be humble enough to know that He created us, and it's for His glory and not our own when we minister and serve, especially when witnessing to unbelievers. We must show them who it's really about, not us but the Almighty Lord.

My pastor and I have talked in the past about how easy it is to put the focus on ourselves, and our human nature doesn't want us to look bad. When I'm playing bass guitar in the church band on Sundays, I have to continue to remind myself that it's not a performance. It's about worship and giving back to God with the gifts He gave me.

Humility is a hard thing to come by in today's world. Nobody wants to be wrong, and everybody wants to be right. When we show the world we are different, it will catch the eyes of some folks wondering how we can be so humble and content putting others first and giving the credit to God.

How can you remain humble in ministry?

MARCH 10

New Again

> I sought the Lord and He answered me and
> delivered me from all my fears.
>
> —Psalm 34:4

Most of us like new. We like new things, new experiences, new people. Some of us want new cars or houses or other things that give us pleasure or satisfaction. A new day is always a wonderful blessing when we're not guaranteed tomorrow. We need to be thankful and willing to cling to the Lord even more as the days go by, especially in the hard times.

Today we closed on our new home. This has been a long time coming for our family. We are now moving to a more central location, and most importantly, it's way closer to our church. My wife and I are both a little overwhelmed with everything, especially the act of moving all our things from one house to another. It's times like these where we know God has made His way for us, and only through Him will our anxiety and worries be lessened.

Often, in times of fear, we want to try to figure things out on our own or run further from God. This is when we must seek Him to find our refuge and strength in His promises. God is good…all the time!

How can your fears and anxieties be lessened through the Lord?

MARCH 11

Hold the Line

> Woe to the world for temptations to sin! For it
> is necessary that temptations come, but woe to
> the one by whom the temptation comes!
>
> —Matthew 18:7

In a world that wants to get further and further from the truth these days, it's not hard to find temptation to sin jumping right out at you. As Christians, we need to hold it together through God's grace to not be the ones that project that temptation in front of anyone else. If we are called to live by example, then we are held to a much higher standard than those of this world.

Everyone is tempted by something. We all have a weakness to some degree. It could be alcohol, drugs, sex, or even more simple things that, when abused, can become addictive. I think as a body of believers, we need to recognize those things others deal with and be an encouragement as opposed to some who can only assist these folks in falling further. I know plenty of Christians who drink alcohol, and I know plenty who don't. Some used to be alcoholics who were very tempted by it, so those are the kind of folks that shouldn't be around another who's drinking, especially if that's another believer.

Accountability is everything when it comes to temptation. This is why it's so important to be a part of the body of believers. It's easy to fall into temptation when walking alone, but when joined in with a body of believers to hold one another to God's standards in the scriptures, it makes a powerful stronghold against sin. Work together, encourage one another, and hold strong to the Word.

*How can you be an encouragement to
each other against temptation?*

MARCH 12

Content in the Calling

*So, brothers, in whatever condition each was
called, there let him remain with God.*

—1 Corinthians 7:24

We live in somewhat of a cutthroat world where everyone is always trying to get ahead. Contentment seems almost foreign to those always chasing success and the dollar. As Christians, this whole passage tells us to be content in whatever the Lord calls us to do. No matter what your race, social status, career, or family life is like, when you have the Lord, what else do you truly need? I don't need to wave a flag in protest because I don't like where life is at. I need to be in prayer with a humble heart, thanking God for where I am because He is the one that brought me here.

We hear constantly about social justice and race wars and everything under the sun like that. What most people, even in the church, don't realize is we're all the same in the eyes of the Lord. When we discriminate on one side or keep the issues alive on the other, then we're not putting God first. When God is first, we have the path laid out for us. It's simpler than we think.

So wherever you are in life, rejoice! God is with you always. This isn't to say that going further in life is a bad thing, but when you do go further, remember who is allowing it. Our pastor always says in the benediction, "You go nowhere by accident. Wherever you go, God is sending you there." Be content where you are but not lazy. Be motivated to get ahead but not arrogant. Trust in the Lord always.

*How can you discern between
contentment and assignment?*

MARCH 13

The Word Will Remain

> I am astonished that you are so quickly deserting him who called you in the grace of Christ and are turning to a different gospel—not that there is another one, but there are some who trouble you and want to distort the gospel of Christ.
>
> —Galatians 1:6–7

Within the sixty-six books of the Bible, there is a lot to learn. So many commands to keep that it may seem impossible to keep them all. Fortunately for us, Christ's triumph over death paid the price for us when we do fail. However, we should make every attempt daily to not sin. One of the worst sins, I personally believe, we could ever commit is to try and change the Word to meet our needs or to fit our agendas. The Word should make you uncomfortable and give you a willingness to change your ways.

In today's society, especially, there are many people in the churches who want to change scripture. Some even think that parts of the Bible are outdated, or they take things out of context to say that certain hot issues are acceptable in the church when it's contrary to scripture. As Christians, we are held to a much higher standard and must keep a stronghold together against the wickedness coming into the church.

I'm sure you can already think of some of these many issues that some churches are allowing within their walls. It's pretty simple, honestly. If God forbids it and it's clearly written in scripture, then we must abide by it. The Word needs to change us, not us changing the Word. It's the same question asked all the time as the serpent in the garden.

"Did God really say that?" Well, my soon-to-be legless friend, yes, He did!

How can you remain faithful to the Word even if your church isn't?

MARCH 14

Sometimes Darkness Can Show You the Light

If we say we have fellowship with Him while we walk in the darkness, we lie and do not practice the truth.

—1 John 1:6

The world is filled with darkness these days. So many people continue to reject God. By action alone, some may not even realize how they reject the truth daily. As Christians, we must stand firm and walk in the light. This life isn't forever, and the light will always win in the end. When you open a closet door, does the darkness jump out at you? Certainly not. The light goes in every time. Go try it if you don't believe me!

In my younger and more rebellious days, I professed to be a Christian, but I sure didn't act like it. I walked in darkness, but I almost felt like I had God as an insurance policy to keep me out of hell after death. What a ridiculous way of thinking. My life was paid for in blood by Christ on the cross, as was yours too. The more we dive into the seriousness of Christ's offering, the more desire we should gain to not only walk in the light but share it with others as well.

Spoiler alert! God wins in the end, and there will be no more darkness. Knowing the ultimate truth, why wouldn't we want to walk in the light if this life is just going to pass on by? If the light's going to win, then that's the side I want to be on!

How can you not only walk in the light but share it as well?

MARCH 15

The Weary May Rise

> Consider him who endured from sinners such hostility against himself, so that you may not grow weary or fainthearted.
>
> —Hebrews 12:3

There's a lot of Christ's examples of where He went through the same things we go through today. For Christians in today's world, it's a very tiring way to be sometimes. It's hard not to get weary when there is so much opposition to us and the church and the scriptures. Jesus sure knew what true weariness was while He was carrying the cross to Golgotha, but He still did it just die on that hill for us.

I think, for me personally, that just being out in public observing can make one grow weary. If you just watch people's actions, what they wear, and what they say, you can sure see a lot of godless people walking around. I'm reminded by being in the Word daily that our Lord will take away our weariness with His promises.

So rise up and fear not. Even when the light seems dim and there's opposition all around, the Holy Spirit burns bright within us. Since Christ walked this earth and never sinned against anyone, even those who hurled insults at Him and put Him to death, then who are we to get so upset and worn down over such little things. Let Him give you rest and take the weariness away.

How can you be encouraged not to grow weary being a Christian?

MARCH 16

Church Ain't Enough

Iron sharpens iron, and one man sharpens another.

—Proverbs 27:17

We're all busy in life. It's just a fact. Even us Christians have busy schedules, and church on Sundays is sometimes all that we have time. I'll put this bluntly. That's not good enough! If we ever expect to grow in the faith, then we must make a conscious effort every day of the week to get into the word and encourage each other in our individual walks with the Lord. We all need accountability and encouragement to be grounded in our foundation with God.

Today was our inspection at our new home. I met our inspector last year for another project, and when we got to talking, we just clicked right into biblical conversation. We both work in the secular world, and it's such an encouragement to me to have conversations like that with him and other working men these days. We started the day discussing the Lord Almighty and praising Him before we talked about anything related to the inspection. Talk about really putting the Lord first. We had a wonderful afternoon, and it was a good pick-me-up during the week.

As the verse says, as believers, we do sharpen one another. Being around unbelievers in conversation that isn't glorifying to God only makes us dull. We must hold onto the Word and encourage each other daily to sharpen our faith more and more.

How can you be like iron sharpening iron?

MARCH 17

The Word Is the Light

Your word is a lamp to my feet and a light to my path.

—Psalm 119:105

The Word is our lifeline. God laid out His guidelines in these sixty-six books for us to turn to at any point in time. The Bible is the number one selling book in all of history, so why shouldn't we, as Christians, take full advantage of it? This holy book is our encouragement and strength to grow closer to the Lord. I carry mine pretty much everywhere.

I should say everywhere, but tonight, I left my Bible in our car, which is parked at our new house since we are still in the process of moving. I felt a little lost not having it and borrowed my wife's Bible to do tonight's writing. It got me thinking, though, if everyone treated their Bibles like a daily necessity, such as their smart phones, no one would go anywhere without it.

Rejoice, for these holy texts are so readily available to us. Read them with purpose and a willingness to understand what God wants to tell you. The more I get deeper into scripture, the more clearly I see God's intentions for us and how much He really loves us. Most people who hate our faith have never truly read the scriptures or made a conscious effort to understand what they have read. This is truly the greatest story in history, and it's a way off planet Earth alive!

How can you make it a priority to carry the Word with you wherever you go?

MARCH 18

Chosen

> When the Lord saw that he turned aside to see, God called to him out of the bush, "Moses, Moses!" And he said, "Here I am." Then he said, "Do not come near; take your sandals off your feet, for the place on which you are standing is holy ground."
>
> —Exodus 5:4–5

If you've ever seen a burning bush talking to you saying it's the Lord and giving you a command, then that'd be pretty easy. For the most part, we don't get these audible and visual commands from our Lord today. This is where tuning our hearts to hear, humbling ourselves, and staying in the Word surrounded by a body of believers comes into play.

After a long day of working at our new house, we got home to our old house, and my wife and I had a check-in conversation with each other. When we moved to our soon-to-be old house, it was definitely for the wrong reasons. Our marriage was struggling terribly back then. We weren't communicating right. We moved here partially for another couple who ended up cutting us out of their lives, and most of all, we weren't considering if this would be glorifying to the Lord. This current move we've been working on has all been about Him. We have accomplished so much in our marriage, we're raising our children in a godly home, and we're only three minutes from church now. We are excited to see the Lord's plan for us in our new home and community, and we plan on serving Him any way we can.

Even if we made a wrong decision, God still used that to teach us. He showed us what was far more important than our own desires. Wherever you are in your faith, God can use you. God can always take a bad situation and use it for good. When you think you're not good enough, just read through scripture and research all those He chose to do His will. Moses felt like he shouldn't be a leader, but God made it happen. He can always do it for you.

How can you live as you are chosen to be a follower of Christ?

MARCH 19

Faith and Works Go Forth

> What good is it, my brothers, if someone says he has faith but does not have works? Can that faith save him?
>
> —James 2:14

Anything in life involves work. Our families, our careers, but especially our faith. Words are nothing without action. If we profess to be a Christian, then it shouldn't be just something we say but something we do. We can't plant seeds in a garden with unfertile soil and expect them to grow without tending to them.

Many years past, I was that man who had the faith but didn't have the works to back it up. I was constantly bringing up faith, but I wasn't living it out. I was judgmental toward people, and I was living in sin. To sum up my faith back then, you could say I was acting like I was walking around with a "get out of hell free" card. Back then, I'm sure people looked at me like I was one giant hypocrite, and they were probably right. Nowadays, I try each day to let my actions be an introduction for my faith.

When folks see you acting different from others, they usually want to know why anyone would go against the grain in today's world. We mustn't just tell the world about our faith. We must show the world our faith through our works. The two will always go hand in hand to work toward living a holier life.

How can you use works to back up your faith?

MARCH 20

Always in Praise

> I will sing praise to the Lord as long as I live; I will
> sing praise to my God while I have being.
>
> —Psalm 104:33

Praising God is easy to do when you feel like you get what you want. The real test of faith is praising God when things don't go your way. Can you praise the Lord even in the midst of a crisis? It's easier said than done, but fear not, because it comes in time, and it's something we all need to do. We need to be aware that even in the worst times, God is still in control, and He always deserves our praise.

This week for our family is already a tough one. We're still in the process of moving, and we have to pack up the rest of our old house for the moving company on Saturday. We still have our normal schedules of work, our oldest daughter's preschool, and taking care of our younger daughter. On top of that, there's a little bit of normal sickness going on, and we're all exhausted and a little cross with each other. Along with all of that, we are truly blessed, and even when things seem very stressful, we're giving our praises to the Lord.

From the outside of the faith, some might say God isn't worthy of our praise, or He's punishing us or being hard on us. Absolute garbage! God always deserves our praise. Even when things seem hard or times are tough, that's what faith is about. Faith to know that His plan is greater than our own, and even if we're in the valley, He's waiting for us at the summit as He guides us there.

> How can you stay praising God even
> when life is hard or exhausting?

MARCH 21

What Not to Change

> For certain people have crept in unnoticed who long ago were designated for this condemnation, ungodly people, who pervert the grace of our God into sensuality and deny our only Master and Lord, Jesus Christ.
>
> —Jude: 4

This is one of the most important things in the faith. We are to change, not the Word! How many churches and folks do you know who have perverted the message to meet their own needs? The letter of Jude explicitly tells us that these people are going to face even more judgment in the end. The Bible is not to be changed no matter what the year is. Some think because of the direction the world is going that the Bible needs to change direction. They will be sadly mistaken in the end.

In my younger single days, amid all the hell I was raising, I did try to go to young adults' groups to try to be around people my own age who were also there to worship. I saw these exact kinds of people at both young adults' groups. Even when I was living in sin, knowing I was doing wrong, I still never tried to change scripture to meet my needs. Some of the folks at these groups were clearly changing the Word of God to fit their own agendas. Needless to say, I didn't stick around these groups.

As we move further into a world that doesn't want God to be a part of it, that's where we need to pull people back to the light. I heard a sermon by Alistair Begg today on this passage, and he said something like, "The gospel is come as you are, not stay as you are." How true that is that we should be changed by the message and not change the message to work around us. Let us be transformed by Jesus Christ instead of making Him out to be what we want.

How can you be changed by the message?

MARCH 22

When All Is Lost, One Thing Remains

And he said, "Naked I came from my mother's womb, and naked shall I return. The Lord gave and the Lord has taken away; blessed be the name of the Lord."

—Job 1:21

When you feel like all is lost, think of Job. Job lost absolutely everything and still remained faithful to the Lord. When we think of earthly things, there's a lot of those things we've become dependent on, but they aren't really necessary in the bigger picture. God just might be allowing those things to leave your life for you to focus on Him more.

I've lost a lot of things in my life—former jobs, former relationships, material things, and so on. As much as it hurt losing those things, some hurting more than others, His plans are far greater than my own. We hurt over those things because of our human nature and attraction to things that sometimes aren't necessarily godly. Job knew that and continued to stay faithful to the Lord, even when everyone around him was telling him to reject God.

When you think all is lost, everything is found. Even when we don't understand it, God is still in control. It's not always best to compare ourselves to others, but there are a lot of folks out there who have lost way more than you have and still press on. My wife's grandmother lost two sons out of her five children, only five months apart of each other, and she's one of the strongest God-fearing women I know. Faith is everything. Our Lord is enough.

How can you still view God as enough even in loss?

MARCH 23

Darkness Closes In

For evils have encompassed me beyond number; my iniquities have overtaken me, and I cannot see; they are more than the hairs of my head; my heart fails me.

—Psalm 40:12

Well, doesn't that sound depressing. If you think you can do it on your own without God, this should sound very depressing to you. You always hear people talk about "following your heart" or "what does your heart tell you?" Like the psalmist says, "The heart will fail you." What we need to be doing is following what God tells us.

I've felt the evil coming over me in years past. I've put myself there, that's for sure. They were things I've done over the years to get me further from God, and the evil was doing its best to get me even further. Even these days, sometimes thoughts alone are hard not to succumb to. There is still good in all that because we don't have to do it on our own. We have a loving God, with open arms, just reaching out for us.

The more these evils come closer, the closer we must run to the Lord. It's easier said and done, and some of these evils are very attractive. That's the thing about sin; it never looks unappealing. We all have good and bad days dealing with this. What's most important is that we cling to the Lord when these things sneak up on us. We don't have to rely on our heart when we have an Almighty God to serve who will never deceive us.

How can you turn this evil around by trusting God?

MARCH 24

The Greater Good of the Lord

As for you, brothers, do not grow weary in doing good.

—2 Thessalonians 3:13

Doing good according to the Bible can sometimes cause us to be tired. It can be very discouraging when you feel like you're trying to follow God's commands but the world is bringing you down. Stand firm in those commands because this life is gone in a blink of an eye, and eternity is so much longer.

Tonight was the last night in our old house. We'll be staying in our new home starting tomorrow, and it's been a crazy ride leading up to it. This move wasn't just a random idea or location. I changed direction a year and a half ago to get my family closer to our church. My wife and I weighed our options, and this has become the best place for us. We've been up late all week packing and getting ready for the movers tomorrow, and it has been very tiring. In a situation like this, it's important to remain strong in the Lord. This was a very prayerful decision we made for over a year, and now it's finally here. God has truly provided for us, and we want to give back to Him.

We don't always get exactly what we want, but when we put God first, we're living the life He's called us to live regardless of the outcome. We need to not live this life just to get rewarded but live a life on earth that we may live in eternity when we pass away. Do good every day and trust in the Lord.

How can you be encouraged over discouraged in doing good?

MARCH 25

One Like the Son

> Beloved, do not be surprised at the fiery trial when it comes upon you to test you, as though something strange were happening to you. But rejoice insofar as you share Christ's sufferings that you may also rejoice and be glad when His glory is revealed.
>
> —1 Peter 4:12–13

Praise the Lord! For even in times of trial and struggling, we can rejoice knowing that our Lord Jesus went through trials before us. It's easy in this life to get upset or angry at things that are very miniscule in the long run. Christ had anger, but He never sinned. Can we do the same? As hard as it may be sometimes, we definitely can.

I feel, in my own life, that sometimes I just want to be mad. The way people drive is enough to get anyone mad. When we let that anger consume us and get us thinking evil thoughts, that's when we must put a stop to it. We must silence our anger with prayer and carry on. If I had a dollar for every time I had evil thoughts about someone that I felt did me wrong, I'd be rich. That is nothing to brag about, and it's all the more reason to repent and not let our anger get the best of us.

As you've heard me say before, this life is so short compared to eternity. What's happening now won't even matter after we're in heaven with the Lord forever. It's so much less draining to just let go and let God be in control rather than hold on to our anger with a tight grip. Trade anger for prayer, and cast your burdens on the Lord.

How can you turn anger into a praise?

MARCH 26

The Lord's Day

> Remember the Sabbath Day, to keep it holy.
>
> —Exodus 20:8

It's a busy world out there. We all have our schedules and daily routines, and sometimes seven days a week isn't enough for the time we think we need. Whether the traditional Sabbath was Saturday or Sunday, we should strive to put a day aside for worship, reflection, and rest.

Sundays for me growing up were for church first and then family. The traditional American Sunday dinner is a great way to wind down the weekend and rest up for the week ahead. Now that I have my own family, I try to implement things like this for my own on this day every week. Being together as a family under the Lord is such a blessing.

Even when we're busy, it's very rewarding to keep this day set aside from our normal weeks. Some folks work on Sundays, and some just don't go to worship. I encourage all of you to set a day aside for worship and rest. Reflect on your days and reset the week for a better one next time.

How can you keep the Sabbath holy?

MARCH 27

Healthy Humility

> Do nothing from selfish ambition or conceit, but in humility count others more significant than yourselves.
>
> —Philippians 2:3

Humility is something everyone struggles with to an extent. If you think you don't, then you definitely do. It's okay that we're all a work in progress with this, but we should strive to be humbler every day. When we put others first, we're also putting God first. When we do things we think are good, we need to do them for the glory of the Father, not ourselves.

How many times do you see people do nice things for others, but they have to post on social media about it? It's not an uncommon thing. Some people love to help the homeless as long as they're recognized for it on a social media platform. This is not glorifying to God at all if you want to take all the credit for yourself. When we're putting the attention on ourselves, then what good is that to the King?

When we do these unselfish acts or lend a hand to those in need, let us think of ourselves as nobodies. We're all just nobodies who are saved by the Almighty God who definitely didn't have to save us. We sinned against God, and there's nothing we can do our own to get back to Him. Jesus is our only way, and that is a gift freely given to us when we don't deserve it. Let's give back and give thanks to God knowing that it's not us who deserves the glory. It will always be Him.

How can you remain humble and give God the glory over yourself?

MARCH 28

Blessed Be

> Blessed be the Lord, for he has wondrously shown his steadfast love to me when I was in a besieged city. I had said in my alarm, "I am cut off from your sight." But you heard the voice of my pleas for mercy when I cried to you for help.
>
> —Psalm 31:21–22

In the midst of trouble, the Lord is present. For those of us who believe, even when hope seems to be lost, we can still be comforted by the Spirit. Even when we feel like we've lost, our hope is not of this world. Earthly losses may occur, but in the bigger scheme of things, it's all right. Life goes on even in trouble. Even if you never fully get over something or someone, God's grace gives us the way to adjust to life without.

Today was our nephew's birthday. He turned four, but he celebrated his birthday away from all the family. He's in heaven because of cancer. I can't even imagine what his parents are going through with this unimaginable loss, but I do know what the scriptures say. That's a perfect example of something you'll never get over. You just have to trust God to get you through the remainder of your life where a piece will always be missing.

When we feel so distant from God as if we are cut off from His sight, we're really not. When a test is going on, the teacher is always quiet. It's time to draw as close to Him as we can and be steadfast in prayer. God is always with us even when we don't know exactly what He's doing. He loves us always even when we're going through a trial. Have faith that He has things under control.

How can you still trust God even in loss?

MARCH 29

Foretold Misfortune

> Thus says the Lord of hosts: Behold, disaster is going forth from nation to nation, and a great tempest is stirring from the farthest parts of the earth!
>
> —Jeremiah 25:32

We can't see the future, but we know what the Lord is allowing to happen because of scripture. If this verse doesn't hit home in today's world and make people believe, then I'm not sure what would. Look around at our world today. There's war, there's hunger, there's hurting. It's everywhere. No one in the secular world wants to say that it's a side effect of sin.

God never intended this world to be like it is, but He gave us free will to do good or evil, and unfortunately, too many choose to do evil with their free will. He knew that not every human would choose to do the right thing. In the end, the war is won by good. Whose side do you want to be on?

Thankfully, there's hope. Not everyone will choose to do evil, but those who walk the path of righteousness will find their strength in Christ. No matter what happens while we're on earth, good or evil, we're gifted our salvation for the life that really matters—life after death.

How can you have hope in disaster?

MARCH 30

Follow Me

> And He said to them. "Follow me, and I will make you fishers of men."
>
> —Matthew 4:19

Follow the Son. When the disciples were called, they gave up everything. Even back then, it wasn't an easy task, but when Jesus called these disciples, they just knew what they had to do. Most of the disciples were eventually martyred for their faith, but they held to truth that Jesus taught them.

My wife and I have been watching the show *The Chosen* about the life of Jesus and those disciples He called. There may be some things typical Hollywood added, but in the show, when He called Matthew, there was a lot Matthew had to lose. Matthew, the tax collector, was shown to be a man of wealth with Roman protection. In those days, it could've meant your own safety. Matthew didn't care. He knew that the life he was living needed to change. Christ calls out to him, and Matthew gives it all up for Jesus.

In today's world, there's not much verbal calling by God but more of a feeling that we get from the Holy Spirit. What are we truly willing to let go of to follow Jesus? It could cost us everything, including our lives. We know, through scripture, that the reward is far greater in heaven than anything on this earth could ever be. Follow Him and grow deeper in your faith. You never know where He'll lead you, but you'll be certain where you'll be after death.

How can you follow Jesus daily?

MARCH 31

Imperfect

Perfect to Change

> Jesus stood up and said to her, "Woman, where are they? Has no one condemned you?" She said, "No one Lord." And Jesus said, "Neither do I condemn you; go, and from now on, sin no more."
>
> —John 8:10–11

Christ didn't come to seek those who are perfect in their own minds. He came to call those who were clearly imperfect, even according to the world. This woman caught in adultery in this passage was to be condemned by other imperfect people. How crazy that just because one sins differently than another that certain sins deserve condemnation while other sins deserve a pass according to this world.

Too many Christians are deceived by a lie that Jesus was all about love. He came to teach us to abandon our old way of thinking and follow Him. Being a follower of His is about being changed from the inside out, not just following Him the way we are. Continuing to live in sin doesn't let the sanctification process proceed. It only keeps us from obtaining our full potential through Christ alone.

It's not all about just loving one another and staying the way we are. It's about a transformation that we go through developing and grounding further into our faith as time goes on. We must make a conscious effort every day to "Sin no more," as He puts it.

How can you be willing to allow God to change you?

APRIL 1

Strong and Courageous

> Only be strong and very courageous, being careful
> to do according to all the law that Moses my servant
> commanded you. Do not turn from it to the right hand
> or to the left, that you may have good success.
>
> —Joshua 1:7

When we think of strength, usually it's in a physical sense. The disciples and other Jews of the times thought that the Messiah was coming to overthrow the Romans and free the Jewish population of Roman control. They were looking for a different kind of strength than what Jesus came to do. He had much greater strength and courage than to just wipe out the enemies of those who follow Him.

To be strong and courageous, a lot of times, means being restrained to not let our emotions get the best of us. To not react out of anger, especially, is an evident sign of being strong and courageous. Being able to withstand the storm is a true test of this. By God's grace alone are we able to hold to this verse.

We must continue to stay on the straight and narrow path. When we don't retaliate. When we don't hate. When we stand firm in the teachings of the scriptures, we are showing courage and strength in this world. People of the world may not understand it, but they didn't understand it back in the days Christ walked the earth. What matters most is that God sees it. Let your actions reflect your faith and how great it will be when we're living in eternity with Christ.

*How can you be strong and
courageous in a biblical way?*

APRIL 2

Hosanna!

> And the crowds that went before Him and that followed Him were shouting, "Hosanna to the Son of David! Blessed is He who comes in the name of the Lord! Hosanna in the highest!"
>
> —Matthew 21:9

Palm Sunday, as we know it by. Jesus enters Jerusalem in His final week on earth before His death. Some of these same people who praised His entry on Palm Sunday will be shouting, "Crucify Him!" on Good Friday. Holy week has begun as we lead up to the cross, burial, and resurrection!

Following Jesus isn't always an easy task. Many of His own disciples had their struggles with following Him, and it led most of them into martyrdom. These people whose tune changed by good Friday are a perfect example of a lot in today's world. When things are going well, we trust God. When they are not going well, some will reject God.

As this holy week begins, let us focus on this love story and follow the Son. When He enters Jerusalem—dead, buried, and rising from the grave—let us continue to walk with Him every step of the way. Let us take time this week to reflect on His teachings and how He loves us so very much.

*How can you take time this week
to embrace this message?*

APRIL 3

The Mission

> Let these words sink into your ears: The Son of Man is about to be delivered in to the hands of men.
>
> —Luke 9:44

The disciples didn't know what He meant by this phrase, but the mission is about to be complete. During this holy week, it's imperative that we take the time to get to know Jesus even more. In only thirty-three short years on earth, He accomplished more than any ruler or king in history ever could have.

In today's society, this verse is still being done in a way. Individually, people trade Christ as their ruler for things of this world all the time. In biblical times, some of the people who saw the miracles and listened to Jesus preach still called for His crucifixion. There are many examples of people still doing that today. We set aside Christ for our own sinful nature to fulfill our earthly desires.

Our sin put the nails in His hands. He was pierced for our transgressions as it was foretold in Isaiah 53. As sad as it really is that He had to go through so much suffering, we can rejoice in knowing that He did it for us. As we walk to the cross this week, let us be ever thankful for what Jesus did for us.

How can you make this Holy Week about Christ?

APRIL 4

Iscariot

"The Son of Man goes as it is written of Him, but woe to that man by whom the Son of Man is betrayed! it would have been better for that man if he had not been born." Judas, who would betray Him, answered, "Is it I, Rabbi?" He said to Him, "You have said so."

—Matthew 26:24–25

Oh, Judas, you had it all. You were one of the twelve, and you blew it! Being one of the chosen twelve, Judas had the life most of us Christians today could only dream of when it comes to being face-to-face with Jesus in the flesh here on earth. Christ knew what Judas would eventually do, but Judas still had a choice.

In our day-to-day life, don't we sometimes betray Christ as Judas did? Have we ever blatantly sinned, going against God's Word when we clearly knew we shouldn't have? In the Gospel of John, the scriptures say that "Satan entered into him," meaning Judas. It doesn't get much eviler than that. We must keep watch to not fall into that same situation where we are being sucked in by temptation so bad. Pray to God and flee the devil.

Another thing we can learn from this is being betrayed by someone we love or a close friend. Jesus loved all His disciples, even Judas. Aside from the prophecy of Him being betrayed and heading to the cross, the fact that He was fully human, as well as fully God, meant He had emotions. He felt sadness, and I'm sure that moment of betrayal was one of His saddest moments. When we're betrayed by someone, I think it's important we forgive just as Christ forgave.

How can you trade betrayal for prayer?

APRIL 5

Healing Power

> The Lord sustains him on his sickbed; in his
> illness you restore him to full health.
>
> —Psalm 41:3

No one likes being sick, and it's a hard interruption to our normal schedules. It's important, while we have slowed down, to give God the glory, even in the suffering.

My whole family came down with something this week, and my wife and I got hit really hard with sickness. Even in this struggle, God is still good. There's still a lot to be thankful for either way. I know this will pass. Even if it's terrible right now, the Lord will get us through.

As you lay down tonight, whether well or sick, pray. Pray for those who are sick. Pray for those especially with terminal illnesses because God can still work miracles. The Lord is faithful even in the hard times. He always is.

How can sickness be used to glorify God?

APRIL 6

The End Is Near

And Jesus said to them, "See that no one leads you astray. Many will come in my name, saying 'I am he!' and they will lead many astray."

—Mark 13:5

You heard it from the Man himself. People, even in the ministry, have led many astray since biblical times. It's important to discern the scriptures and seek the right biblical council to weed out these false teachers who come with an agenda of their own that's not the Gospel.

In the summer of 2022, my wife's side of the family and us attend a week-long camp meeting. Every year, an evangelist comes to speak every night of the week. This particular year, there was one of the worst speakers I have ever had to sit through. This false teacher perverted the gospel and came with his own agenda that he made more important than getting the message across. We didn't even attend all the sessions because what he was preaching was definitely not biblical. It's sad that so many go this path to use the gospel for their own gain.

For those newer to the faith, it may be hard, at first, to discern right from wrong. When scripture makes you think, makes you uncomfortable, and makes you question your own life, that's how you know you're in the right place. Jesus even spoke about life on earth not being easy for those who follow Him. This life and these miniscule issues we have are nothing compared to life in heaven for eternity. Let's get through it serving Him and obeying His teachings and not worry about all the problems of this world.

How can you discern who may be leading you astray?

APRIL 7

It Is Finished

> Then Jesus, calling out with a loud voice, said,
> "Father, into your hands I commit my spirit!"
> And having said this He breathed His last.
>
> —Luke 23:46

The curtain has been torn in two, the disciples are in hiding, and darkness shrouds the earth. On that day, the feeling of despair His followers must have felt was pretty strong. They walked with Him for so long, hearing and obeying His teachings, just to see it end like this.

As Christians, I feel like sometimes we don't fully understand the severity of the crucifixion. Aside from the immense physical pain that Jesus went through, are we always grasping the true meaning? When Christ hung on that cross, He physically became sin. That's the sin for all of time. Those then and us now. Christ wasn't killed by man, but He freely gave up His life.

I pray you reflect on this day for what it really means. The greatest love story ever is about to take the biggest turn in history. Right now, His scattered followers probably thought they lost. They probably had their doubts and that they would be next. Satan was laughing with delight thinking he won, but Sunday is coming.

How can you take in the death of Christ for it's true meaning?

APRIL 8

Prophecy Fulfilled

> He was despised and rejected by men, a man of sorrows and acquainted with grief, and as one from whom men hide their faces he was despised, and we esteemed him not.
>
> —Isaiah 53:3

Oh, what would we do without the book of Isaiah? It was written around seven hundred years before the coming of Christ yet foretold His teachings and how the world would take Him. Prophecy isn't a word we think about in day-to-day life, even as Christians, but it's important to recognize all the prophecies that came true in scripture.

Jesus went to the cross to fulfill the promises God gave us. Even if He could have chosen a different path at any time, He willingly laid down His life for us. The people of the world at that time did reject Him and must have thought they were in control of His destiny. Even in today's world, that prophecy is still being fulfilled as people still reject Him today.

For us, when we're rejected because of His name, we can only count it as pure joy. People will hate you for many things, but if I'm going to be hated for something, then what better way than the name of Jesus. It doesn't matter in the long run if we are hated on this earth. All the disciples, except John, eventually went to the grave because they professed Jesus and wouldn't falter from their servitude to Him. Rejoice in knowing that those who have gone before you in the name are now in paradise with Him for eternity!

How can you see a fulfilled prophecy as a praise?

APRIL 9

The Best News Ever

He is not here but has risen. Remember how he told you, while He was still in Galilee, that the Son of Man must be delivered into the hands of sinful men and be crucified and on the third day rise.

—Luke 24:6–7

Alleluia! Christ is risen indeed! On this wonderful Easter Sunday, it's been a joy to celebrate the resurrection of our Lord. For all Christians, this is the focal point of the truth. Without the resurrection, it's all meaningless. Jesus conquered death itself! This means we will conquer death and rise again with Him in eternity.

When you truly get to know Jesus, you start to feel a way that you never would have as an unbeliever. Anyone can look at the bloody crucifixion and feel sorry about it, but not everyone is looking at as themselves being saved from death. Christ bridged the gap that was opened back in the garden of Eden by Adam and Eve as we refer to it as the "fall of man." Sin entered the world and left us hopeless.

Let Jesus restore your hope. May He be the Lord of your life. Only He can grant you what you are looking for. Even if you're not looking for Him, He is your way out of whatever situation you may be in, especially getting out of this world alive again. Christ is risen. He is risen indeed!

How can you make Christ the Lord of your life?

APRIL 10

Lord of All Creation

And the Lord God planted a garden in Eden, in the east, and there He put the man whom He had formed.

—Genesis 2:8

Back when the earth was fresh off the holy press, it must've been complete bliss. He created Adam to work that new creation. Can you imagine how beautiful it was? As Christians, we can look around anywhere outside and see God's handiwork involved. For those who don't believe it's impossible to deny a creator when you look around at the earth.

Today was a beautiful day in our area. I had the day off, and my wife took a short trip to the office. When she returned home, we took our two daughters to the local park to play. So many children and their parents were out enjoying all the sunlight and the fun. I myself could only rejoice and be thankful for a day out in the creation with my family. Our Creator is one excellent artist. What a blessing to be enjoying His creation.

We all need little reminders daily of God's presence. Being outside and walking in what He made is an excellent reminder that no matter how alone you may feel or how distant you may feel from Him, He is always with you. Even when we don't see Him, He's there. Think of the wind. We cannot see it but always feel its presence. If we tune our hearts to listen, we can always feel God's presence, especially in His creations.

How can you be reminded of God's presence by His creation?

APRIL 11

Let No One Stand against Me

> No man shall be able to stand before you all the days of your life. Just as I was with Moses, so I will be with you. I will not leave you or forsake you.
>
> —Joshua 1:5

When God makes a promise, He keeps it. So many days go by that we face challenges of many kinds, but here is our peace that God is with us. When God has a plan in mind for someone, we might wonder how it will be possible or what might get in the way, but it's all in His works. He will surely make a way.

In my own life, there have definitely been those I've encountered who I may have thought stood in my way or opposed me. Even in those troubled times, God was showing me that He's still with me. It's always been a struggle for me knowing that there are people who have deliberately tried to wrong me. Even I need daily reminders that no matter what anyone could do to me, they can never take away my salvation and peace I have in Christ.

So going forth, rejoice in knowing that God is with you. There's a much bigger plan at hand and as you live day to day. Even when dealing with those people who you may think are standing against you, there's a much bigger God standing with you to get you through. Be at peace with His plans for you and let Him guide you. Even knocking on death's door is only the beginning for those who believe.

How can you be at peace knowing God is much bigger than all those antagonists we face?

APRIL 12

Sin No More

> So whoever knows the right thing to do
> and fails to do it, for him it is sin.
>
> —James 4:17

We've heard Jesus say it in the gospels. "Sin no more!" He meant it when He said it, and now that we know what is sin, we must avoid it at all costs. Thankfully, we have those scriptures to show us the sins of this world and how we must avoid them. Temptation is everywhere, but once you know the doctrine, it's even more important to run as fast as you can away from those desires of the flesh.

In my younger days, I blatantly ignored the scriptures on certain issues. I justified my actions, in a way, by openly admitting the things I was doing weren't good for me. I didn't stop doing them, though. I only fell deeper into sin. I remember that on some Sundays in church, I knew the message was meant for me, but by the next Saturday night, I was living a life where one couldn't tell I was a Christian. Something had to change.

As you grow deeper in your faith, be rooted in the scriptures to withstand the winds of temptation that can easily surround you. As the world draws further away from God, it's all the more reason that we, as Christians, must cling as tightly as we can to Him.

How can you understand more what sin is?

APRIL 13

Social Mercy

> Therefore, the Lord waits to be gracious to you, and therefore He exalts Himself to show mercy to you. For the Lord is a God of justice; blessed are all those who wait for Him.
>
> —Isaiah 30:18

We hear constantly, in today's world, cries for justice. If people actually knew what that meant, they'd be begging for mercy. We live in a very divided America where some people want justice for certain groups for things that happened way in the past. That equates to no forgiveness. When we truly believe in the scriptures, God's got things under control. Who are we to be impatient and not let Him do His works?

I've noticed that even Christians have fallen into this trap of what the world calls social justice. We as Christians need to have nothing to do with this. We're called to obey the Lord and trust Him. There is always some action we can take, but that's our own individual action of being kind and being supportive of those in need. When we promote unforgiveness and fueling fires of the past, we're going against what God tells us to do.

What's the answer, you ask? When we're promoting love and peace and forgiveness, we're the real social justice warriors. What if we loved our neighbors a little more? What if we showed mercy to those who are different from we are? We're all created different, and we all deal with different things in life, but if we all read the same scriptures, there should be no division. Let's look to seek mercy rather than justice and wait on the Lord.

> How can you look more at mercy than
> justice dealing with today's issues?

APRIL 14

The Weight

> Brothers, if anyone is caught in any transgression, you who are spiritual should restore him in a spirit of gentleness. Keep watch on yourself, lest you too be tempted.
>
> —Galatians 6:1

Everyone in this world has different things they're tempted by. Even those in the church have different trials and things they struggle with that may be harder for them to deal with than others. What's important is to come alongside those with a merciful attitude and help them through it. Too often, churches get a bad name for being judgmental and too critical of folks that may be struggling with sin.

For me, I grew up in a youth group where this kind of negative unbiblical behavior was way too prevalent. I fell into temptation in high school with many different things. I knew that what I was doing was wrong, but I was so entangled in sin that I needed help getting out of it. I was met with great hostility when I came forth for help. Looking back now, I realize what a terrible example of the scriptures that leadership team was. Once I got out, I learned from their mistakes in the way I treat people.

We must continue to be kind and supportive. However, if someone is going in a direction that will be a temptation to your own walk of faith, it's important for us to know when to walk away or direct the individual to stronger biblical support than ourselves. We're all living in a broken world where many troubles will come our way, and us Christians need to unite for one another and not continue to divide the body of believers.

How can you be gentle with those struggling?

APRIL 15

The Celebration Continues

He said to Him the third time, "Simon, son of John, do you love me?" Peter was grieved because He said to him the third time, "Do you love me?" and he said to Him, "Lord, you know everything; you know that love you." Jesus said to him, "Feed my sheep."

—John 21:17

When Jesus rose from the dead, He paved the way for us and gave us a mission. Simply, "Feed my sheep," as He commanded Simon Peter. At the time, Peter might not have known what this meant, but he did just that as we read further into the New Testament. Easter may be over this year, but the celebration is never over.

Today we celebrated Easter at my in-laws' house. We had to reschedule because of sickness. Even though we're six days after Easter, it's important to remind ourselves that the resurrection is something to be celebrated every day. Christ's offering of Himself on that cross paid the price for all of us.

Rejoice every day for what Christ has done for us. Easter is something that, as Christians, we should be reminded of daily. We now can conquer death as Christ did and rise from the dead with Him. We will rise and be with Him in eternity in heaven. So feed His sheep and tell the world of this promise He has made and will keep for us. Keep on celebrating the wonderful news of Christ's resurrection!

How can you be reminded of Easter every day?

APRIL 16

Who Can Come?

But Ananias answered, "Lord, I have heard from many about this man, how much evil he has done to your saints at Jerusalem. And here he has authority from the chief priests to bind all who call on Your name." But the Lord said to him, "Go, for he is a chosen instrument of mine to carry my name before the Gentiles and kings and the children of Israel. For I will show him how much he must suffer for the sake of my name."

—Acts 9:13–16

When the Lord told Ananias that Saul was going to be called by the Lord himself, old Ananias sure had his doubts. It's easy for us to be subconsciously judgmental in today's world when it comes to who we think is a good Christian or who can be a Christian. God can truly use anyone to do His will. Even the worst of the worst like Saul, whose mission was to hunt down and kill followers of Jesus.

The kingdom has room for all those who believe, repent, and turn from their wicked ways to follow Jesus. At any point in time, someone can make that choice and have their slate wiped clean. Some folks are fortunate enough to be raised in a Christian home with a solid foundation from the start. Others may find Him later in life after they've lived a life of sin and have become aware of their wrongful way of life. Some even find Him on death's door like the thief on the cross who was crucified next to Jesus. It doesn't matter when your conversion occurs, just as long as it occurs before death.

So when we see those wicked people in today's world who slander the name of the Lord and His followers, it's important to realize that at any time, God could call them to follow Him. The Lord may just use you to bring them on board just like He called Ananias to minister to Saul. This is all the more reason that we need to live out God's commands in love and be an example for those who are lost in darkness. I know it's hard because even I fall into those judgmental thoughts about others, but I pray God uses me as well to help bring others to Him.

How can you be willing to minister to those evil folks in this world?

APRIL 17

When There's Nothing Else to Say...Praise!

*Oh, how abundant is your goodness, which
you have stored up for those who fear you
and worked for those who take refuge in you,
in the sight of the children of mankind!*

—Psalm 31:19

Sometimes we just don't know what to say to God. Whether good bad or indifferent, we don't always have something to say. It's important in those times to just praise His name. God is always good. Even when we are thankful deep down but don't really know how to say it, let us look to the scriptures for guidance.

It's easy to get too comfortable in life sometimes. When we feel like we don't have anything going on or we're not in need of anything at the moment, it's easy to forget to praise the Lord. Everything and every day, His blessings and mercies flow, and we must give credit where credit is due. God's goodness is truly abundant even when we don't realize it.

When we fear God and come to Him with a humble heart, we're praising Him. I pray all who read this can think of this verse as we all may forget to be submissive to the Lord on occasion. May we take refuge in Him always and encourage others to do the same.

*How can you take the time to
praise the Lord daily?*

APRIL 18

No True Atheist

> The fool says in his heart, "There is no God." They are corrupt,
> they do abominable deeds; there is none who does good.
>
> —Psalm 14:1

Here's a good lesson for sharing the good news with someone who calls themselves an atheists. There's no such thing as an atheist, first of all. For I am convinced that anyone who claims to be an atheist is still influenced by scripture whether they want to admit it or not. Everyone is influenced by scripture. People who talk about morality claim to be atheists. Where does one get morality from? Scripture! If atheists actually believed themselves, there would be no need for morality because there's no doctrine that prevents it to fall back on!

In my life, I've come across many people who call themselves atheists. When conversing with them about their beliefs, the bottom line is they either don't want to believe in God so they just deny His existence, they're mad at God for something that happened to them, or a Christian was mean to them so they deny His existence, or they truly just don't know if He exists so they deny His existence altogether. It's always one of those three things. If people truly did their research to try to disprove God's existence, they would end up believing in His existence.

So for us who do believe, it's important we treat these people with gentleness. Most of them have been wounded by believers, and that fuels their hatred for God. We can make a difference by showing them the true nature of the Gospel. God's love, God's law, Christ's teachings. When we truly know Christ, we realize He's everything we've been looking for. Don't be a fool, as the scripture says!

How can you minister to a so-called atheist with gentleness?

APRIL 19

I See Grace

> But he said to me, "My grace is sufficient for you, for my power is made perfect in weakness." Therefore I will boast all the more gladly of my weaknesses, so that the power of Christ may rest upon me.
>
> —2 Corinthians 12:9

No one likes to be considered weak. In our world today, it's all too common for people to be too power hungry, and weakness is not an option. On the contrary, weakness in us just allows God's grace to flow even more. We're to be humble and kept in check that God may take all the glory. We must be out of the spotlight. Grace is unmerited favor. God's pretty good at giving that out!

It's our nature to want to put the focus on ourselves. We subconsciously want power and to be in control. As Christians, to sum it up in one word, surrender. We must surrender those things to not be afraid of failure or weakness. In my own life, I'm weak at a lot of things. Some of these things have kept me down for a long time, but I am free in Christ. His glory will continue to increase in my life, and all the credit I give to Him.

It's not an easy path to walk, but we can remind ourselves daily of the grace that is shed upon us by Him. When we choose to follow Christ, let's put Him in the spotlight and step back. Our weaknesses will seem very small compared to the grace of Christ. He's got this covered, so rejoice in His grace and do not be afraid of your own weaknesses.

How can you embrace His grace?

APRIL 20

Prayer Power

> Is anyone of you suffering? Let him pray. Is anyone cheerful? Let him sing praise.
>
> —James 5:13

This verse is a constant reminder that in good and bad, God deserves our attention. Our prayers go a long way. We all know that God can take care of things deep down, but we do have our doubts on occasion whether He will or not. Regardless, lets lift those prayers and praises up to Him every day.

Over two years ago, a customer that I had gotten to know pretty well was diagnosed with a form of cancer. He's had other operations as well since then. When I used to deliver to the mill where he'd work, we'd always sit and have conversations over coffee. After getting to know him and hearing his story on the last day I was delivering there, before I went to a different route, I asked him if I could pray for him. I stood there in that dirty old mill office with my arm around him, asking God for healing and protection for him. Today we spoke, and he's cancer-free! In the midst of all his happiness, he thanked me for that prayer over two years ago. We both know who the real credit goes to!

Hearing of God's healing in His life got me thinking that this verse is an endless loop. When we suffer, we ask for healing. When we're healed, we praise, and then it repeats. Let's keep that in mind and always ask God for healing and praise His name no matter what comes!

How can you suffer and praise all the same?

APRIL 21

Yet to Come

Then the sixth angel blew his trumpet, and I heard a voice from the four horns of the golden altar before God, saying the sixth angel who had the trumpet, "Release the four angels who are bound at the great river Euphrates." So the four angels, who had been prepared for the hour, the day, the month, and the year, were released to kill a third of mankind.

—Revelation 8:13–15

Well, isn't that scary? This is why the time is now to be on the right side of history. Revelation is filled with the prophecy of the end times, but unlike other books of the Bible, it hasn't happened yet. It was only shown to the apostle John in a vision from God. When we dive into this book, it gets even darker for those who don't believe.

Strange things are happening in this world. These four angels in these verses were locked up under the Euphrates River in the Middle East. This very river has started to drain, and there's been video footage online of some sort of structure underneath. Noises were heard of moaning and rattling chains. It's easy for us Christians to look at this and compare it to scripture, but it's definitely enough to make an unbeliever think.

As you explore this book and God's prophecy and promise, may you be at peace being on this side of the cross, knowing what God has in store for us who believe and walk in His ways. The Lord is faithful in promise, whether it's good or bad. The good or bad part just depends on which side you're on.

How can you discern the knowledge of the end times and be ready?

APRIL 22

One Way Out

> No temptation has overtaken you that is not common to man. God is faithful, and He will not let you be tempted beyond your ability, but with the temptation He will also provide the way of escape, that you may be able to endure it.
>
> —1 Corinthians 10:13

As we've continued to talk about before, temptation is everywhere. For Christian folk in today's world, it's an even bigger burden to carry when we're trying to walk in the footsteps of Christ. It's an ongoing battle that we must be heavily guarded against. Temptation comes in all forms, and it's important to figure out what we are tempted by and how to avoid it. There's always room to run far away from it, but let's not get too close that we may be drawn in by whatever tempts us.

Today, after a union meeting with some of my coworkers, I felt myself being tempted to slip into some old habits. It made me think of times when I wasn't acting like much of a Christian, even though I always believed. I realized how easy it would be for me to fall way back to the mess I used to be. While nothing ended up happening today, I felt very uneasy about it, and I just knew that I am weak enough to make poor decisions if I ever end up in the wrong situation. That's conviction at its finest. Don't go down roads that are hard to climb back up.

The devil is everywhere trying to destroy you. He knows he's lost the war, but he will try to win every battle against God he can. It starts with destroying God's followers and leading us down paths that we shouldn't be on. Guard yourselves in the scriptures and praise the Lord daily. Avoid temptation at all costs and know when to run away. It's easier said than done sometimes, but it's not impossible. Don't give the devil any reason to pull you under.

How can you avoid situations where you might be tempted?

APRIL 23

One Small Spark

> And He said to them, "Go into all the world and proclaim the gospel to the whole creation."
>
> —Mark 16:15

The world is a big place with many people. Unfortunately, a lot of people just don't want to believe in the gospel, and it can be very discouraging to us to sometimes hold back from sharing the good news. Be that as it may, God commands us to go out into this world and share what we know. You never know who it might make an impact on. Sometimes, it just clicks with people who have lived very sinful lives. When some have seen the light, they become an unstoppable force for the Lord.

Today in church, we had a speaker from Ukraine come to preach. She was in an orphanage and received a box from Operation Christmas Child many years ago. It's a ministry that sends donated gifts to children around the world. She shared her story about how this brought her to Christ. Such a small act by those of us who send boxes, but a huge impact can be made on those who receive them. Her ministry today is all about keeping up with sending boxes and sharing the message.

So wherever you go, be reminded that many may hear the message just because you shared it with one person. There are endless opportunities every day if we tune our hearts to hear the Lord's command. Pray for courage and strength. Pray that the Lord makes you fearless to go out into the world and share the good news of Christ. You never know who He'll put in your path.

How can you go into the world with an attitude of preaching the Word?

APRIL 24

The Next Generation

> Remember your leaders, those who spoke to you
> about the Word of God. Consider the outcome
> of their way of life, and imitate their faith.
>
> —Hebrews 13:7

We're all taught the Word from someone. Most people don't have an "I saw the light" conversion. It often starts out slow when we're being taught by someone older and wiser in the faith. It's important we learn as much as we can from our pastors or youth leaders or any other spiritual leaders that we may teach the younger someday.

Growing up in a Christian household, I had the foundation from a very young age. While I don't remember a specific date or time for accepting Christ, I knew when I was old enough to understand faith. That's when it was my own. My own walk and not someone else's. For years, I did youth work. We went on mission trips, we had weekly meetings, and we had simple, unorganized, and spur-of-the-moment fellowship where I got to pour into kids what I had learned over the years.

When we know Jesus and we continue to grow more, then we need not hide it and pour into those who don't know Him. Everyone who comes to the faith comes at different points in their lives. We need to be open and ready to pass that information on, especially to those younger than us. When we all pass, we need a new group of Christian people to share the message after we're gone. Be open-minded in the way of looking for opportunities to share the good news with those younger than you are.

> How can you take time to be a Christian influence
> to someone younger in the faith?

APRIL 25

Jesus Loves the Little Children

But Jesus said to them, "Let the little children come to me, and do not hinder them, for to such belongs the kingdom of Heaven."

—Matthew 19:14

Children are a gift from God. I believe it's everyone's responsibility, especially the parents', to make sure these little ones know Jesus. Back in the book of Matthew, the disciples rebuked these children, but Jesus intervened. Everyone, big and small, no matter what age, deserves to know Jesus.

This afternoon, my wife and younger daughter went to visit my wife's sister and her family for dinner. I got to pick up our older daughter after work, and it was just the two of us at our house for the evening. My little three-year-old daughter loves the show *Listener Kids*. It's all Christian music for younger kids, and she is learning all these songs and loves to sing them all. We spent this evening singing and praising the Lord through these songs. For a three-year-old, she doesn't fully understand the faith yet, but we love it that she's on the path to the right foundation. It's a beautiful reminder to me as I hear her sing, "I am a C-H-R-I-S-T-I-A-N!"

For those of you who are parents, teach your kids young. Read them Bible stories, teach them those songs, and don't just pray for them. Pray with them. Kids want our attention, and what better attention to give them than interacting with them with godly songs and conversation. These little ones will one day be teaching their little ones, so introduce them to Jesus at a young age.

How can you introduce kids to Jesus?

APRIL 26

An Eye for Compassion

You have heard that it was said, "An eye for an eye and a tooth for a tooth." But I say to you. Do not resist the one who is evil. But if anyone slaps you on the right cheek, turn to him the other also.

—Matthew 5:38–39

Retaliation is something we all feel like we want to do when we've been wronged. We feel like we need justice and someone else needs to pay for their wrongdoings against us. It's pretty black and white and hard to avoid when it comes to the words of Jesus himself. Jesus actually goes on to tell us to love our enemies and pray for those who persecute you.

In many situations have I found myself not retaliating. Some of those have bothered me that I didn't, but in my heart, I know I did the right thing. It's easy to want to seek vengeance in some situations, but to walk in the path of the Lord, we must obey His commands. Let us not seek to be in own form of control, but let the Lord handle our oppressors.

This life, as I've said in previous entries, is so short compared to eternity. Nothing in this life will even matter anymore once we get to heaven. Those daily burdens and little meaningless situations really don't matter in the long run. Why get so upset over things we can't control? Trust in the Lord and walk in His ways each and every day.

How can you resist the urge to retaliate against someone?

APRIL 27

Not Our Hands but His

> Rejoice in the Lord always; again I will say rejoice. Let your reasonableness be known to everyone. The Lord is at hand; do not be anxious about anything, but in everything by prayer and supplication with thanksgiving let your requests be made known to God.
>
> —Philippians 4:4–6

This one will somewhat go along with yesterday. The Lord is faithful, so why should we worry so much? It's so easy to get anxious about things in today's world. We're slammed with so much excess stress, whether it be work, family, or any other drama that may come our way. Nevertheless, we need to immediately commit it to prayer. I think sometimes it's a love and hate relationship with those anxious feelings. We want to get better, but we also want to feel distressed. It may sound crazy, but I've encountered many folks like that, and I've been one myself.

In my own life, I've had many anxious feelings. I've always felt like I'm looking for the next best thing in life. Anxiety can be like swimming for the surface and the water keeps rising. You're almost there, but you're holding back in a way. These are things we need to let go of that are weighing us down. When we make decisions in anxiety, stress, or anger, they are never thought through completely. Prayer is our way out of our situation.

When we pray before we make a rash decision, because of whatever it may be, we start gaining peace. When we look at the bigger picture that God has given us, we react to things with a different outcome. We must be set apart from the rest of the world as

Christian people. One of the biggest things unbelievers will look at when it comes to Christian folk is how we react toward others in times when we feel we've been wronged. If you're like me, you've screwed up in this area. We can't take back things we've done or said in these situations, but we can always strive for a better tomorrow to make things right.

> How can you make prayer a priority in times of anxiety?

APRIL 28

Engage and Encourage

> He who dwells in the shelter of the Most High will abide in the shadow of the Almighty. I will say to the Lord "My refuge and my fortress, my God, in whom I trust."
>
> —Psalm 91:1–2

It's so easy to get discouraged in the secular world these days. Thankfully, we have our Bibles to read for that encouragement we need so bad. When we engage God's Word, we can get peace of mind through anything. Engaging the Word encourages us so when we engage others, we may encourage them.

It doesn't take much in this world to show a little kindness. As Christians, we want give people that same encouragement we have. As the verse says, God is our refuge, so why wouldn't we want to share that peace with others? I had an opportunity that the Lord laid on my heart to be that encouragement for someone today. I felt Him telling me yesterday there was something I needed to do for someone, and I ran with it. Even if those things we try to do for others aren't recognized by them, it is certainly recognized by God.

So in all you do, let the Lord be your refuge. Be encouraged by His Word and be willing to use it to encourage others. The Psalms are a beautiful book of God's promises. Read up and go forth. As you are taking in His Word, learn from it and share it. You never know who you'll encounter who really needs that refuge and fortress God has promised us in Him.

How can you engage and be encouraged by scripture to lead someone else there?

APRIL 29

Watch Your Mouth

> Let no corrupt talk come out of your mouths, but only
> such as is good for building up, as fits the occasion,
> that it may give grace to those who hear.
>
> —Ephesians 4:29

When we think of corrupt talk, many things come to mind. Swearing, cussing, dirty jokes, and the like are all things that weaken our witness. Those of us working in a secular workplace can have a big impact without even mentioning the gospel. It's how we carry ourselves. It's how we treat others and the words we use.

In my profession of being a union truck driver, the phrase "mouth like a trucker" is something that can get the best of us in the field. If I'm professing to be a Christian and everyone in the workplace knows it, then how am I any different if I join in the same language and actions as everyone else? I've been there on occasion, and it's always been instant conviction of me thinking, *You know, you shouldn't have said that.* Thankfully, there's grace, and we can strive for a better tomorrow with God's guidance.

When you are different in the secular workplace, people definitely notice. People want that peace that we have even if they don't know that the only way is through Jesus. Be an example and go against the grain at work and wherever you may be. When you don't talk bad about people behind their backs, when you don't complain constantly about the job or the boss, it will not go unnoticed. The tongue is very dangerous when used for the wrong reasons. Let's use ours to glorify God in our speech each and every day.

How can you think more before you speak?

APRIL 30

What's Next?

And when He had said these things, as they were looking on, he was lifted up, and a cloud took Him out of their sight.

—Acts 1:9

For the disciples who had walked with Jesus in physical form throughout His ministry, they had the commands, but I'm sure they felt a little lost without their teacher. These men were so privileged to be able to be a part of Jesus's ministry on earth, but they had to continue carrying the fire after He made His departure to heaven. Eventually, all of them, except for John, were martyred for their faith, but at that point, I'm sure it crossed their minds, *What's next?*

Fast-forward to our times and we see a world slipping further from God. We as Christians should strive every day to figure out what God has next for us. He is in control, and whatever is next is for His glory. Even when all the disciples were being murdered for their faith, they never faltered in their beliefs, and it didn't matter in the end because they knew where they were headed after death. Between life and death, though, we always wonder what's next. Discerning God's Word will help us understand His plans for us.

I personally get anxious about things. Starting another week is always something I get anxious about. The good old Sunday night blues, as I call them. Starting work for the week always seems difficult with whatever may be going on, but I know I'm not alone. I know there's a loving God who has the plans laid out for this life He's blessed me with. I will look at work as a blessing, not a curse. I will do my best daily to see where He's leading me. It's a hard thing to process sometimes, but the Lord is ever faithful in His promises. Let Him show you what is next.

How can you discern God's plan for what's next?

MAY 1

Don't Look Back

And He overthrew those cities, and all the valley, and all the inhabitants of the cities, and what grew on the ground. But Lot's wife, behind him, looked back, and she became a pillar of salt.

—Genesis 19:25–26

The Lord's angels gave strict commands to Lot and his family. Don't look back! There are certain things better left in the past, no matter how appealing they still may look. The city of Sodom was a place of sin. The folks in that town rejected the truth for an unnatural and ungodly way of life. I'm sure all that looked pretty appealing to them until the fire rained down from heaven. Lot's wife looking back reminds us that what's in the past can sneak up on us and try to destroy us.

Memories are something we all have, good and bad. Both can be harmful for us if we hold on too tight. When we look to the past, sometimes we are so engrossed with memory that it can hold us back from a brighter future. Little bits of the past that we learn from and use to grow help us for a better future. When we just dwell on those things and can't move past them, that is when it becomes a problem. When those bad memories sneak up from guilt or shame, God's grace is sufficient to remind you to think otherwise.

Rejoice for the good memories and learn from the bad ones, but don't look back as to want to be there instead of the present. The here and now that God has given us truly a gift. Be thankful for this season of your life, and if the Lord blesses you with another season in the future, be thankful then as well. Let God's plans for your future unfold, whatever has happened is past.

How can you protect yourself from the past?

MAY 2

Christian Stereotyped

> For what have I to do with judging outsiders? Is it not those inside the church whom you are to judge? God judges those outside. Purge the evil person from among you.
>
> —1 Corinthians 5:12–13

One of the most used phrases against Christians from unbelievers is "Do not judge." Here's your scripture that actually proves they're right. I hate to break it to you, but yeah, it's true. When it comes to those unbelievers, we have a huge responsibility but also opportunity. This honestly makes it so much easier when we take judgment off the table in witnessing to those outside the church. We just show love and share the good news. I think when you come to someone with the message without a condemning attitude, it's a lot easier to capture their attention.

A lot of us Christians get accused of being hypocrites, and here is a perfect example of why. I sure have, and I will admit that I once was this judgmental type. Just because I have repented of my sins and given my life to Christ doesn't mean I've never sinned. I've sinned, and I've sinned bad just like the unbelievers. The only difference is I've accepted the truth. I need a Savior. We are called to share the message, not judge them for their sin. That is the Lord's territory.

I just had a conversation today with a friend of mine who doesn't necessarily want to believe because of all the hypocrisy and threats of going to hell from preachers. While we don't want to be judged by others, let us in return not judge God based on the poor portrayals of the faith by man. The message is pretty simple when broken down. "Love God, love others, and try to be good," in the words of Phil Robertson. God will help you with the fine details.

> How can you keep judgment off the table when witnessing to an unbeliever?

MAY 3

Be Wise

Who is wise and understanding among you? By his good conduct let him show his works in the meekness of wisdom. But if you have bitter jealousy and selfish ambition in your hearts, do not boast and be false to the truth.

—James 3:13–14

Wisdom is something the world is truly lacking in. Unwise decisions are constantly made in society today. We must use our actions over words to show our wisdom. Some folks who may seem wise are only doing what they do for personal gain or their own agenda. Let us use our wisdom to glorify the Lord.

When we look at society today, there are a lot of wise people. So many scholars and academic folks seem to be very wise. When some of these people who don't know God use this wisdom for their own gain and point people on the wrong path, they are definitely being false to the truth. A poor uneducated man who knows the Lord is far wiser than a rich educated man who claims there is no God. Don't be deceived by status or wealth on who would truly be the wiser one.

Wisdom comes from the Lord. When we use the wisdom He's given us for His glory, we are giving back to Him for the blessings He's given us. When we use it for our own agenda, personal gain, or going against God, we are taking the truth away. Be wise in your freedoms, your choices, and your actions. Ask the Lord for wisdom in His way.

How can you use the wisdom God has given you to glorify Him?

MAY 4

Not of This World

> We know that we are from God, and the whole world lies in the power of the evil one.
>
> —1 John 5:18

You ever see some serious tragedies on the news and so many people always say, "Where was God?" God's right here with us, but He's allowed the evil one to have his power in this world. Most of the people you usually hear ask this question either don't believe or have very little faith. Our scriptures sent to us straight from above can give us peace of mind in any situation. This is why the world is as bad as it is. The evil one has a foothold in many folks' lives, even folks within the church.

It has always been a hard concept for me personally. I want people to think like me. I see people committing evil in this world, and it blows my mind how people can be so cruel to one another and not feel an ounce of compassion or pity for those they are cruel to. I also need to be reminded that the evil one does have power in this world, and he's deceived so many hearts since the dawn of time.

For us Christians, knowing this makes it simple for us. Don't be of this world, but prepare for the kingdom of heaven. For the day of the Lord grows nearer as each day passes. We just need to share the message and ask the Lord for us to be used to help save as many souls as possible. The evil one has a strong grip, and the sins he tempts us with don't ever look unappealing. He preys on our weaknesses, and in those weaknesses, may the Lord be our strength.

How can you walk in the light in a world ruled by the evil one?

MAY 5

Restoring Reality

> He drove out the man, and at the east of the garden of Eden he placed the cherubim and a flaming sword that turned every way to guard the way to the tree of life.
>
> —Genesis 3:24

Before Adam and Eve ate from the tree of the knowledge of good and evil, this world was exactly how God intended it to be. It was perfect! When they brought sin into the world for the first time, they were done. No more tree of life to eat from for to live forever. God's plans for us, however, are that we can live forever if we accept the gift of His Son.

Jesus isn't just in the word. He is the Word! Everywhere in the Bible, the scriptures point to Him. Without Him, the rest is just a nice story or guidelines we should try to follow. God restored our reality through Jesus's death, burial, and resurrection. We now can live forever with Him in eternity. We will all die in this life, but that new life goes on forever!

When you get discouraged or feeling down because of a situation, just remember God has the bigger picture. When Adam and Even sinned at the beginning of time, we are all still affected by. It's all the more reason, knowing that sin is forgiven, to do our best for Him.

How can you live differently in a secular world?

MAY 6

Surrounded by Believers

> And let us consider how to stir up one another to love and good works, not neglecting to meet together, as is the habit of some, but encouraging one another, and all the more as you see the Day drawing near.
>
> —Hebrews 10:24–25

What better place is there to be than surrounded by believers? Togetherness is something we sometimes lack in making a priority. Church on Sunday is great and definitely necessary to grow, but what about the rest of the week? It's hard to be around believers 100 percent of the time because of careers in the secular world and being out in public. However, are you spending too much free time with unbelievers? It might be time for a little self-analysis.

Today we had a birthday party for our younger daughter who will be two in two days. We hosted it at our house and had mostly family and a few close friends over. I looked around at everyone there. It was wonderful to see this little body of believers gathering to celebrate our little one. Being together as a body of believers, big or small, can do so much for any believer. Birthdays are once a year, but we are looking for even more opportunities to keep close in the body of believers so we may encourage others and be encouraged ourselves.

It's exhausting at times with work and family to add one more thing to our already busy schedules, but it's something we must make time for. Fellowship with other believers can go a long way. Over the years, I've weeded out pretty much everyone who wasn't good for me to be around. All those folks who don't want to take the message seriously can easily drag you down to a place you don't want to go. Be with those brothers and sisters in the body of Christ and be relieved of this world's issues for a while.

> How can you make meeting together with
> other believers a high priority?

MAY 7

Outbound Defiler

And He called the people to Him again and said to them, "Hear me, all of you, and understand: There is nothing outside a person that by going into him can defile him, but the things that come out of a person are what defile him."

—Mark 7:14–15

I would encourage you all to read the full passage to understand this even more. These verses can be confusing because even though many things go into our minds every day, it's still important to not fill our minds with filth. It's even more important to not be influenced by things that can come out as a poor example of the faith. We must be diligent that no matter what comes our way, we reflect Christ in our actions.

Working in the secular world, especially in a trucking environment, leaves a lot of room for the kind of filth you don't want to hear coming into your mind. When you hear these things that you sure can't unhear, what do you do? You don't engage in certain conversations. Just because you're hearing a certain kind of talk does not mean you should talk the same. When unbelieving men get together in a secular workplace, there's a lot of cussing and talk about women. Don't chime in and be like they are.

We should always guard our hearts and our minds with what we take in, but those things that we just end up hearing without warning are reminders of who we need to be. We need to be followers of Christ and not defile ourselves with things of this world. Sometimes it's hard to be who we're meant to be, but we must make the attempts daily to be set apart from the rest of the world.

How can you watch your words and actions as to not defile yourself?

MAY 8

Feed the Birds

> Look at the birds of the air: they neither sow nor reap
> nor gather into barns, and yet your heavenly Father
> feeds them. Are you not of more value than they?
>
> —Matthew 6:26

This passage is really about our worth in the sight of the Lord. If God takes care of our little winged friends in the air, then aren't we far more important to Him than the birds? When we worry, as this passage goes on to say, we're not gaining anything. We're causing ourselves unnecessary stress, and we need to put it in the hands of the Lord.

Today was the birthday for not only my wife but also our second-born daughter. I took off work to be with the whole family today. The four of us went to the aviary today to see all the species of birds. I always seem to stress myself out when it comes to the last day of a long weekend. I always think too far ahead about work the next day, and I'm usually distracted from living in the moment. What better a place than to be stopped in my tracks and reminded of this verse when I'm surrounded by birds.

So wherever you are in life, do not worry. I've struggled with this my whole life, and I need to be reminded of this daily. Enjoy the days God has given you, and don't miss out on those precious moments with your loved ones. One day, they may not be there. God is in control, and He loves us. Live and love better every day for Him.

*How can you put off worry to
live each day to the fullest?*

MAY 9

When You Were Young

Let no one despise you for your youth, but set the believers an example in speech, in conduct, in love, in faith, in purity. Until I come, devote yourself to the public reading of Scripture, to the exhortation, to teaching. Do not neglect the gift you have, which was given you by prophecy when the council of elders laid their hands on you.

—1 Timothy 4:12–14

This one goes out to the younger readers. If you were blessed to be raised in a Christian home, my prayer for you reading this right now is that you do not stray. When we're young, we think we know it all. We have most definitely thought at some point that we could do things better than the way we're being told. We might think otherwise even when it comes to scripture. Even when we're saved, we're still tempted by sin. Mistakes can still get made by us. It's important that we learn from those and come back into the light instead of drifting further away from the Lord.

I myself was fortunate enough to be raised in a Christian home. However, that all shattered for me when my parents divorced, my mother remarried a year later, and then we moved two hours away. My whole life was flipped upside down when I was heading into my ninth grade year of school. Even though I had the foundation, I was weak after everything I went through. I never stopped believing, but I stopped following and listening how I should. That time of my life set me on a path where I would continue to dig myself deeper into a hole for many years. Many years later was when I finally started climbing out of it and got to where I am right now, writing to you!

Not every day is easy. Temptation is still everywhere from what I used to be. Flooding my mind over the years with things that go against scripture can take a toll on anyone, even if they don't believe in scripture. I encourage all of you growing up in a Christian home. Trust God with your foundation. Build your future upon His promises and be steady as to not get dragged into sin that will drag you even further from the Lord. I always told my youth group kids back when I was in the ministry, "Learn from my mistakes before you make them yourselves!" By God's grace, even if you have screwed up like me, you will make it. He will make a way for you.

How can you keep a solid
foundation made on the Lord?

MAY 10

The Mark of the True

> Let love be genuine. Abhor what is evil; hold fast to what is good. Love one another with brotherly affection. Outdo one another in showing honor. Do not be slothful in zeal, be fervent in the spirit, serve the Lord.
>
> —Romans 12:9–11

We think of all these things that seem so simple but are so hard to do. Once we really dive into God's word, getting to know Him more and more every day, these things go back to being pretty simple. The thing about it is if we're truly upholding these verses, then people will see the light through us by our actions without us ever saying what we believe in. Walk the walk. Don't just talk the talk. True leaders lead by example, not just enforcing rule and law by mouth.

When we see leadership today on smaller scales such as workplaces or even churches, do we see real leadership? Are our leaders following these commands? If we all did these things, would the world not be a better place? We can't control others' actions, but we sure can control our own. True love is without condition. When evil is being done to you, do not retaliate with more evil and love even more because of it. When we love with that brotherly affection, there is so much power and encouragement in that. If we tried to outdo each other in honor, we'd always be striving to do better. All of this adds up to serving the Lord better each day.

In today's world, these are hard things to live by. Evil is around every corner, trying to get us to sway to the other side. Stand firm, my friends, and trust in the Lord to guide you. Serving God in this life and giving up those desires we have is a small price to pay for an eternity in paradise with Him.

How can you hold to these specific commands every day?

MAY 11

Pride Path to Destruction

> And he will spread out his hands in the midst of it as a swimmer spreads his hands out to swim, but the Lord will lay low his pompous pride together with the skill of his hands.
>
> —Isaiah 25:11

When we think of pride, a lot of things come to mind. The biggest problem with pride is that it's a feeling of pleasure or satisfaction from one's own accomplishments. Being too proud of what you're doing takes away what God is doing. When folks are especially proud of their actions that are completely unbiblical, that's when pride becomes even more of a problem. A prideful attitude lacks all humility. To be followers of Christ, humility is the name of the game.

What we have in life, as Christians, we know comes from above. The Lord giveth, and He taketh away, as scripture tells us. We can always strive to work harder, to be better providers, to have bigger houses, and so on, but when we don't acknowledge God's hand in all of that, we become too prideful. It's not our actions but the will of the Lord for us to have those things. This is where faith and works go hand in hand. Work hard to be successful in life, but don't stop having faith just because things are going well. It can all change in the blink of an eye.

Even in the Christian world, people can get too conceited. We saw it in the gospels with the Pharisees. The proud sit in church every Sunday, and some do not recognize their own sin in this area. It's a reminder we all need to hear. Seek humility and ask God to help you recognize the areas of life where you may be a little too proud. Show more of Him and less of yourself every day.

How can you be too proud about things?

MAY 12

Unashamed

> For I am not ashamed of the gospel, for it is the power of God for salvation to everyone who believes, to the Jew first and also to the Greek.
>
> —Romans 1:16

Living unashamed of the gospel takes great sacrifice. We must deny everything to truly follow our Lord. Today's world is a hard one to be unashamed in. Society wants to cancel Christians and silence us as much as they can. We see it all over the media and in the way people react to our faith. I think God's blunt message for us in all that is "Who cares? I am enough." This is all prophecy, and it's happening today just as the scriptures said. When we see this kind of cancel culture wanting to take us out, it's nothing that we can't be prepared for through scripture.

When we're out in public or around a group of people who don't believe it can be somewhat intimidating to bring up scripture, so many call it "offensive" or "intolerant," which couldn't be further from the truth. The narrative about us believers has been lies fed to people who believe them. We know that heaven is just around the corner for us, no matter what stage of life we're in. Why not live in a way that's pleasing to the Lord? Christ lived the ultimate unashamed life by laying it down for us.

Don't be afraid about what people will say. Some will hear the truth and mock it. Some will reject it. Some folks are even afraid of the truth, even if they won't admit it, and become very hostile when it's brought up. Those who live in darkness are scared the light will reveal their true colors. We have simple commands from the Lord to follow. Let's live this life unashamed of the Gospel and go forth serving the King wholeheartedly.

How can you strive to be unashamed in the eyes of the Lord?

MAY 13

Rest Stop

> Let us test and examine our ways, and return to the Lord!
>
> —Lamentations 3:40

Anybody here like to be wrong? I would safely assume not. Let's face it. When we're in the wrong, it's not always an easy thing to admit. We get caught up in our selfish ways that we just long to be right and make any excuse we can to prevent others from thinking otherwise. We sometimes hit every dead end possible and still don't want to admit we were wrong. How do we move forward without it? As Christians, the Lord is far more important than us being right about something that doesn't really matter in the end.

I'd like to say I have this figured out, but I sure don't. It's a learning process for me as well as to take a step back and examine myself. In dealing with any relationship, especially a marriage, this has to be done almost daily. When our ways truly aren't the Lord's way, then we need to be the ones to examine the error of our ways and truly return to Him.

Whatever life throws at you, be humble enough to examine yourself. When we don't look at our own wrongdoing and change, we'll start to see the effects of it eventually. We grow more miserable, we ruin relationships, and we stray further from God. All that being said, why do some folks still hold on to being right? We've all seen and maybe even been those types of people to an extent. Even if you've lacked in this in the past, every day is a chance to make it right.

How can you examine yourself daily to keep in check with the Lord?

MAY 14

Us and Them

So Peter opened his mouth and said: "Truly I understand that God shows no partiality, but in every nation anyone who fears Him and does what is right is acceptable to Him."

—Acts 10:34–35

Our pastor preached on this passage today. Our world we live in today is very divided. The sad part is that there are some groups of people who preach so much about diversity that it backfires in a way and makes people more divided. As Peter said in this verse, none of those backgrounds matter if they follow this command. People come from many different backgrounds because of race, religion, ethnicity, upbringings, and so on. It doesn't matter where we've come from. It's where we're going once we decide to follow Jesus.

For those of us believers, the biggest thing we have in common with unbelievers, from a spiritual perspective, is that we all need God's grace. With us and them both needing that, the only difference is that believers know they need it while unbelievers don't know. When we share the message with someone, we don't need to be the ones trying to change them. We need to share the message so the message changes them. This lays out easy instruction for witnessing to unbelievers. Follow Jesus. He'll do the rest.

We are not the judges of those outside the church. That's God's turf, and He'll deal with those people accordingly. We don't need to look at their past or present and cast judgment upon them. We're just called to tell them the good news about Jesus. We don't need to worry about their sin. We don't need to worry about their background. It doesn't matter what their politics are or sexual orientation or what kind of religious background they come from. God will handle all that. We just need to show them why they need a Savior and who He is. Jesus is the way.

> How can you focus on sharing Jesus without passing judgment on someone?

MAY 15

Highs and Lows

> But seek first the kingdom of God and His righteousness,
> and all these things will be added to you.
>
> —Matthew 6:33

In every season of life, there are high and low points. Even for me writing to you, this year has already had highs and lows. I often think of a heart monitor picking up a healthy heartbeat. There's a little give up and down, but not too much to be unhealthy. The same is true for our spiritual health. A little give is normal, but drastic or erratic changes are unhealthy. We must seek our Lord always to stay on a not so much shifting path.

When I was younger in youth group and also a leader as well, every year, we would take a week-long mission trip. It was always in July, and we traveled to other cities to minister to different groups of people. When we would come back, it would be a big spiritual high. We were always so pumped up and ready to take on our hometown to share the good news, but the high would eventually wear off. Some of us, myself for sure, would hit lower points than usual. It was like a crash and burn effect. Trips, as such, should be a step up in your faith, not just a week-long high that fades away with the wind.

Fortunately, we have it laid out for us by our Lord. We should be seeking His kingdom daily. This life is full of highs and lows every day. We must not be too high or low about anything. It takes balance in life, even in this. I've been the person who was on fire for the Lord on Sunday morning after I had just been drunk the Saturday night before. I look back and realize how big of a fool I was in those days. Keep things in close, and be consistent on how you live every day.

How can you keep your highs and lows close?

MAY 16

Death

The Beginning

> Do not marvel at this, for an hour is coming when all who are in the tombs will hear His voice and come out, those who have done good to the resurrection of life, and those who have done evil to the resurrection of judgment.
>
> —John 5:28–29

Death is looked at with so many different perspectives. Some people fear it, some people want it, and some people are at peace with it. The real peace of mind is Jesus when it comes to death. As He rose from the dead, so will we one day. We will all rise from the dead, but to face what? Well, that depends. If we chose to follow Him, it's pretty clear in scripture that heaven bound we go. It's those who don't know Him and have lived a life of sin that should truly fear death.

Being the giant nerd that I am, to quote Master Yoda, "Death is a natural part of life. Rejoice for those around you who transform into the force. Mourn them do not. Miss them do not." If we just replace the Force with Jesus, then this is perfect! We don't have to fear death or miss those who have passed that have given their lives to Jesus. We will all die eventually, one way or another. We don't know the hour it will happen, so being ready is crucial to get out of this world alive.

God's given us a true gift in His Son, Jesus. We have the free will to decide whether to follow Him or reject Him. God doesn't send anyone to heaven or hell. He's laid out the way for us to get to either one by our own decision. We're all in this world together, so showing more people the way to heaven is something we must strive to do as Christians. For what do we have in this life that can compare to greatness of heaven? As for me, I'm sticking with the truth. Heaven sounds like a much better deal, and to walk a life of restraint is a small price to pay to get there.

How can you be at peace with death?

MAY 17

Good, Bad, and Judgment

> For God will bring every deed into judgement, with every secret thing, whether good or evil.
>
> —Ecclesiastes 12:14

Every deed we do, good or bad, in secret or in public, big or small, will be brought to light by the judgment of the Lord. In our own lives, it's easy to think that the good will outweigh the bad. Unfortunately for us, only one bad deed has already outweighed the good. When Adam and Eve sinned against God, sin entered the world and condemned us all to death. Just one sin took it all away from us.

On the bright side, those sins were taken away from us. By God sending His Son, Jesus, to go to the cross to pay the price for our sins, our slates were wiped clean. God gives us many second chances in life. By His grace, we have daily opportunities to make things right with Him. This verse is a good reminder to be consistent in the way we live. When we behave the way we would in church throughout the week, we aren't putting on a face for anyone. We're living as we should be.

Thankfully, God's given us a promise that the final judgment will come down to one thing. Do we know Jesus or not? I think of the thief on the cross. His bad deeds were many, but Jesus said he could come to heaven. Others have done great deeds like giving to charities, helping others, and so forth. Even in all those things, that doesn't get you into heaven. Knowing Jesus is our only way out.

How can you live a consistent life?

MAY 18

Known by Fruit

> Beware of false prophets, who come to you in sheep's clothing but inwardly are ravenous wolves. You will recognize them by their fruits. Are grapes gathered from thornbushes, or figs from thistles?
>
> —Matthew 7:15–16

False prophets are a topic we truly can't get enough of. Today's world, just like back then, is filled with them. It's so important for Christians today, especially newer believers, to watch out for these kinds of people. Most false prophets are in the ministry for themselves. I've personally experienced people like this who have a lust for power and control. They twist the scriptures and try to use God as a weapon to get others to do what they want them to do. We must always be humble enough to seek biblical council from those wiser than ourselves. We just need to make sure we're hearing true biblical council.

I've been around many church folk my entire life, and I can tell you that not all of them were good. I found myself right in the middle of a church divide, and one of the two men doing the dividing was my youth leader at the time. This man used youth ministry as a means to control others. Most adults were beyond being controlled by him, but many of the youth took what he said, hook, line, and sinker. He wanted to know every detail of everyone's lives, and many youth left the group over his behavior. Most of the many youth who left the group eventually stopped believing. He may have been the only example of church they'd ever been a part of, and now most of them turned away. Someone like this focuses way too much on the law and not the love of God.

So when we see church leaders acting like this, it might be a good idea to find another church. Never settle for someone who focuses on too much law without love or too much love without law. That's just one example, but there are too many others out there. When you see a thriving church with a Bible believing and preaching pastor, that is where you want to be. Let us also be known by our fruits too. How we treat others, how we behave in the secular world, how we speak. The list goes on. We want to show others God's glory in us that we may reflect Him.

> How can you show others who
> you are by your fruits?

MAY 19

Church outta Church

> For where two or three are gathered in my
> name, there am I among them.
>
> —Matthew 18:20

Organized Sunday worship is a wonderful thing. It gives us time to learn and grow in our faith. When we're part of a good Sunday school class or we hear in-depth sermons being preached, we know we're in the right place. We know that we're growing in our faith when we're a part of a good Bible-believing church. However, that's only on Sunday mornings for normal church worship. For some of us, that may be all we can do as far as getting together with other believers is concerned, but we should definitely seek a way to be in fellowship and the Word more than just Sunday mornings.

My best friend was over tonight on a last-minute invitation. We have both known each other for over a decade and have continued to bounce off each other for encouragement in our faith. After we had dinner and our girls went to sleep, he, my wife, and myself went to our basement and had a wonderful time covering many topics of discussion. Amid the model trains running in the background, we dove deep into biblical conversation about almost every big subject going on in the world today. We're always in church on Sunday mornings, but this is a great example of fellowship and encouragement outside of church.

Wherever you go, you find believers. Sometimes you don't have to look very far. Even if you meet a complete stranger who's a believer and you share a word of prayer, you are gathered with them in the name of the Lord. We as believers should really seek to be involved with other believers to be in fellowship throughout the week when we're not at church. We all need encouragement, and we all need to be reminded to follow God's commands. Someone on the same faith level as you and someone who isn't afraid to gently remind you when you're wrong is a true believer.

> How can you make time for fellowship
> on a weekly basis?

MAY 20

The Church Has Left the Building!

> For you were called to freedom, brothers. Only do not use your freedom as an opportunity for the flesh, but through love serve one another.
>
> —Galatians 5:13

Our freedom in Christ is something we should take great care of. We have a greater responsibility to use the freedoms God gave us to give back to Him. When we use our freedoms to gain things of the flesh or glorify ourselves, we're only losing opportunities to serve God. If we take the gifts that are given to us and live a life pleasing to the Lord, we are much more successful than living a life to please ourselves.

Today was our annual Church Has Left the Building Day. It's an outreach day into the community where we volunteer our time and our talents to serve God by serving others. We gave out free lunch and delivered furniture. Some made blankets, and others did projects inside the church. It's a wonderful time to be together as the body of Christ and serve Him by our work. I got to go clean windows with another church member at an elderly church member's home. She doesn't get to church much anymore, and she's in her nineties. It may not mean so much to most, but it was greatly appreciated by her.

Wherever you are in life, no matter what's going on, be the church outside of the building. Even though this church event was a one-day-per-year thing, we as Christian individuals can go out into the world and serve the Lord any day. It doesn't have to be an organized event. In our everyday lives, the Lord gives us opportunities to minister to others and serve Him. The body of believers have a charge to look for was to serve Him daily.

How can you be the church in the world?

MAY 21

Idolatry in Impatience

> When the people saw that Moses delayed to come down from the mountain, the people gathered themselves together to Aaron and said to him, "Up, make us gods who shall go before us. As for this Moses, the man who brought us up out of the land of Egypt, we do not know what has become of him."
>
> —Exodus 32:1

This refers to the golden calf the Israelites made to worship while Moses was up on the mountain receiving the Ten Commandments. The Israelites, who had already seen God's promises, grew tired of waiting. They waited through the enslavement of the Egyptians, which the Lord got them out of, but they felt they should do this their own way. They were impatient in the Lord's timing and thought their way would be better. Does this sound familiar? It should.

In our world today, people don't melt their gold and make something up to worship. They do it in other ways. It's so easy to get caught in idol worship in everyday life. Our lives our constantly busy, and we all have our responsibilities and commitments, but it's almost too easy to put that ahead of the Lord. When we think of our youth who have dreams of being professional athletes who may miss church regularly and fall farther from the Lord, this is only one example of things that can become idols in our lives.

When we don't put God first and we try to fill our voids with things of this world, we will never truly be fulfilled. It's okay to have responsibilities, interests, or hobbies, but we must not let those things become our idols that take us away from growing closer to our

Lord. Set apart time for Him daily, as hard as that may be, and gain knowledge and understanding through His word. Seek Him first and do not gain a false comfort from things of this world.

How can you discern what may
be an idol in your life?

MAY 22

Shifting from the Truth

> The fear of the Lord is hatred of evil. Pride and arrogance
> and the way of evil and perverted speech I hate.
>
> —Proverbs 8:13

In our world today, sin is no longer done in secret. On the contrary, it's paraded down the streets to be welcomed with open arms by society. As Christians, we must stand firm on God's teachings to be able to discern right from wrong. Some, unfortunately, have welcomed sin even into the churches. It's a terrible thing to be using the word of the Lord to steer folks in the wrong direction, but it does happen far too often.

I've come across many people in the world who are enslaved by many different sins. I, too, was once one of those people. One of the biggest misconceptions with sin is that all sin is dealt with in the same way. While sin may be sin no matter how big or small, there is a huge difference between struggling with sin and accepting sin as normal. When someone is legitimately struggling with sin and seeking the right biblical help for it, that's normal and the right way to go about it. Too many folks, even church leaders, have thrown out certain scriptures to meet their own sinful needs. It's the same as the garden of Eden when the serpent questioned Eve, "Did God really say that?"

So what are we to do? I especially think of those new and impressionable to the faith who may not know better just yet. It's important that we seek the right biblical council and find the right church to be in. We must be seeking church leadership who preach the whole Bible and not leave out things that are crucial in today's world. Pride, arrogance, and perverted speech are a deadly combination for a false doctrine. It's so easy to get tangled up in a mess like that, especially in a church. Be guarded in the Word and guided by the Spirit to stand firm on the teachings of the Lord.

> How can you be on the watch for pride, arrogance, and perverted speech (especially in church)?

MAY 23

Guiding Light

And the Spirit said to Phillip, "Go over and join this chariot." So Phillip ran to him and heard him reading Isaiah the prophet and asked, "Do you understand what you are reading?" And he said, "How can I, unless someone guides me?" And he invited Phillip to come up and sit with him.

—Acts 8:29–31

When Phillip met that Ethiopian eunuch, the Spirit gave him instructions. Phillip was supposed to share the good news of Christ with this eunuch. The eunuch was reading from the prophet Isaiah, which is the foreshadowing of the gospel. He needed Phillip to guide him through the scriptures to be able to learn what he was reading. We all need that guidance from people who are wiser in the scriptures than we are.

The people in our world today who mock Christianity and try to disprove it or cut up the words clearly just don't understand the message. Anyone can read the Bible and misinterpret it to make it say pretty much anything they want. When anyone with an open mind seeks the right biblical council and understanding in reading the scriptures, it would be hard for them not to believe. We must come to folks in love in sharing the good news and present the message in a way they can understand.

Everyone is learning when it comes to the Bible. Some of us may have studied it for years, while others may be opening it for the first time. What's important for us who have gained knowledge is that we share the correct doctrine to guide others to the truth. False prophets are everywhere, perverting the Word. We always want to steer others in the right direction of our faith.

How can you be a guide to the scriptures for someone new to the faith?

MAY 24

The Grand Illusion

Therefore God gave them up in the lusts of their hearts to impurity, to the dishonoring of their bodies among themselves, because they exchanged the truth about God for a lie and worshiped and served the creature rather than the Creator, who is blessed forever! Amen.

—Romans 1:24–25

    The lusts of our hearts rarely look unappealing. In a world today drifting further from the Gospel message, it's easy to be caught up in our desires and be tempted to disobey God. As a Christian in the world today, there's much to be done to guard yourself from trading the truth for a lie. There are always people we're around with who would love to drag us away from the truth. We have a huge advantage, though, as we don't have to be close with those types. Even on our smartphone's temptation can easily creep up on us.

    Over the years, my circle of close friends has gotten smaller and smaller. I've realized that having church friends and secular friends is a hard balance. My wife and I now have a very small circle only consisting of believers. It's easy to hang out with folks who are like-minded as you. When we invest time in those who refuse to believe and want to drag us to their levels, it can be more of a trap that gets us further from the truth. God calls us to share the good news with these people, but we are not obligated to be around someone who doesn't want to make the necessary changes in their life. He will do the rest once the seed is planted.

    Friends, go out into this world with the truth in your heart and be willing to share it with those around you. Take time to step back and look at your own life as well in the areas where you've fallen short of keeping the truth. As I'm writing this to you now, I think of some of the times I disobeyed. When we do it our own ways and not God's way, we end up worse off in the long run. Even if something may make us temporarily happy, it's a false happiness if it goes against the truth. Stick with the Word, obey God's commands, and walk the line while you're on earth. There's a much better reward in store than what could come out of this world.

How can you stay true to the scriptures?

MAY 25

Children of God

> Behold, children are a heritage from the Lord,
> the fruit of the womb a reward.
>
> —Psalm 127:3

"See what love the Father has given us, that we should be called children of God." Our pastor makes that statement after every baby baptism in our church. I always say it with him while I sit quietly in my seat. It's a beautiful reminder that our little ones are such gifts from above, a true blessing created by our Lord. Even the tiniest form of a child within his or her mother's womb is one of the greatest gifts anyone could ever receive.

Today was our oldest daughter's end-of-the year presentation for preschool. The preschool is actually part of our church, and it's the same one I went to when I was younger. To see our daughter getting the foundation of Christ taught to her at a young age is a great blessing. As she learns about our Lord in school, we as parents are reinforcing those teachings at home as well.

This world is such a corrupt place that children need a strong foundation from the beginning. When we raise our children in a Christian home and keep them active in the church through Sunday school and youth group, the more knowledge they will gain of the message. As parents, we only have eighteen short years with our children before they graduate high school and head off into the real world. How we direct our children in that short time will affect the outcome of their future. We hold a great responsibility in raising these little ones right. Even if you don't have children of your own yet, you can still be an influence in leading kids to Christ.

How can you teach kids about Christ?

MAY 26

Wrong Road

> There is a way that seems right to a man,
> but its end is the way to death.
>
> —Proverbs 16:25

How many times do we make big life decisions without prayerfully considering them first? It's something that we don't always think about, but we need to keep ourselves in check and do things God's way. It may not always be black and white or an easy choice to make, but we must be willing to surrender our ways to His. Try as we might, we don't always make the best decisions for ourselves with our worldly views of understanding what may be best for us.

We tend to think we have it all figured out. We play out scenarios in our heads of what we think our lives should be like. We're manifesting something in our minds that can eventually let us down if it doesn't happen. I've wrestled with this throughout my life where I want something so bad but don't put God first in making a decision. It's easy to make decisions that only benefit us and don't necessarily glorify God. We must constantly be mindful of our actions and where our choices might lead us.

When we end up on the wrong road, we may find a very superficial happiness temporarily, but in the long run, we won't be fulfilled. I myself have made countless decisions over the years that have put me on the wrong road and led me to pain and suffering. We need to keep our eyes on discerning the Lord's plans for us and not falling into our own ways which may not be good for us.

How can you walk the Lord's path over your own?

MAY 27

Leave the 99

> What man of you, having a hundred sheep, if he has lost one of them, does not leave the ninety-nine in the open country, and go after the one that is lost, until he finds it? And when he has found it, he lays it on his shoulders rejoicing.
>
> —Luke 15: 4–5

When something is lost, even if you have many of whatever it is, you only care about the lost one at the moment. God cares about all His followers, but every time someone who is lost and without Him comes into the faith, there is much rejoicing to be done. I've had opportunities to pray that prayer of salvation with folks, and what a feeling that was to see a soul get saved firsthand. We as Christians need to be willing to leave those who have heard the message and turned to Christ and go after those that are lost. It's easy to stay within your comfort zone of Christian friends, but we need to be willing to reach out to those who don't know Christ yet.

Today, unbeknownst to us, our youngest daughter went out the back door, down the deck steps, and up the driveway out into the street. My wife and I thought the other one was watching her. We got a knock at the door from our neighbor, and it was a police officer who just happened to be driving by when our little lady escaped. She's only two and obviously had no idea where she was going. As scared as we both were when we found out, we were so relieved that she was safe. God protected her in that time when we didn't even know she was out of the house. The one that went missing was found, and there was much rejoicing to be had in our house, even if we still felt a little sick over the situation!

The people of this world are all meant to follow God and spend an eternity with Him. Unfortunately, some don't believe it, and some just don't want to believe it and will reject it in a very hostile manner. God wants all His lost sheep to be found. We as Christians have a big responsibility to lead the lost to Christ and rejoice when they are found in Him.

How can you minister to the lost?

MAY 28

Step by Step

> But I say, walk by the Spirit, and you will not gratify the desires of the flesh. For the desires of the flesh are against the Spirit, and the desires of the Spirit are against the flesh, for these are opposed to each other, to keep you from doing the things you want to do.
>
> —Galatians 5:16–17

How do we walk in the Spirit when the flesh is tempting? More than likely, if you want to do something that goes against the Spirit, it's probably looking real good. Sin is something that is rarely unappealing. If we could see sin in an actual form, it would probably look pretty ugly or sick. When we walk with the Spirit and understand those things that aren't good for us, then may we stay as close to the Spirit as possible to avoid these things of the flesh.

Everyone struggles with something. It doesn't matter what it is or to what degree the struggling is, but everyone has their own cross to bear. When it comes to those things we are tempted by, we need to know how to avoid them. God leaves us a way always, but the closer you get, the harder it is to find that way out. Some things can be addictive, no matter what they are. Statistics say that when someone tries heroin for the first time, they can become immediately addicted. I believe that can be the same for a lot of other temptations in this world. I lost a cousin to that specific temptation of heroin. I myself would never touch it, which made it no temptation for me, but to him, it had him hooked all the way to the grave.

We're all different in what can tempt us and pull us into the flesh away from the Spirit. We need to avoid these situations that can get us into those things at all costs. The Spirit is our guide. May we strive every day to be closer to Him and become less of the flesh.

How can you walk in the Spirt every day?

MAY 29

Love Forever

> Greater love has no one than this, that someone
> lay down his life for his friends.
>
> —John 15:13

The first thing that comes to mind with this verse is probably military related. Today being Memorial Day this year, we are remembering those who gave their lives for our freedom in America today. Generations past and present have paid the ultimate price to keep us free. That's the kind of love God wants us to have. When Jesus gave His life up for us on the cross, He paid the ultimate price for our sins so that we could be free and that the gap between us and God could be closed.

People give their lives every day protecting others. When we value someone else's life more than our own, we walk in the footsteps of Christ. The love that He gave us, by giving up His life, is something we should be willing to do for others. We could never amount to the impact that He made on the cross, but we may end up in a situation where we will save someone else by giving up our own life. It's scary to think about and somewhat unlikely that we will find ourselves in those situations. I think as Christians, we always have to be willing and ready if the time comes, and we're never going to be fully ready.

As believers, we know for us that departing this world just means an eternity in heaven with Jesus. Our earthly lives may pass, but a heavenly life awaits us for eternity. Do not fear death yet greet it as a friend when it comes your way. Even if you find yourself losing your own life to save someone else, that's the kind of love Jesus wants us to have.

How can you be willing to lay down your own life to save others?

MAY 30

Roll with the Changes

> God is not man, that He should lie, or a son of man, that He should change his mind. Has He said, and will He not do it? Or has He spoken, and will He not fulfill it?
>
> —Numbers 23:19

In an ever-changing world, we must be conscious of what does not change. God's promises and His faithfulness to us never changes. We may not always get the answers we want. We may be suffering and not see His greater plan for us, but rest assured, whatever we're going through is going to be part of His plans for our life. We may not understand it while we're going through it, and some things we may not ever understand. Have faith, friends, and be comforted knowing God's plans are greater than our own.

Things change throughout life. The four seasons are a simple reminder of change. Today was the day we closed the sale of our old house. We lived there three and half years, and this marked the official end of an era. For the buyer and her little girl we met today, this marked the beginning of a new era for them. Even though we couldn't wait to be fully moved into our new home, it was somewhat bittersweet to be finally saying goodbye to the first home we bought. It was a much-needed change for our family, but God remains constant in it all.

Whatever season of life you may be going through, God is with you. Change isn't always easy, but if God never changes and we are with Him, then what should we fear? No matter where you are in life, some sort of change is inevitable. The important thing is that we put our faith in the One who never changes and always has our best interest in mind, even when we don't see it.

How can you be strengthened in faith by change?

MAY 31

Unclean No More

> While He was in one of the cities, there came a man full of leprosy. And when he saw Jesus, he fell on his face and begged him, "Lord if you will, you can make me clean." And Jesus stretched out His hand and touched him, saying, "I will; be clean." And immediately the leprosy left him."
>
> —Luke 5:12–13

According to the law of Moses, lepers were unclean. To make matters worse, one could become unclean by being around a leper. Society back then would've shunned people with leprosy for fear of catching it themselves. When Jesus healed this man with leprosy, He made him clean of his disease but also showed us how we are made clean through Him in the eyes of God. Our true cleanliness comes from Christ's sacrifice on the cross. He paved the way for us to be clean of our sin.

We often subconsciously judge who we think is clean or unclean in our society according to what scripture tells us. The problem is, we are not the judge. Regardless of what anyone has done, he or she can be made clean through Christ. Everyone gets a chance on planet Earth to accept Him as their Savior and Lord so they may be resurrected with Him. We were all unclean of sin, whether we recognize it or not.

You will meet a lot of people in your life. Some will get it, and some won't. Some will embrace the truth while others reject it. What's important is we share the message with those who don't know the truth and let God do the rest. We can live clean pleasing lives to Him, or we can live dirty self-pleasing lives. The reward for a clean life is far greater than a dirty one!

How can you embrace the cleanliness you have in Jesus?

JUNE 1

At the Cross

So Pilate, wishing to satisfy the crowd, released for them Barabbas, and having scourged Jesus, he delivered Him to be crucified.

—Mark 15:15

Right before Christ was led away to be crucified, this was Pilate's predicament. Do the right thing or do the easy thing. Pilate chose the easy way out. It is said that the same people who welcomed Jesus into Jerusalem were calling for His death. Even if Pilate could've done what was right, or even before that, if Judas would've done what was right, the cross still needed to happen. Everything points to the cross.

Throughout scripture, everything must come down to Christ's death, burial, and especially His resurrection. Without all that, the rest of the Bible is only just simple guidelines that don't really have the depth they would need without the cross. When we go through scripture, especially when sharing the good news with others who haven't yet heard it, we must bring everything to Jesus and the life He lived. The cross is ugly yet beautiful. It's a reminder of the pain and suffering our Lord had to go through so we don't have to. Eternal life and being raised from the dead with Christ only comes because of what He did on that cross.

I'm always reminded of the season of Easter and how fun it can be, especially now that I have children. It's important, though, that we not lose sight of what happened in biblical times to give us Easter. We need to keep that Easter message alive and well and be reminded of it daily. The battle was won that day not by fighting but by surrendering. We must surrender to Christ daily. Let us look to that cross with thankfulness and a stronger desire to follow the one who paid the price for us. Jesus.

How can you be a witness to others bringing the message down to the cross?

JUNE 2

Ain't No Good Life

> I have said these things to you, that in me you may have peace. In the world you will have tribulation. But take heart; I have overcome the world.
>
> —John 16:33

The age-old conundrum that the world just doesn't understand. Who could ever have peace in tribulation? Even for us Christians, it's sometimes hard to have that peace, but Jesus gave us all the answers we need. It's not going to be easy, but it becomes easier to get through when we have that peace of Christ. I could not imagine living in this world and not having the peace of Christ. The peace people think they have without Christ is all an illusion.

Things of this world will try to pull us away from God. It becomes more evident as the days go by that the world is trying hard to go against God and His people. We hear of this cancel culture trying to silence the name of Jesus and all of Christian people. When we see this happening, it's hard not to be discouraged, but in an even more powerful way of thinking about it, Jesus foretold of this in His teachings. He was rejected by the people of this earth, and so are we.

Fear not, friends, because this story has the happiest ending of any story. Christ has already overcome this world. All He wants is us to make the choice in our free will to follow Him. One day, everyone will confess the name of Jesus whether they planned to or not. Let us do our best to follow Him even in times of this tribulation the world puts us through.

> How can you have peace in this world during tribulation?

JUNE 3

Fish

> When they got out on land, they saw a charcoal fire in place, with fish laid out on it, and bread. Jesus said to them, "Bring some of the fish that you have just caught." So Simon Peter went aboard and hauled the net ashore, full of large fish, 153 of them. And although there were so many, the net was not torn.
>
> —John 21:9–11

I've always found this to be some of my favorite verses in the Bible. Being an avid fisherman most of my life, I've always thought that if I didn't believe in Christianity, this would be the verses to get me hooked! Who wouldn't wanna have a fish fry with our Lord? Even if we can't have a meal with Jesus in person today, we should always make Him the head of our time together. Whether it be a meal or a get-together or doing something fun, let us let Christ be the head of our groups.

Today I had the chance to get out and do a little fishing. I always keep the "fishers of men" verse in mind. Today I got a chance to share the gospel with an Indian fellow who practices Hinduism. The fishing was secondary at that point, and it was time to share the news of Christ. In his religion, Christ is just considered another deity, but not the only one. He was somewhat receptive, and I am keeping in touch with him. God gave me an opportunity to be unashamed and share the message. After that, I got to talk to another Indian couple who were third-generation believers. His father ministers in India passing out Gideon Bibles. We fished together and talked faith while we filled their bucket with the fish we caught. They already heard the good news, so the least I could give them was some fish!

For me, when it comes to my passion of fishing, I imagine what it must have been like for those disciples who were fishermen to be able to fish and eat with Jesus. I find fishing a wonderful way to witness to others. When we have interests or hobbies in our lives, it can be a great way to minister to others. No matter what kind of group or activity you participate in, God is calling you to use those passions as a way to minister to others. Everyone needs to hear the message, and we all, as believers, can use what we have to relate and connect to different people. God gave us gifts and talents, and this is just one way we can use them to serve Him.

How can you use your passions, hobbies, talents, and gifts to share the message with others?

JUNE 4

The New Reality

> Flee from sexual immorality. Every other sin a person commits is outside the body, but the sexually immoral person sins against his own body. Or do you not know that your body is a temple of the Holy Spirit within you, whom you have from God? You are not your own, for you were bought with a price. So glorify God in your body.
>
> —1 Corinthians 6:18–20

This is a big one that most people don't like talking about. However, if scripture makes you feel uncomfortable, then it's doing what it's supposed to do. We are called to recognize and come to terms with our own sin, and sexual sin is so widespread in today's world. When we sin against others, it's bad enough, but in this case, we're sinning against our own bodies. If Christ paid the price for us and the Holy Spirit has come upon us, then our bodies truly are a temple of God. Why should we continue to defile them with sexual sin?

Sexual immorality is not limited to just one way or act of sex. Many acts in today's world can fall under sexual immorality. I had a conversation with someone today about a subject that fits under this. This person said it was "the new reality." That couldn't be further from the truth. This so-called reality we're living in is not the right way of doing things. People are blinded by their emotions to think that sexual immorality isn't that bad. Almost as if they think it's not hurting anything. Sex was designed by God as a gift to husbands and wives within the boundaries of marriage. Anything unrelated to that is sexual immorality. It's black and white, yet so many people, even in the churches, feel the need to change that.

No matter the year, God is still God, and His Word rings true. It's easy to just accept a person's sin and have nothing to say as they go on sinning. What's difficult is to challenge them to sin no more and make the necessary changes in their lives to repent and go the direction God wants us to go. These people are not to be despised; they are to be loved. Christ loves them just as much as He loves us. We're all God's children, whether we accept it or not. Let us pray to be courageous enough to help those out of this sin that can easily ensnare people and blind them from the truth. That's what really being an ally in today's world is.

> How can you be guarded from sexual immorality and help others out of it?

JUNE 5

What a Friend We Have in Jesus

> But now thus says the Lord, He who created you, O Jacob, He who formed you, O Israel: "Fear not, for I have redeemed you; I have called you by name, you are mine."
>
> —Isaiah 43:1

Oh, does that lyric ring true. What a friend we truly have in Jesus. Jesus came to call us as friends through His teaching, life, death, and resurrection. Of all the different faiths in the world, there has been no greater love story than God coming down in human form as His Son, Jesus, to offer His life up for us. God came to get down on our level and relate to us as friends. It's often hard to relate friendship with God, but when it comes to worship, would we relate better with a deity that's a malicious dictator or a loving friend?

Getting to know Jesus is everything when it comes to our faith. Without Jesus, the scriptures would be nothing but good rules to follow. In my own walk of faith over the last few years, it's become more evident that I need to get to know our Savior more every day. I need to walk in His footsteps and follow His teachings. It's not always easy, but it's so rewarding when we buckle down and look toward what He wants for our lives.

It's not always going to be easy. Jesus tells us in scripture several times that it will get difficult to follow Him. We must be willing and ready and always be faithful to Him no matter what. When we look at what the disciples went through as a cost of following Jesus, we can see that they followed Him all the way to their own deaths. Can we ever imagine what they are doing in paradise with Jesus now? They may not have fully seen it back then, but they sure see it now as will we someday.

How can you view Jesus as a friend?

JUNE 6

Working for the Lord

But if anyone does not provide for his relatives, and especially members of his household, he has denied the faith and is worse than an unbeliever.

—1 Timothy 5:8

No one always likes the work they do, and work is definitely not spelled F-U-N! Work is a necessary part of life. Even most of those outside the faith work and provide for their families. How would we look to the world if we don't want to work or can't hold a job do to our own lack of discipline? God has given us all gifts and talents to do something with. When we use those to make our livings and provide for our families, we as Christians must give all the credit to the Lord. For those of us working in the secular world, as most of us are, God can use us just as much as people in ministry. We're all called to minister no matter where we are or what we do.

We live in a society today where every politician up for election makes a pitch about creating jobs. The problem is, a lot of jobs are out there, but people don't want to do them. In my field as a union water delivery driver, I've seen so many people come and go in the short five and half years I've been working there. When it comes to laboring with our hands, not everyone wants to do that. I didn't attend college, and this job fell into my lap ten years after high school. I have had good and bad times there, and when I wanted to throw in the towel, God was whispering, "Stay a little longer. I'll work it out." And He did! When we put our faith in Him, especially when we work, He's working things out for us.

When I first got married, I wasn't the best provider. I was working two part-time jobs and drinking my money away. After four months of a strained marriage and sinking financially, a change had to be made. I started at my current job three weeks later, and here we are today. God is there to help you through the hard times. When we make the steps to live according to scripture, He's there to guide us. It's not always easy, and the answers we want aren't sometimes the ones we get, but God always knows best.

How can you work in the secular world still holding to God's teachings?

JUNE 7

Sleeping in the Spirit

> In peace I will both lie down and sleep; for you alone, O Lord make me dwell in safety.
>
> —Psalm 4:8

Rest is something we don't always get enough of, and eventually, it can catch up with us. This is a good reminder that we need to be taking care of ourselves to be ready to do our Lord's work. We often need a full recharge to reset ourselves and get the rest we need. Sometimes that only happens when we reach full exhaustion and are forced to slow down. You moms out there especially need your rest. My hats off to all that you do.

Sometimes between work and responsibilities at home and kids and everything else that takes up our time, we become overloaded. We're running on fumes and don't even know it sometimes. Our whole family felt that this week. We're all sick with something this week, and it's been a struggle to keep our chins up. Even in these times, when we wonder what God is doing, He is still faithful. God is still looking out for us even when we don't feel it.

So whatever is going on your life, make time to rest. Sometimes we need it more than we know. Take the time get recharged and pray for rest from the Lord. With Him in our lives, He is all the rest we need.

How can you make time to rest in a busy world?

JUNE 8

Just Faith

> Now faith is the assurance of things hoped for, the conviction of things not seen. For by it, the people of old received their commendation. By faith we understand that the universe was created by the word of God, so that what is seen was not made out of things that are visible.
>
> —Hebrews 11:1–3

We don't always have the answers. The world tells us we just blindly follow. Faith is all we need, though. When we have that conviction in our hearts of what the Lord has done for us, then we don't need to see to believe. We can see through greater understanding in scripture. When we dive into the word and really break it down verse by verse, it's a good way to enforce our faith learning more about God's word.

What can we do to strengthen our faith in this world? Being involved in church and Bible study are two things that will really help. This world tries to tell us all kinds of lies, and we must be grounded in scripture to combat the lies of the enemy. Faith is also that peace of mind we have knowing we need not worry about those things God has already taken care of.

So wherever you are in your Christian journey, have faith. It's easier said than done sometimes, and we often have our doubts to what God is doing, but He has our best interest in mind. Keep fighting the good fight every day, and keep your faith strengthened through scripture, prayer, and accountability. Just like the wind moving through the air, we cannot see it, but we see its effects. Just like God who we cannot see, but we see His effects. Keep the faith, friends.

How can you strengthen your faith?

JUNE 9

Authority Always

> Be subject for the Lord's sake to every human institution, whether it be to the emperor as supreme, or to governors as sent by Him to punish those who do evil and praise those who do good. For this is the will of God, that by doing good you should put to silence the ignorance of foolish people.
>
> —1 Peter 2:13–15

Authority is everywhere that we must submit to. When we obey the law of the land and submit to authority in whatever situation, we're ultimately submitting to God's authority. We know as Christians that his authority is most important, so we need to try our best to submit to authority on earth here. We all have teachers, bosses, church leaders, and so on that we are subordinate to. A true testimony of our faith is submitting to those authorities.

Some folks can do this no problem, and others will struggle with this all their days. We need to recognize where we are with authority. Are we respecting and submitting? Are we just being defiant? Do we think we know better? I know, at times, I've had to answer yes to all three of these questions. It's a hard think when we don't always trust our leadership, but if we're trusting God, then what do we have to fear?

So wherever you are in this area of life, you're probably a work in progress like me. God's giving us daily chances to get better at this, and we can always trade our ways for His. It's not always easy submitting to someone who we probably know better than, but that's all the more reason to trust God that He's going to take care of it and make a way for you.

How can you work on respecting authority?

JUNE 10

Does It Matter?

> What causes quarrels and what causes fights among you?
> Is it not this, that your passions are at war within you?
> You desire and do not have, so you murder. You covet
> and cannot obtain, so you fight and quarrel. You do not
> have because you do not ask. You ask and do not receive
> because you ask wrongly, to spend it on your passions.
>
> —James 4:1–3

If we just flip on the news or look at social media, we will see these quarrels taking place. Most of the time, these quarrels are meaningless, and it's just the passion to be right that has people so angry that they have to get the last word in or belittle someone else online because they don't have to face them in person. Ultimately, people are fighting because they don't know God. If we do know Him and we are acting like this, then how are we any better?

We mustn't let our passions get in the way of our relationship with the Lord. It's okay to be passionate about certain things, but let's just keep in mind that these things come from God, not to take His place. When some of these things start getting in the way and we want to hold on so tight, we must ask ourselves if these things really matter or not. Nothing matters that much if it is something that will interfere with your relationship with the Lord.

Passion isn't always a bad thing. It's a tool that can be used for good or bad. When we pray, pray that we'll be passionate about growing closer to God. Passionate about learning scripture better. Let us not fight like the unbelievers who don't know God. May we be the examples out there to share the good news by our actions. When we obey and do the right things according to this scripture, people will notice. God's followers have made Him look bad generation after generation. We still will, but will we recognize that and push on to do the right things? That's what really matters.

How can you discern when passion is in the wrong direction?

JUNE 11

Time Flies

In the morning sow your seed, and at evening withhold not your hand, for you do not know which will prosper, this or that, or whether both alike will be good.

—Ecclesiastes 11:6

Time is such a tricky thing. No matter what we do, we can never catch it, and it's always slipping away from us. For our time on earth God has blessed us with, let us use it well to give back to Him. God didn't create us to be lazy, nor did He create us to work ourselves to death. We are to have balance between work and rest and the most important things in the middle, our relationship with Jesus and then our loved ones.

I've never been good at managing my time as well as I'd like to. My career doesn't have set hours, and as I have a commercial driving position, I could be done a different time every day. Fortunately, it's usually early afternoon, which gives me a lot more time to spend with my wife and children than most people in a job like mine. With my wife working from home and my somewhat shorter schedule, it's easier to manage work, followed by family time and household responsibilities, and ending the day with a strict bedtime for all of us. Sometimes it doesn't always go how we planned, but sometimes we need a little change.

God sure has blessed us with time, and we need to make the best of it while we have it. One day, it will all be gone. We don't know the hour or the day, but it will come. Let's live that out daily to our Father in heaven to thank Him for the gift of our time He's given us. Let us love one another more as well, even those distant family members we might not be close with. Work, rest, and love always. Get to balancing that every day and see the gradual improvements in your life. God is with you.

How can you balance your time right to please the Lord?

JUNE 12

He Knows

The woman said to Him, "Sir, give me this water, so that I will not be thirsty or have to come here to draw water." Jesus said to her, "Go, call your husband, and come here." The woman answered Him, "I have no husband." Jesus said to her, "You are right in saying, 'I have no husband'; for you have had five husbands, and the one you now have is not your husband. What you have said is true."

—John 4:15–17

In those days, the Jews and Samaritans didn't really associate with each other. This woman at the well, who lived a shameful life even for Samaritans at that time, had to come during the day to get water to avoid ridicule from others for the life she was living. She had a lot of shame to hide. What a perfect time for our Savior to be there to help her turn this life around. The living waters He spoke of was the perfect attention-getter!

Sometimes in our own lives, we come across people who we can tell are struggling or searching just by having a short conversation with them. We don't need to know every last detail about them to know that they need Jesus, and they need Him bad just like we do. God knows the true depths of their hearts and minds. We need to be loving and judgment-free toward them to be able to share the same good news that Jesus shared with this woman at the well. It doesn't matter what kind of past someone has had. What matters is what they are going to do about it for a better future. A true healing can only be found in Jesus.

So when you're out in public and have that opportunity to strike up a conversation with someone to share the message with them, don't worry about what they've done. It's not for us to be the judge but to show them the way out of whatever kind of life they may be living. Everyone who doesn't know Jesus is full of shame from the life they are living, whether they will admit it or not. We just need to show them how they can live a life where they don't have to feel that way. They need the Way—Jesus.

> How can you share the message with someone
> without making them feel more ashamed?

JUNE 13

Reserved Freedom

> Therefore let us not pass judgment on one another any longer, but rather decide never to put a stumbling block or hindrance in the way of a brother. I know and am persuaded in the Lord Jesus that nothing is unclean in itself, but it is unclean for anyone who thinks it unclean. For if your brother is grieved by what you eat, you are no longer walking in love. By what you eat, do not destroy the one for whom Christ died.
>
> —Romans 14:13–15

Freedom to do many things in Christ comes with a lot of responsibility. Some of our freedoms must be reserved for certain crowds or company. Some folks may not be okay with certain freedoms being exercised around them. We need not be the ones to cause these folks to stumble in their faith. If we as Christians are causing other Christians to stumble in their faith, then how are we any better than the rest of the world? There are enough unbelievers out there who want to tempt us and want us to fail. That's the kind of behavior we should stay away from.

I think this all ties in with the different temptations we all have too. Some Christians drink alcohol responsibly, and most don't find anything wrong with that. Some others, however, might have been alcoholics at one point, so should we put that temptation in their path by drinking around them? Certainly not! If that is something you do responsibly, you are free to do it, but be prepared to give up that freedom if a situation arises where you are around someone who may struggle with it. These boundaries we need to set for ourselves on occasion are meant to strengthen our witness and overall unity with one another of the faith.

So whatever you do in life, be conscious of how it could affect another believer. Let us not be the reasons for one another to stumble. We must be encouraging and uplifting to one another especially through our actions. When we set limits for our freedoms by using biblical principles, we have everything we need. Too much freedom can eventually backfire and have the opposite effect. We can be free to make the right choices and be the right examples, but we don't want to end up slaves to sin or our own desires that lead us and others down wrong paths. Be there for one another, and live lives pleasing to the Lord.

> How can you hold back some of your
> freedoms when a situation arises?

JUNE 14

There's Always a Choice

Jesus answered them, "Did I not choose you, the twelve? And yet one of you is a devil." He spoke of Judas the son of Simon Iscariot, for he, one of the twelve, was going to betray Him.

—John 6:70-71

We don't often feel sorry for Judas, who made the greatest mistake in all of history because of his own selfish desires. Judas still could have made the right choice no matter what happened. It would have ended up being someone else that betrayed Christ. To think that Judas was lucky enough to walk the earth with Jesus and be a part of His ministry. He was one of the twelve apostles, and that would have been an amazing privilege to have. Nevertheless, Judas made his choice over his love of money. No matter how involved someone is in the faith, whether it's just going to church or being a part of a ministry, it doesn't matter if the foundation of the individual is not solid in Christ.

Over the years of my volunteer work in youth groups and camp ministry, I met so many different people. I stood alongside some of the people sharing the gospel with kids, leading Bible studies, memorizing scriptures, and trying to build off each other to strengthen our faith. Some of those people now don't believe at all. They made their choices, and you have to wonder, was their faith ever really there at all? Who would make the choice to trade the key to salvation for a lie unless they never really believed at all? I pray that these folks find their way back to Jesus, but they have to be the ones to make that choice.

When it comes down to us as individuals and our own walks of faith, we must be in a constant state of self-analysis. We always have the choice whether we are going to truly follow Jesus or not. When we keep on the righteous path and stay away from sin, we're making the right choice. We don't want to ignore God's teachings for our own desires just to get a thrill, especially when we know the truth. We always have a choice to turn back to Jesus even up to the very end of our lives, but why wait until then? We're not guaranteed tomorrow, so make that choice to follow Him today and never look back!

How can you choose Jesus daily?

JUNE 15

Torn Down to Rebuild

> Then the word of the Lord came to me: "O house of Israel, can I not do with you as this potter has done? declares the Lord. Behold, like the clay in the potter's hand, so are you in my hand, O house of Israel."
>
> —Jeremiah 18:5–6

Throughout life, we make mistakes as human beings. We tend to go down wrong paths and then have to backtrack and go down the right path. We exhaust ourselves with our own desires, only to realize the Lord's way is better than ours. Like the potter with the clay, the Lord needs to mold and reshape our ways of thinking. When the clay is still soft if a mistake is made, it's easy to rework it and start again. The harder it gets…well, the harder it gets. When we become hardened in our own ways, the harder it is for us to get back on track.

Sin can easily entangle us. I struggled with certain sins for years, and it took a long time to be able to come back down the path I should have been on all along. The further we get down the wrong path, the further it is to break those bad habits and sin that we have got ourselves into. God is there for us the second we turn around, but it takes a lot of work to get back where we need to be. We must be steadfast in prayer and scripture reading and have faith to get back on the path where God wants us.

Humble yourselves, friends. Don't be too devout about anything unbiblical that you aren't willing to change. Anyone can be reshaped and have a fresh start if we trust in God to guide us and let go of those things that are trying to keep us misshaped. Sin is hard thing to deal with, and it tends to cloud our vision as to what is right. Cling to the scriptures and ground yourself in prayer. Have faith because it does get easier.

How can you recognize when you need to be reshaped?

JUNE 16

I Am the Church, You Are the Church

What agreement has the temple of God with idols? For we are the temple of the living God; as God said, "I will make my dwelling among them, and I will be their God, and they shall be my people."

—2 Corinthians 6:16

One song our pastor loves to lead us in goes like this: "I am the church, you are the church, we are the church together. All who follow Jesus, all around the world, yes, we're the church together." It goes on to say, "The church is not a building, the church is not a steeple, the church is not a resting place, the church is the people." Tying this song into this verse is to tell us that we as individuals of the faith are the church. It's not just a place we go. It's a conscious action we take when we go out into the world every day.

Being the church isn't always easy. It's not about standing on the street corner with an open Bible preaching to everyone who walks by. It's about having the courage to stand up for our faith no matter where we are. We want to be ready, willing, and able to share the good news of Jesus with anyone who is willing to listen. We need to lead by example and let our actions do the talking more than anything. Being in that church building every Sunday, surrounded by believers, is a great and necessary thing for our faith to grow. We need to take what we learn and go out into the world with it.

We're only in church for a couple hours on one day of the week. What are we doing with the other six and a half days? God is calling us to be the light in this dark world out there. We need to seek Him and His teachings every day and look for those sweet opportunities to go out and actually be the church every day. We may not always feel we're ready for that, but God can use anyone to get His message out there. Could it be you today?

How can you be the church in the world today?

JUNE 17

Attention Please

"If they will not believe you," God said, "or listen to the first sign, they may believe the latter sign. If they will not believe even these two signs or listen to your voice, you shall take some water from the Nile and pour it on the dry ground, and the water that you shall take from the Nile will become blood on the dry ground."

—Exodus 4:8–9

When God wants your attention, He will get it regardless. When the Israelites were enslaved in Egypt, Pharaoh's heart was so hardened that he needed these signs to get his attention. When he still refused, he faced the ultimate pain of losing a child. God got his attention then, and he let the Israelites go. When he still wouldn't listen after that, he lost his armies to the Red Sea.

Flash forward to today and look at those things that we go through in life, but sometimes we still won't turn back to God. I've met a lot of people who live hard lives but won't even take the chance with faith to make their lives even easier. Some folks struggle willingly. They won't turn back to God even though we, as Christians, can see all the signs. God is loving but also jealous. He gives us the free will to reject or receive Him. I'd much rather receive Him for Him than to reject Him and risk His wrath.

Whatever kinds of struggles we all may be going through, just know that they are not in vain. We have a Savior who wants us to choose to follow Him no matter what we are going through. Only through Him can we truly have peace by giving Him our attention as best as we can. It's not an easy thing, and sometimes we can be mad at God for what we're going through. When that is the case, we must be willing to surrender to Him and cast our burdens on the cross. He's there for us always through the good and the bad.

> How can you tell when God is
> trying to get your attention?

JUNE 18

A Father's Love

*And I will be a father to you, and you shall be sons
and daughters to me, says the Lord Almighty.*

—2 Corinthians 6:18

For Father's Day, I'd like to look at our heavenly Father who has called us all His children. As a father myself, it's a great yet very rewarding responsibility. Children are a gift from God, and it's our duty as men to be the spiritual leaders of our families and be the examples of the faith God has called us to be. It's an everyday affair once you have a family. No matter how tired or burned out you may feel, you must press on toward fighting those spiritual battles around you to keep your family grounded in the Spirit.

For some of us, fathers are a touchy subject. Some may not have had attentive God-fearing fathers that led a life that was a poor example of a spiritual leader. Fortunately, we have a heavenly Father that loves us and is always there for us no matter what. In those scenarios of growing up with fathers who weren't the greatest examples, it's crucial that we learn from their mistakes and go the other way when it comes to our own families. Every generation has a chance to break the cycle and start anew.

Whether you have children or not, or if you had a father in your life or not, this day is a celebration for everyone. Our heavenly Father is there with open arms, and He deserves our attention and praise. We may be let down by man, but one thing for certain is that our Father in heaven will never let us down no matter where we end up in life.

*How can you find something to
take out of Father's Day?*

TIMOTHY A. MILLS

JUNE 19

Why?

> And at the ninth hour Jesus cried with a loud voice, "Eloi, Eloi, lema sabachthani?" which means, "My God, my God, why have you forsaken me?"
>
> —Mark 15:34

We hear a lot of people say, "You should never ask God why." That could not be further from the truth. When people think that, it's almost as if they have a modern-day Pharisee way of thinking. There are plenty of times we ask God why. It's not that we're not trusting in Him. It's that we don't completely know the plans He has for us. Whether we ever know them or not, we can rest assured knowing that He's in control, but it doesn't hurt to wonder and ask why. Even the Son of God asked the Father why as he was hanging on the cross.

In my own life, I have seen the answer to the why when it's come to certain situations in my life. Other times, I haven't seen it. Whether we've discerned God's plans or not, we must still be faithful in prayer to Him. We must still strive to live a life pleasing to Him. As Jesus said on the cross, "Why have you forsaken me?" That didn't make Him turn away from God. That didn't make Him live any less of the life than He did. Even at the end of His life, He still remained faithful to the Father.

So wherever you are in life or whatever you may be going through, it's okay to ask God why. It's okay to wonder what God is doing. We just need to have faith in His plans even when we don't fully understand them. Even in tragedy, there is still a greater plan at hand. God loves us so much, and even when we feel like He's not paying attention, He's got things right where they need to be.

How can you ask why and still have faith?

JUNE 20

Drifting Away

> I have gone astray like a lost sheep, seek your servant, for I do not forget your commandments.
>
> —Psalm 119:176

Oh, what a world we live in these days. Everything seems to be drifting further from God. Even Christian folks have their struggles. We're not perfect people either. We've just found the truth and want to adhere to it. The problem with our sinful nature is that sin always looks appealing. It can be far too easy for us to slip up in a moment of temptation even when we know the commands God has given us. It's important for us not to be led astray by anything. We should avoid situations that are likely to make us stray.

I've been in this battle in my own life. Even when I knew something was wrong, there were times I just blatantly ignored God's commandments. I didn't forget them. I just chose my own desires of what God would've wanted for me. There are still consequences of those actions today, not just for me but for anyone who sins knowing it's a sin. I never lost my faith while I was astray. I just put it on the back burner, which was also not right either. I've felt God's presence in my life and how He is still using me as a servant even when I didn't serve Him right at all.

We're going to mess up in life. We're going to need God's grace, and that's what the cross is for. We just need be conscious of what we're doing. We need to keep watch and be guarded that we might not be led astray by the evil things of this world. Being in constant prayer and in the Word of the Lord every day is the way to a solid foundation. If you've been led astray, fear not. There's a loving God waiting for you to come back with open arms.

How can you tell when you're being led astray?

JUNE 21

I Have You to Thank

Ascribe to the Lord the glory due His name; bring an offering and come before Him! Worship the Lord in the splendor of holiness, tremble before Him, all the earth; yes, the world is established; it shall never be moved. Let the heavens be glad, and let the earth rejoice, and let them say among the nations, "The Lord reigns!"

—1 Chronicles 16:29–31

Sometimes we just need to thank God and give Him the praise He is owed from us. The whole passage is titled "David's Song of Thanks." We need to do just that every day. Give thanks to the Lord for what He has done for us. When we look at Christianity as a whole, it's not about anything we could do to earn our way into heaven. It's God's grace and the cross. Other religions focus on what we can do to earn our way into the afterlife. Not one other involves a god who laid down His life for us that we may be free from a fate worse than death—sin.

Every night, when we pray before bedtime as a family, I always thank God for the many blessings He's given us. I make a point to always say, "Even the ones we may not know about or take for granted." God is blessing you even when you don't know it. I am a commercial union driver, and coming home every afternoon is a blessing. Thanking Him for my safety every day is just a small thing that can easily be forgotten. Just when you think He's not doing anything, He's doing everything.

Take some time every day to just thank God for who He is and what He's done. You'll find it good for the soul to just praise our loving Creator even in times of trouble. This world is full of things that will continue to let us down. Why not put our faith in someone who will never let us down? There's one way off this third rock from the sun. That's Jesus.

How can you take time daily to just simply thank God?

JUNE 22

Clearly Think, Wisely Choose

> Therefore, preparing your minds for action, and being sober-minded, set your hope fully on the grace that will be brought to you at the revelation of Jesus Christ.
>
> —1 Peter 1:13

The mind is a terrible thing to waste, they say. Wasting it can consist of filling it with things that aren't good for you. If anything comes to mind that could pull you away from God and it clearly says it in scripture, that's where the sober-minded direction comes in. To be sober-minded isn't just exclusive to not being under the influence of alcohol. Anything that could cloud your vision of God's plans for you would exclude you from being sober-minded.

The title of this entry comes from a phrase my one uncle always says. To clearly think and wisely choose anything takes thought and prayer. When we don't think something through and don't choose wisely, we may be in for a pretty bad time. Years ago, when alcohol was a problem in my life, I realized that I could not clearly think or wisely choose when under the influence. I made countless bad decisions that cost me in the long run. This was a struggle I had for years that God delivered me from. Being sober-minded is a lot better than having your vision clouded.

Whatever decision you may come to, let it be discerned with prayer, and make a choice that's pleasing to our Lord. Some things are pretty black and white and easy to know that making the wrong choice would go against scripture. Other choices we come to may take a lot of prayer and discernment to make the right decision. Do all things that are pleasing to the Lord and know His grace when we fall short.

How can you clearly think and wisely choose according to God's will?

JUNE 23

Rain

> If you walk in my statutes and observe my commandments
> and do them, then I will give you your rains in their
> season, and the land shall yield its increase, and
> the trees of the field shall yield their fruit.
>
> —Leviticus 26:3–4

A lot of people don't like the rain. It's true. However, we need the rain to bring life. I have personally always loved the rain. To me, I always reflect on the rain and the growth that it brings. When it rains outside and there's not much to do, it's a perfect time for spiritual growth and self-analyzation. We cannot have the nicest weather without the rain. Just the same in our lives where we cannot be completely spiritually grounded without growth. The Word of God is the rain we need.

To be able to yield spiritual fruit, we must have our figurative rain. To be recognized by our actions over our words, we must grow constantly and serve in the ways God would want us to serve in. A lot of people claim to be Christians and constantly let everyone know they are. This is okay, unless you are not living according to a Christian life. I would much rather not say I'm a Christian but actually show it in my daily behavior. We must continue to grow and trust God in our witness to others.

No matter how old you are or what experience you have, there's always room for growth. We must be humble enough to know that we don't know it all, and we need to grow and be faithful to the Lord. When we walk in His steps, people will notice something different about us. When that spiritual rain comes upon us, let us grow closer to God and be better witnesses in our daily lives.

How can you recognize when you need spiritual growth?

JUNE 24

Gifts of Blessings

> Every good gift and every perfect gift is from above, coming down from the Father of lights with whom there is no variation or shadow due to change.
>
> —James 1:17

Have you ever received a gift that you know, clear as day, could only be explained as a godsent blessing straight from above? It's an amazing feeling when we receive those blessings and have hearts of gratitude for our Lord. It's important that we look at these gifts and think of ways we can give back and use what we have to bless someone else. The phrase "paying it forward" comes to mind. When we have a chance to bless someone else because we've been blessed ourselves, we should never pass up that opportunity.

Our family is a part of a Christian camp where we lease sites and stay in camper trailers. It's become a home away from home that I was introduced to by my wife, who grew up there. We had just purchased a new used camper this past year and opened it up for the first time yesterday. Over the winter, it must have leaked, and there was a broken waterline along with no electrical power. We were feeling a little bit in despair, wondering how we were going to afford the repairs and also get it ready for the camp meeting week in a month. My wife had posted on social media just a little bit about our dilemma, and another couple we camp with came to our aid and just gave us a newer camper at no cost. We knew just then that the Lord used them to bless us right at the perfect moment. We, in turn, were giving our fixer-upper camper to another family in need and helping them get it ready. What a big deal that was for us!

When we receive while still giving thanks and looking for ways to pay back, we have an awesome God who is making ways for us. Never be too greedy for yourself and want to always receive and never give back. The Lord does amazing things, and He has many blessings in store for those who follow Him.

How can you receive thankfully
and give back faithfully?

JUNE 25

Faith outta Fear

> For by grace you have been saved through faith. And this is not your own doing; it is the gift of God, not a result of works, so that no one may boast.
>
> —Ephesians 2:8–9

For generations, Christianity has been weaponized to scare people into believing. Most people who have experienced that kind of treatment reject it completely. There's plenty of people out there who have been mistreated by Christians who leave the faith altogether. Too many church leaders sometimes act like they are the ones doing the saving of people when, in fact, the credit needs to go to Christ. This verse shows us that we're all equal and we cannot make our own way. It's always God's way.

I grew up in a very dysfunctional youth group, and my faith was not my own. I was under the leadership of a control freak who would scare kids into believing by twisting scripture to make them feel horrible for the things they did. We would go on mission trips, and sometimes, other youth groups would be there. This man would bad-mouth the other groups all week like we were the only true Christians and everyone else was unbiblical. This is how easy Christianity can be weaponized, and people only believe out of the fear of disobeying man and not God. When I got out of that group and I started to make all kinds of bad decisions because of the new freedom I had, I knew my faith was not my own. I was riding on the coattails of this very destructive individual.

Whether you have accepted Christ as your Savior or you are still unsure, don't base your faith on fear of not believing. Base your faith on Christ and what He has done. The cross was the greatest rescue mission and love story because Christ laid down His life for us because he loves us so much. He doesn't want to see one of us lost. Let us give Him the credit and live for Him because we love Him, not just because we want to stay out of hell. We have the freedom to make the right or wrong choices. Let's choose Christ every day.

How can you believe out of love for Christ over fear for yourself?

JUNE 26

The Right Side

> And let us not grow weary of doing good, for in
> due season we will reap, if we do not give up.
>
> —Galatians 6:9

    Doing God's will isn't always an easy task. He's laid out commands for us, but we struggle at keeping them. As Galatians tells us, it will pay off. Now we shouldn't just do things with the motives of what we're going to get out of it. We should desire to do these things to serve the Lord. That's the real prize. Anything we may receive as a blessing is just a bonus after that. We always have a choice because of our free will. It's important that we discern the right choice through scripture.

    Last week, while coming back from my route, I was about fifty feet from the gate when I noticed something on the ground. I stopped to find a brand-new, shiny red pair of bolt cutters with the tag still on them. What man out there doesn't want more tools?! I put them in my work truck and pulled around the side of the building preparing to take these home. As I was putting my bag in the car and getting ready to leave, I changed my mind on taking these home. Instead, I took them in my boss's office and left them with him in case someone came to claim them. Well, today, one of the workers in the plant came to me when I got back to tell me that a tractor trailer driver did claim them. He left them on the back of his trailer when he departed, and they fell off. I didn't get a chance to meet this driver, but he was very appreciative. My coworker told me he was very relieved to have them returned to him.

So when a situation like this may arise, think of how it might affect someone else. You might not see the earthly outcome, but the heavenly outcome will be so much better! When your foundation in Christ is solid, the true reward is knowing that we served Him in a situation like this. We're not looking for a great recognition or something else we may get out of this. Our desires need to be about doing what is right by Him. Let's try to be better at that every day.

How can you look for little ways to do the right thing every day?

JUNE 27

When the Hurt Feels Too Much

> The Lord is near to the brokenhearted
> and saves the crushed in spirit.
>
> —Psalm 34:18

It's easy when we're hurting to try and rely on our own ways to fix things. While some earthly things may give us temporary comfort or take our minds off the hurt, only God can take our pains away forever. It's easy in a world like today to get discouraged. The more I see people out in public interacting, sometimes the more short fuses and hatred can be seen. People clash over silly things that don't matter in the long run. People struggle with depression and anxiety, and sometimes the weight of that is just too much for us to bear. When we cry out to God, He is right there waiting for us.

Sometimes the people we love hurt us the most. I think it's safe to say that we've all tried to help a loved one see a potential danger they may be heading toward and they lash out in anger because they don't want the help. We're the ones left hurting, and in the end, if they don't heed the advice, they are too. In times like these, the Lord is our only hope. We can't always avoid heartbreak and broken spirits, but that's where faith comes in to get us through.

We often lack the motivation to cry out to God in these situations. When we're that overwhelmed, it may be just exhausting to pray. Nevertheless, that is the only true way for healing in times of hurt. God loves us so much, and no prayer is too small or too much for Him. When we don't even bother asking, what good are we expecting to get? If God created the earth in six days, who's to say He won't answer your prayers? You never know until you get on your knees and lift those prayers up. His grace is sufficient.

How can you still cry out to God in prayer when suffering hurt?

JUNE 28

Winners and Losers

For whoever would save his life will lose it, but whoever loses his life for my sake will find it.

—Matthew 16:25

Life seems to be all about competition. In this world today, it's all about gaining for yourself as much as you can of whatever it may be. People high up in the corporate world are sometimes fueled by greed, and money is what they can't ever get enough of. When we're winning in the world, are we always winning in God's eyes? If our motives in life are to please ourselves, we'd be winning by a worldly standard. In turn, we would be losing and losing bad by God's standards. We must bring every gain we have to scripture to see if we're still within God's commands.

In my field of work as a teamster, there is always something going on with contract negotiations within the international union. This year, our union's biggest company, UPS, was considering a strike vote over unfair wages. The higher into management one could go in this company, the more money one would make. Some individuals are believed to be making millions themselves. The union was mocked and insulted for asking for higher wages. What if just one of those guys in the highest level of management agreed with the union on wages? What if one came forward and said they didn't need to make that much money and taking care of others was more important? That would be losing out on things in our own life for doing something pleasing to the Lord. I'm not against those in high positions making money, but is that money going to glorify the Lord?

Whatever we do in life, we must be willing to give up earthly things for heavenly things. When we lose our lives on earth, as believers, we are only finding ourselves deeper in the love of Christ. To truly win on earth is to live a life pleasing to the Lord and reject those things that go against scripture. A life of restraint on earth brings great the reward in heaven.

> How can you win with God
> while losing to the world?

JUNE 29

Promises We Can't Keep

Peter said to Him, "Lord, why can I not follow you now? I will lay down my life for you." Jesus answered, "Will you lay down your life for me? Truly, truly, I say to you, the rooster will not crow till you have denied me three times."

—John 13:37–38

Do we ever make promises we can't keep? Most of us have at some point in our lives. When we make promises to God, I'm sure sometimes He may chuckle knowing that we cannot keep some promises by our own accord. Only through a commitment to Jesus may our promises be kept through Him. Peter must have been mortified when Jesus told him what he was eventually going to do. Still, Peter, knowing this, denied his teacher three times, just as Jesus said. That's why the cross needed to happen. We can't always keep our promises, so Jesus paid the price for us to receive God's grace.

Every year, when I was in youth work, I used to go on a mission trip. I always viewed that as the end and the new beginning of what I call the Spiritual Year. I always took that time to reflect on the past year. The whole year of youth group was building up to that week. Many years went by that I came off the trip with a spiritual high that only faded away, and I was right back to living the life I shouldn't. Most of us have found ourselves in those situations where spiritual highs don't really have us grounded in our faith and we end up getting off track. While trips like these are important, it is more important to make a step up in our faith and be even more solid coming off a mission trip.

Even though Peter did this horrible act, where do we think he is now? He's in heaven right now, and thanks to God's grace, that sin doesn't matter anymore. The price has been paid, and we are saved by grace. When we truly repent and come back to the Lord, there's nothing stopping us from amping up our relationship even more. Be humble, and do not be conceited or in the mindset that you can make a deal with God and promise Him something you can't deliver. Stay in the Word and get to know what Jesus has done for us.

How can you understand that some promises we make to God can't be kept?

JUNE 30

They Can't Stop Us

> For me to live is Christ, and to die is gain.
>
> —Philippians 1:21

In the world today, we have many religions but only one true way to heaven. Christ paid the price for us so that we may live in eternity with Him. Now the biggest worry a lot of people have in life is that they are afraid of death. I think everyone has a mild fear of how we're going to die, but a lifetime in heaven with Jesus is a far greater reward. What shall we fear when Christ has laid it all out for us?

The fact that there are other religions in this world always makes me wonder why Christianity isn't treated the same. In mainstream media and society today, who do people want to censor? It's always the Christian folk and the name of Jesus. They don't ever talk about Buddha or Mohommed in a bad way. Why is that? I firmly believe it's just man's attempt to rebel against God. People hate Christianity because it brings their sin to light. They have serious trouble coming to terms with not being in control. They can't reconcile their own sin. Only Jesus can do that. Some people get driven completely mad when they can't be in control of every aspect of their lives. It's a lot easier and less stress to surrender to Jesus.

You will meet these hostile folks in life. It's just inevitable to come across these rebellious people. We need to try to get the message to them, even if it's just a short sentence that God will do the rest. No one gets out of this world alive. It's the most important decision of our lives to choose Christ. So even if they ridicule us, slander the name of Jesus, or even if they kill us, the Christian folk and the power of Christ can never be stopped. We win either way.

How can share the truth with others on what happens after death?

JULY 1

Always a Fight

> But as for you, O man of God, flee these things. Pursue righteousness, godliness, faith, love, steadfastness, gentleness. Fight the good fight of the faith. Take hold of the eternal life to which you were called and about which you made the good confession in the presence of many witnesses.
>
> —1 Timothy 6:11–12

When we accept Christ as our Savior, we're given a peace like no other. However, we may not truly realize that we are instantly thrown into battle because the enemy hates the fact that he's lost us. The devil tries to throw many stumbling blocks in our way to hinder our relationship with God. We must be in constant watch of these things that may tempt us to stray. Everyone on earth has something they struggle with and can fall into temptation with easily. The devil knows these things, and he will never stop trying to get us.

When we make a confession of our sins and choose to follow Jesus, we must do everything we can to avoid the temptations of this world. If we choose to follow Christ, then we need to stop following things of this world. When we're professing to know Christ but our actions aren't changing, we're going to fall right back where we were. Some relationships we have with unbelievers can be a hindrance. In our family, my wife and I have cleaned up our circle over the past few years, and we are now only close with other believers.

Do not be discouraged. Even the trials of this world will come to an end. When we make our commitment to Christ and live lives pleasing to the Lord, then we are going to be raised from the dead with Christ for an eternity in heaven. Many things in life, good and bad, will come and go, but God's promises last forever.

How can you be on guard for a spiritual battle every day?

JULY 2

Distorting the Truth

> When they had gone through the whole island as far as Paphos, they came upon a certain magician, a Jewish false prophet named Bar-Jesus. He was with the proconsul, Sergius Paulus, a man of intelligence, who summoned Barnabas and Saul and sought to hear the word of God. But Elymas the magician (for that is the meaning of his name) opposed them, seeking to turn the proconsul away from the faith.
>
> —Acts 13:6–8

I would encourage all of you to read more of this section. Acts 13:1-12 will help with the bigger picture. You can't get to be any more of a blasphemer with a name like Bar-Jesus. His real name is Elymas, but he took the other name, which means "son of Jesus" in the Hebrew language. We all know Jesus didn't have children! This false prophet was trying to find favor in the Roman proconsul by spewing lies. As scripture says, the Roman proconsul, Sergius Paulus, summoned Paul and Barnabas to hear the truth. He wasn't called a man of intelligence for nothing! Paul later goes on to rebuke this false prophet, who ends up with temporary blindness. Paul actually calls him "Son of the devil!" That's pretty serious!

The truth still gets distorted today by people. Many unbelievers today will try to distort the truth simply because they don't understand. When we're grounded in the faith, that's something we don't have to worry about as much. They just don't have the knowledge we have and let other unbelievers influence them to hate the truth. What we really need to be on guard for is when people in the church distort the truth. Further into the scriptures, especially in the letter of Jude, it explains to us the penalties for those who pervert scripture.

Far too many churches today are trading the truth for a lie to water down the Gospel message and not offend anyone. Places like this are only taking their congregations further from God's true message for us. We can't pick and choose which scriptures to follow and which to reject. It's back to the garden of Eden all over again when the serpent said to Eve, "Did God really say?"

Friends, be on your watch. You never know when this could be happening in your own church. If it happened back then in the book of Acts, then it's still happening today. Seek the right biblical council. If something said by a church leader doesn't coincide with scripture, then it's probably something that we need to look further into. We need to seek wisdom and the context of the scripture to fully understand what the Lord is telling us. As a body of believers, we truly need to grow closer to the truth. Only understanding God's teachings will show us the way to live a more holy life pleasing to Him.

> How can you be spiritually in
> tune to spot a false prophet?

JULY 3

Put Boasting Away

Thus says the Lord: "Let not the wise man boast in his wisdom, let not the mighty man boast in his might, let him who boasts boast in this, that he understands and knows me, that I am the Lord who practices steadfast love, justice, and righteousness in the earth. For in these things I delight, declares the Lord."

—Jeremiah 9:23–24

How often do we see people of the categories of the first verse in the world today? It's pretty common to see this kind of boasting come forth just about every day. So many people we may see on television or online think they have it all figured out. They think because of where they have gotten in life that their wisdom is something they have achieved and look at some others as beneath them. Even people with physical strength tend to be the same way. I'm sure everyone can think back to their school days and recall some not so nice kids who bullied others just with their size.

We as Christians need to be humble with these things God gives us. Whether wisdom or strength or anything else, it's important that we not go around boasting about what we have done. We need to direct the credit where credit is due and give it all to God. When we've been blessed with anything, how we act about it toward others must reflect Christ. A humble heart is always a better way to share the message with those that notice something different about us.

When we walk in the paths of love, justice, and righteousness as the Lord tells us, we are setting an example for the world to see what sets us apart from the rest. Being too proud or too boastful about our own accomplishments can easily turn others away from the faith. We're called to be humble in submission to the Lord's teachings. May we show the world we truly are different by taking that wisdom God has given us and use it to glorify Him.

How can you choose humility over boasting?

JULY 4

Let Freedom Ring

> For freedom in Christ has set us free, stand firm therefore,
> and do not submit again to a yoke of slavery.
>
> —Galatians 5:1

Freedom comes in many different meanings for many different people. In America today, just about everyone is about freedom. When we celebrate our independence from Britain, there is a lot of American joy throughout this country. Much bigger joy than that, however, comes from our freedom in Christ. We may be able to live our lives way more freely than any other country, but none of that matters if we don't have true freedom in Christ. Our freedoms in America today must be held with great care because one day, they may be gone. Our freedom in Christ is forever.

It's okay to be patriotic, but we don't want it to become a religion. For many on any side of politics today, it's their most important mission to win an election or get their right candidate in office, but when Christ is not at the head of those thoughts and actions, we don't have true clarity on how to vote or act when it comes to patriotism. I think being patriotic is something very special in America. It's a love for our country and the principles it was founded on. These principles of religious freedom we have are something we take for granted every day. In other countries, one could be jailed for mentioning the name of Jesus. We have it so good in this country, and we must give credit to our Almighty God for the freedoms we have.

Whenever we raise the flag, it's important that it's still below the cross. We're allowed to like our country, but we must still put God first always. None of this freedom we have would be possible without Christ's ultimate offering of His life on the cross. Let us truly never forget that.

How can you be patriotic and still have God above all else?

JULY 5

Homegrowing

> Now therefore, fear the Lord and serve Him in sincerity and in faithfulness. Put away the gods that your fathers served beyond the River and in Egypt, and serve the Lord. And if it is evil in your eyes to serve the Lord, choose this day whom you will serve, whether the gods your fathers served in the region beyond the River, or the gods of the Amorites in whose land you dwell. But as for me and my house, we will serve the Lord.
>
> —Joshua 24:14–15

When we think of our church homes, it's pretty easy to guess who we serve there. What about our own homes? If we're only in church getting spiritually fed for a few hours on Sunday, what are we doing for the rest of the week? If we are not using our homes to serve the Lord with our families together, then something needs to change. We don't have to go too extreme, like opening our homes to the homeless, but we do need to be in prayer together as a family. We need to be in the Word every day and discuss it among husbands, wives, and children. Growing together in the faith is how we keep our families stronger.

One of my favorite quotes about our faith comes from Allistair Begg (I may have used this in a previous entry, but it's far too important to not repeat). "For Christianity to have an impact on this world, it must revolutionize our home life." How true is that? If we're involved in church and serving in specific ways there but our home life is lacking, then what good are we really doing? If you fight with your spouse because you were at church too long serving, then it may be time to step down for a bit and fix things at home. The family unit is far too sacred to take lightly.

However you serve the Lord, serve Him at home with your families the most. Whether you're married with children in a house or you're single in a one-bedroom apartment, make that home a place of dwelling for the Lord. When we take what we're learning in church and apply it at home, we have better home lives. When we're in the Word and in prayer, we are further grounding ourselves in the faith. We have less risk for falling away when we're serving at home and growing together.

How can you serve the Lord at home?

JULY 6

Never-Ending

> Can you find out the deep things of God? Can you find out the limit of the Almighty?
>
> —Job 11:7

These are two questions that can't really be answered by us. Fortunately, knowing God's plan for us, we don't have to worry about these things or try to figure it out. Faith is what we rely on. We don't have to see God to believe. Some folks out there, who I like to refer to as "too smart for their own good," just can't wrap their brains around God. Almost as if they think they're too smart for that or their knowledge has already surpassed needing God in their lives. People like this have a rough time with surrender. We know, as believers, that's what it's all about. We must keep Christ in the spotlight and not ourselves.

There are too many people who don't believe in anything that can't be explained scientifically. Knowledge of things that are explainable is what they rely on. Faith is something they struggle with because of the surrender aspect. Faith starts out as not 100 percent knowing something is true, hence the phrase "leap of faith." What the intellectual types of people don't realize is that they have more faith than they realize. When they get on an airplane, they have faith in the pilot to fly the plane safely. When they eat at a restaurant, they have faith in the staff to make sure the food isn't spoiled. When they go to a doctor for a life-threatening disease, they have faith in the doctors to diagnose and medicate the condition. They just need to put their faith in the One who really matters.

Throughout life, we may think we have it all figured out. We may think our own knowledge is going to get us through. We make plans about life and goals that we want to achieve. The old saying goes, "If you want to hear God laugh, tell Him your plans." When we don't have faith in God and we try to go through life with our own understanding, we're not going to get the best outcome for our lives. We sometimes think we know things or even know best, but if it's not aligned with God, then it's not His plan for us. Remember this, friends. "Where human knowledge ends, faith must take over." We don't know it all, and when we truly surrender to the King, faith is all we need.

How can you believe in God on faith alone?

JULY 7

A Hero Emerges

After the death of Moses the servant of the Lord, the Lord said to Joshua the son of Nun, Moses' assistant, "Moses my servant is dead. Now therefore arise, go over this Jordan, you and all this people, into the land that I am giving to them, to the people of Israel."

—Joshua 1:1–2

Oftentimes, when a great leader passes away, we wonder who will take their place. Even though God is number one, these people sometimes become our heroes on earth. In the church, when a pastor retires or is called to another church, there's always that uncertainty of *What's next?* Even if we may not fully understand why one of our spiritual leaders may be called away, we need to have the faith in God to bring a new leader forward. After everything Moses did with the Israelites, I bet they were a little bit lost. I would think they would have even questioned Joshua's ability to lead at first. We do this with politicians, church leaders, anyone in a new position in our lives. If the leader is being led by God, then what do we need to worry about?

Change can be a harder thing to deal with in life for some more than others. What doesn't change is God, so when faced with new leadership, we must go straight to the scriptures. Our church has a wonderful spiritual leader. Our head pastor is very gifted and blessed at what he does. However, he won't be there forever. In a denomination, as a whole, who has proclaimed to accept things that aren't biblical, our pastor has made sure to make it known that we don't agree with everything the entire denomination speaks of. It makes me wonder, though, when he's gone, will someone come in who wants to change these scriptures of controversial issues? I pray that's not so.

Heroes come in all forms, but a true hero stands up for the faith. A true hero submits to God and stands firm on the scriptures. When God calls us to rise up and lead, we must heed the call. Joshua had some big shoes to fill when he took over Moses's leadership. If God led him to that position and Joshua trusted in God to equip him to be the leader he needed to be, then the people needed not worry. When God calls someone to do something, we need to be ready and willing. We could end up like Joshua, carrying the fire on after a great leader. God can take you places you would have never dreamed. Faith in him is everything.

How can you respond to God's call to lead by His principles?

JULY 8

If I Traded It All

> And He sat down opposite the treasury and watched the people putting money into the offering box. Many rich people put in large sums. And a poor widow came and put in two small copper coins, which make a penny. And He called His disciples to Him and said to them, "Truly, I say to you, this poor widow has put in more than all those who are contributing to the offering box. For they all contributed out of their abundance, but she out of her poverty has put in everything she had, all she had to live on."
>
> —Mark 12:41–44

We don't often see our church brothers' and sisters' financial gifts, but you can bet that there are some very devoted to tithing and giving to the Lord. We don't need to compare ourselves to what others are doing, but we need to be conscious of Jesus's words on giving. This poor widow gave everything she had to the offering box. These words can teach us that it isn't even about money. It's about giving it all up for the Lord.

When we look at our daily lives with schedules and families our careers and only a couple of hours a week in church, then how are we able to fully give ourselves to the Lord? Even in the secular workplace and wherever you may be, it's important that we fully devote ourselves to the Lord. In our words and in our actions, we can give it all. It's easy to get caught up in the desires of the flesh by giving into temptations that do not honor God. We must do our part daily to stay in the Word and, in prayer, be grounded in our faith as to not be hindered by the things of this world.

Whenever you give, give it all. Not necessarily financially speaking. Give to the Lord your all in your Christian walk with Him. It's not always easy, and some days can be a struggle, but that's all the more reason to cling to Him more. We offer ourselves in surrender, just as Jesus did on the cross. We are walking through the faith with servants' hearts. May we always be willing to trade all the things of this world to strive for what matters most. Jesus needs to be our number one priority.

> How can you trade all the things
> of this world for Christ?

JULY 9

When the Truth Hurts

> We are from God. Whoever knows God listens to us; whoever is not from God does not listen to us. By this we know the Spirit of the truth and the spirit of error.
>
> —1 John 4:6

If the Bible isn't making you feel awkward at all, then you're probably living the life God has called you to live. Those who become highly uncomfortable and offended by scripture only have these feelings because of their own sin. The Spirit of truth allows us to confront our problems and work toward holier living. The spirit of error only puts a wedge between us and God by us letting it get our earthly feelings in the way of the truth. When we take scripture for exactly what it is and don't try to change it to meet our own needs, that's how we are supposed to live. God gave us the guidebook, and we need to trust in Him and obey.

One of our backup preachers at church preached on Acts 13 very recently, and it was one of the most truthful sermons I've heard when it comes to today's controversial issues. I heard that there were some folks in our church that day who were crying in the back of the sanctuary because they were upset at the content of the sermon. They were offended because they disagreed with what he was preaching on. What he preached on was straight out of the Bible, and he covered some touchy topics of today's world. If someone is getting that upset over scripture, then it's because they would rather hold onto their own sin and worldly views of certain issues. The Bible brings these issues to light. Even if the Bible doesn't directly come out and say it, the answers are there about most of today's issues. What if we tried to obey instead of trying to change scripture?

I've always said presentation is the key to sharing the message. We must present it in love and truth. Sometimes, no matter how you say it to someone, they are going to get offended. If you live in darkness, you will be offended by the light. Far too many people have a death grip on their own sin and refuse to let go. They follow false prophets in the church that affirm their own sin and don't tell them to change. We must strive every day to be a more biblical body of believers. When we hold fast to the truth God has given us, life becomes a lot simpler. When we get to a point in our faith where we know what is right and refuse to go outside the boundary line, a much better life is there for us.

> How can you hold to the truth
> no matter what the issue?

JULY 10

The Wide Body of Believers

> John answered, "Master, we saw someone casting out demons in your name, and we tried to stop him, because he does not follow with us." But Jesus said to him, "Do not stop him, for the one who is not against you is for you."
>
> —Luke 9:49–50

There are many different churches out there. The ones that do preach the Bible faithfully are such a blessing to be a part of. I feel like we all get into the habit of subconsciously thinking, *My church is the best*. It's not supposed to be a competition in the vast body of believers. We're all serving one purpose, and that is to further the kingdom. We all need to be a part of a church where we are learning; go where you grow, I always say. We can try different churches until we find that one, but we need to keep in mind it's not that one church is wrong over another just because we have our opinions on how they do things.

You've heard me talk about the youth group I grew up in. We would go on mission trips, and sometimes there would be other youth groups with us. Our head leader often mocked these other groups because he felt they weren't doing things right. Many of the kids in our group would join in as well. I look back on that nowadays thinking what a poor example of Christ we were to those other churches. When it comes down to it, if a church—or youth group, in this case—is preaching the Bible and kids and adults alike are growing in their faith, then we must do well to get along in peace and fellowship while we're on this planet.

Don't let silly unbiblical opinions divide you from one another. This body of believers we're in is all over the world. Just because someone worships a little different from you doesn't mean they are doing it wrong. Everyone has different ways of connecting with God. If we're all accepting Christ and we continue to follow the message of the cross, then little traditions or methods really don't matter in the eyes of the Lord. God wants our attention. May we continue to work toward unity of this giant body of believers.

> How can you embrace other ways of worshipping God outside of what you do?

JULY 11

Belief Unseen

> Thomas answered Him, "My Lord and my God!" Jesus said to him, "Have you believed because you have seen me? Blessed are those who have not seen and yet have believed."
>
> —John 20:28–29

I'm sure you've heard the term *doubting Thomas* when it comes to certain people and the faith they have. The apostle Thomas hadn't been there when Jesus first appeared to them after He rose from the dead. Even though Thomas was one of the twelve chosen apostles chosen by Jesus Himself, Thomas didn't just believe on faith. He had to see it for himself that Christ had risen from the dead. He wanted that living, breathing truth that Christ conquered the grave. I wouldn't say Jesus held this against him, but He makes a point to commend those who believed without having to see the proof.

In today's world, Jesus isn't walking in the flesh where we may see and touch Him physically. However, there is much proof out there to be seen of God's existence. Not every conversion happens by a full-blown godsent miracle. Faith must proceed for one to be able to see God's promises. Faith is the belief in God with strong spiritual convictions that we don't need proof. We are convinced by scripture and teaching that what we believe in is true.

It's far too easy to be looking for proof in the wrong places when you already have a chip on your shoulder about God. We're living in a world that wants to censor and cancel the church and any talk of God. As Christians, it's so important that we hold true to our beliefs and do our best to share this message with others. A lot of unbelievers only look at God from a worldly standpoint, and without faith, they will never be convinced otherwise. We need to explain in truth and love the greatest story of all time. God is always here for us, and even those who don't believe have every chance to make it right with Him before it's too late.

How can you believe without seeing?

JULY 12

Nobody Knows

Therefore, stay awake, for you do not know on what day your Lord is coming. But know this, that if the master of the house had known in what part of the night the thief was coming, he would have stayed awake and would not have let his house be broken into.

—Matthew 24:42–43

There's a lot of things we can be sure of when it comes to God's promises. What we'll never know is when He's coming back. Christ's return will truly be amazing. If nobody knows about when, the time is now to get ready. As the scripture says about the thief, if you knew your house was going to be robbed, wouldn't you be waiting with a weapon or have the police there to stop the robber? Absolutely we would. We wouldn't just leave our doors unlocked and wait for someone to come in. We would be taking the proper precautions. The same is true for our faith.

Being ready is a process we can work on every day. We may not even live to see the day Christ comes back, but we must live like it could be tomorrow. When we walk in the spirit every day and live the lives God calls us to live, then we're readying ourselves for Christ's return. I've heard a lot of people putting off church because they don't think it's the right time. They don't think they're ready to make the commitment. I've heard some younger folk say they want to live a wild lifestyle because they know they'll have to clean up their act later in life. Well, why not start now? Why not begin a relationship with Christ that will last forever? The deeper we go into the faith, the more we understand how crucial it is that we get right with the Lord.

At whatever point you may be in your faith, don't be discouraged. Everyone is on different levels. What's important is that we lay the right foundation in Christ and build on His teachings. Most conversions don't result in a drastic lifestyle change right at the start. It may be a process that takes several years or even decades. We're all growing and learning over time. Let us continue to ready ourselves as if the Lord's return is now.

How can you ready yourself for Christ's return?

JULY 13

There Will Be a Day

> For behold, the day is coming, burning like an oven, when all the arrogant and all evildoers will be stubble. The day that is coming shall set them ablaze, says the Lord of hosts, so that it will leave them neither root nor branch.
>
> —Malachi 4:1

It's a sad thought to think about this. When the trumpet sounds and Lord comes back, there will be many people who never believed. To some, believing is just too easy that the message of Christ seems like it should be way more complex. A lot of people who have never known that kind of love have ground their heels in and await their own destruction in due time. Our presence in this world is a mission to bring these people to the light before it's too late. Even if it isn't in our lifetime, the Lord's day will come.

God can always do miracles to turn someone's life back to Him. We know, for sure, that anything is possible when it comes to His many wonders. Unfortunately, not all will be turned to Him. Someone you love will be on the wrong side at the end. In my years, I've had the opportunity to share the gospel with many people, and I've seen some spit it out and reject it. Could they still come to Christ eventually? Absolutely! It's just so hard seeing someone reject it when we know what the penalty will be if they do. In the end, no matter which side we're on, we're going to bow and confess Christ as Lord.

Tell the world what Jesus has done for us. Even if they don't listen, the seed is planted. God can do the rest. When we love and live the life God has blessed us with in a manner pleasing to Him, we set an example for the rest of the world to follow. When we're joyful in every occasion, people can't stand that because deep down, they want that joy and don't believe it's possible. It's *very* possible! In love, tell everyone who will give an ear to hear about the good news of Jesus Christ before the clock runs out.

> How can you be loving in warning those of the end times?

JULY 14

From the Inside Out

> Likewise the Spirit helps us in our weakness. For we do not know what to pray for as we ought, but the Spirit himself intercedes for us with groanings too deep for words.
>
> —Romans 8:26

I am weak, but He is strong. We've heard that line in "Jesus Loves Me." When we really get down to it, all accomplishments we have come from God. When we think we're doing things, we need to recognize that our strength comes from God. In any situation, give credit to the King. When we pray, we're often stumped on words. Sometimes we're so overwhelmed that even asking God for help can be difficult. Even when we don't have the words, the Spirit is there interceding for us. We have the Spirit in us as believers. From the inside out, let us constantly be in prayer to the Lord.

Life can knock us around a bit from time to time. We have a lot on our plates in today's world. When we go around the clock for our daily lives for however long, we are eventually going to crash. Sometimes we just need to stop and pray, and even when we don't have the words, the Spirit does for us. I'm reminded of a picture of a letter I saw on social media. It simply says, "Dear God," followed by several tearstains, and concludes with "Amen." Sometimes, that's all we can get out. God knows our needs, and He knows our hearts, and when we truly desire Him, He is there to listen to those wordless prayers.

I encourage all of you to make time to be in the Word every day. Make time to pray. Stay involved in a church. Most of all, put God first in everything. That can be easier said than done. When life overwhelms you and you find yourself not having the words to pray, remember that God is bigger than that. He knows your heart, and He knows your needs. Let the Spirit that lives within you be your guide.

> How can you rely on the Spirit when you
> don't have the words to pray?

Debt Forgiveness

Who is a God like you, pardoning iniquity and passing over transgression for the remnant of his inheritance? He does not retain His anger forever, because He delights in steadfast love.

—Micah 7:18

When's the last time a debt collector called you to tell you they paid your debt off because they love you? I'm gonna go with never for me, and I'm sure you'll all answer the same. This verse asks the unworldly question of "Who is a God like you?" *Unworldly* is the key word because in today's world, we don't often hear of people who just get their debts cancelled, whether it be financial debt or not. God loves us way too much to hold our pasts against us. Every day is a chance to make it right with Him and obey His commands.

We've all sinned against God one way or another. Even before we were able to sin, we inherited the generational sin from our parents. When Adam and Eve were cast out of the garden for the first sin ever committed, we were separated from God for that moment. Humans can do nothing in the light of earning our way back. We were originally created to be flawless, but we had a choice. Adam and Eve chose wrong. Even if we have made the wrong choice, we can still make the right choice next. Unfortunately, it only took one to separate us from God.

The cross had to happen so the price would be paid for us. When Jesus, who never sinned, laid down His life for us, the debt was forgiven. We were destined for eternal separation from God, but Jesus interceded on our behalf. When we think of these worldly things that we feel entitled to, we must be quick to remember the freedom that was bought at a hefty price for us. Forgive those around you who you may feel have wronged you. Go and sin no more, because your Father in heaven loves you enough to pay the price for your freedom from sin. Forget your past as the Lord has forgiven you. Make the right choice and follow Him.

> How can you give freely knowing your debt has been paid?

JULY 16

Run Free

> For if you forgive others their trespasses, your heavenly Father will also forgive you, but if you do not forgive others their trespasses, neither will your Father forgive your trespasses.
>
> —Matthew 6:14–15

    I think if all of us took a poll on things we wish Jesus never said, this would be at the top of the list. Forgiveness is something we all struggle with to some degree. We all have a tendency to feel like we're owed something by someone who's wronged us. We desire vengeance against people who have mistreated us. All we're doing by holding onto those feelings is keeping ourselves locked up. We're enslaved to these feelings when we're unforgiving. If God is forgiving us for all our wrongs over and over, then who are we to withhold forgiveness from someone else?

    Forgiveness isn't even a one-time thing. When you feel like another has wronged you in some way, forgiveness may be a long process. Whether someone asks for forgiveness or not, if we confess that we forgive them, it might take some time. We may be mad all over again about the situation a few days later. We may need to keep praying to God to help us forgive. We truly can't do it on our own without Him. In this world, you are going to be wronged by someone, but in turn, you will wrong someone else in some way. I think this is a perfect example of the old golden rule "Treat others the way you want to be treated."

    Believe me when I say that this has always been a struggle for me. If you are going through this, then you are definitely not the only one. This is a hard thing to deal with because sometimes, we just want to be mad. We may think we're hurting the other person when we connive and plot against them. More than likely, they've probably already forgotten what happened. Let it go, and may God's grace free you from your own prison and allow you to run free.

How can you forgive as Christ forgave you?

JULY 17

The Word of the Lord

All Scripture is breathed out by God and profitable for teaching, for reproof, for correction, and for training in righteousness, that the man of God may be complete, equipped for every good work.

—2 Timothy 3:16–17

Oh, scripture, what can you tell us? Scripture can tell us everything we need to know about God and then some. Within these sixty-six books can be the biggest mystery yet so simple that a child could understand it. This sacred Word we've been given is exactly how God intended it. No more and no less could it be. We have the guidebook to walk us through life. To hear these teachings can be the biggest blessing we ever receive. As believers, if we hope to grow, we must be in the Word every day. Just as plants need water, we need the living waters of the Word to rejuvenate us and restore our souls.

It's a common argument with people who think there are things left out of scripture. We all, at some point, may wonder, not question, why God didn't add some things in there. Some of us, I'm sure, wish He left some things out! It's okay to have these questions, but it must not pierce the armor of your faith to the point where you have doubts about all of it. My personal question I'll have to ask the day I get to heaven is, Where and what did Jesus do from age twelve to thirty? It's just a wonder that I have. My faith would not be contingent on whatever that answer may be.

God breathed out these words just as He did in the Creation story. What is in scripture is what is supposed to be there, and what is out is left out for a reason. This is where our faith must be strong. We must rely on that for what we don't quite understand in scripture just yet. We also must not try to change scripture for the things we struggle to accept. Teachings also must be discerned and passed down through the generations who also discern and study these sacred words. We're all in this process of understanding scripture together. May we grow closer to God in our reading, and may we be unashamed to tell others about what we find in these Words.

> How can you have the faith to accept the scriptures for what they are?

JULY 18

Praying with Urgency

> If you then, who are evil, know how to give good gifts to your children, how much more will the heavenly Father give the Holy Spirit to those who ask Him!
>
> —Luke 11:13

No surprise that we are evil people. We've sinned against God, and we've been separated from Him ever since the dawn of time. Jesus mended that relationship by paying the price for our sins on the cross. We have been given a gift to have a relationship with our Father in heaven who loves us dearly. God is there for our daily needs. We must not be ashamed to get on our knees and pray for those needs.

What's very important to remember as Christians is that when we pray urgently, we also need to pray humbly and not out of greed. Even when we are praying for those specific needs, sometimes God's answer is still no or "I have something greater in store." When we pray for loved ones to be healed, one would think God would do that, but it's not always His will. Regardless of whatever His will may be, we are just called to pray. We are called to trust in Him, that He is hearing our prayers. Sometimes those things we pray for come back with the answer from God, saying, "I am enough." We don't always need what we pray for, but we always need God.

Don't think that because God didn't answer a prayer that He is any less loving. I know plenty of people who have lost loved ones after they prayed for years for healing. God didn't give them the answer they wanted, but their faith in Him still had no doubt. My personal take is that God always wants to hear our prayers, even when He already has something else in mind. It's about trusting His plans over our own. Have faith and believe. Whatever you are going through, don't do it shaking your fists. Do it on your knees in prayer. Talk to your heavenly Father daily. If God is willing to send His Son to die on a cross for your sins, then how much do you think He cares for you? Do not worry when you don't get the answer you want because God will meet your needs in ways you never dreamed. God is greater than that!

> How can you make prayer a bigger priority for your needs?

JULY 19

Keep the Fire Burning

> Whoever walks with the wise becomes wise, but
> the companion of fools will suffer harm.
>
> —Proverbs 13:20

Walking in this world alone can be hard. When we're walking through this world as Christian people, it's even harder when we keep the company of unbelievers. We are often in regular fellowship with these people, and it will eventually take a toll on us. If we have shared the gospel with these folks and they've rejected it, we need to walk away. If we have been silent about our faith because we don't want them to view us differently, then we need to examine ourselves and either share our faith or walk away. Let us walk unashamed of our faith and tell all who will hear.

Being together in this vast body of believers is so important for us to keep on God's righteous path. Personal in-depth relationships can never be truly fulfilling if it's a believer with an unbeliever, especially one who has rejected the truth. In my own life, I had these kinds of relationships with unbelievers. Guess what? They're all gone. We need to do everything we can to surround ourselves in fellowship with other Christians with every opportunity we receive. For those of us, like me, in the secular workplace, it can be a struggle maintaining your faith. When we're surrounded by foul language, unfair treatment from our bosses, or even temptation to join that crowd outside of work.

Wherever you are in your faith, be together. Don't just go to church on Sundays for a social hour. Grow together, learn together, and feel together. I'm a union guy. I know what can be done when people stand in solidarity facing opposition. Get involved in other ways. Read your Bible daily. Discuss it with those other believers. If you have the opportunity to be a part of a midweek Bible study, I strongly encourage you to make it a priority. Check in with one another and ask how others are doing. Build one another up and encourage others to stay on the right path. Ask for help. Be humble enough to know you need encouragement. Most of all, talk to God together. Prayer is so powerful, especially when it's a loud resounding chorus of people praying together. God is always with us, but He's also given us fellowship with other believers. Take advantage of that. Keep the right company.

> How can you avoid toxic relationships and cling to the body of believers?

JULY 20

Ridin' the Storm Out

> And He said to them, "Why are you afraid, O you of little faith?" Then He rose and rebuked the winds and the sea, and there was a great calm. And the men marveled, saying, "What sort of man is this, that even winds and sea obey Him?"
>
> —Matthew 8:26–27

If you're like me, you would wonder what the disciples must have felt when they watched this firsthand. How awesome it must have been to see this, but also how terrifying. I'm sure some of them might have been glad to know He was on their side and for what might happen if He wasn't. Christ performed many miracles during His time on earth. The literal storm He calmed wasn't the only storm He came to calm. We all go through times in our lives where the storm of spiritual warfare rages on within us. What must we do to ride it out?

At our camp meeting this week, there was a tornado warning. When you're camping, a tornado coming is never what you want to hear. As the storm raged on outside the auditorium, the entire attendance was found inside, dry and warm, singing praises to the King. We joined in fellowship and prayer to ride out the storm. I'm sure some people have anxiety in these situations, but we sure rode it out together. It got me thinking of the power of prayer and worship. When we have those spiritual storms in our life, we must commit it to the Lord. Every day can be a battle, and the storm can rage on for seasons of life. Our faith and trust need to be put in the Lord.

Whatever kind of storm you may be going through, always remember that God can calm it. Our spiritual burdens can be lifted through our prayers and praise to the King. Especially as believers, we need to be on our guard to keep watch for these storms rolling in. Sometimes you can prepare, and sometimes you can't. You don't always get a tornado warning in a spiritual storm. Wherever you are in that storm, Christ is reaching to pull you out. Christ can calm that storm in you. Won't you reach out and take hold of his hand?

> How can you accept Christ's help to pull you out of the storm you're in?

JULY 21

Sweet Emotion

Is anyone among you sick? Let him call the elders of the church, and let them pray over him, anointing him with oil in the name of the Lord. And the prayer of faith will save the one who is sick, and the Lord will raise him up. And if he has committed sins, he will be forgiven. Therefore, confess your sins to one another and pray for one another, that you may be healed.

—James 5:14–16

The truth is, we're all sick. We're all ill from something called sin. Sin came into this world around the dawn of time, and everyone is infected with it. We, on our own, can't shake it off. There are no pills to take to get rid of it. No doctor can surgically remove it. It's ours because we messed up. Fortunately for us, Christ took that burden away from us. We now can have our relationship with Him and spend eternity in heaven. That part is 100 percent figured out. Because of sin though, we are going to have flare-ups and outbreaks in this life where the burden is hard to bear. We can get so overwhelmed that we truly can't do it on our own. Prayer is a powerful weapon against sin. When a body of believers comes together, marvelous things can happen through collective prayer.

Tonight was our last night at camp meeting for the week. Our evangelist offered anointing and prayer for anyone seeking the Lord's anointing. I myself was in that long line of believers, and it's something I've never done before. To me, it always seemed too religious or just symbolistic. The more I embraced the moment and saw many others come forth, the more it made me realize this is one of God's commands. Who are we to say what God will or won't do when we pray? When we humble ourselves and surrender to Him, we have all the potential to receive His blessings when He wills it. Tonight really taught me about being faithful and obedient to His teachings. It's something I think we all need to fine-tune in our spiritual walks with Christ.

If you have the opportunity to be anointed in the name of the Lord, I strongly encourage you to step up and take it. If you are physically or mentally sick or just suffering the side effects of sin, seek this kind of spiritual help. Scripture is very clear on this command. You may even find yourself anointing another who is struggling someday. God wants to hear our prayers. He wants our faithfulness when we come to Him. Believe and go forth. God will hear you.

How can you be healed by being anointed?

JULY 22

Faith Like a Child

I have no greater joy than to hear that my
children are walking in the truth.

—3 John 1:4

Oh, the little ones. When children praise God, it's a beautiful sight. It's even more beautiful to see parents taking the time to teach their children about Jesus and the good news He brings. Children seem to always be watching what we as parents do. Even if you don't have children, believe me, there are children watching your example. My two daughters love to put my wife's and my shoes on and walk around in them, stumbling and sometimes falling. There's a big deeper meaning than that. They want to be what they see and hear. As Christian parents, we want to hear them praising the Lord, and we need to be the ones they learn that from.

We finished up our camp meeting week with the presentation of the children who participated in "Kid's Corner," as they call it up at camp. All the children were divided into tribes according to their age. One member from each tribe got to get up from and share a "God sighting" that they experienced during the week. Our four-year-old daughter was one of these children. When it got to be her turn to share her God sighting, she proudly said, "My mommy and daddy." (Queue the tears!) She is seeing, at a young age, her parents behaving in a godly manner. Like most parents, we don't always get it right, but my wife and I make a conscious effort every day to live out our faith.

Whether you have children or not, be an example. Even in your church, there are kids struggling that don't have godly parents to guide them. As Christians, we must set an example for everyone, especially children. Children are a true gift from God, and they are the next generation to carry the fire for the faith. Those older in the faith must always be willing to teach the younger in the faith so we might all burn brighter together. May we all take that very seriously in our faith and guide these little ones to the light of the world.

How can you be a better example of Christ for children to follow?

JULY 23

Flying Stones

> But Jews came from Antioch and Iconium, and having persuaded the crowds, they stoned Paul and dragged him out of the city, supposing that he was dead. But when the disciples gathered about him, he rose up and entered the city, and on the next day he went on with Barnabas to Derbe.
>
> —Acts 14:19–20

If there's only one thing we could ever take out of the book of Acts, it's that God can take one of the vilest human beings and us them for His glory. The apostle Paul was no saint before the Lord got ahold of Him. The irony in these verses comes from Acts 7. When Paul was still called Saul before he knew the Lord, a man named Stephen was stoned to death for enraging the crowd by preaching the good news of Jesus. Saul ravaged the churches before He came to know Christ. He was the one casting the stones, and later on, it happened to him for the same reason that he was doing it to others.

Throughout life, I feel like we all have been on both sides of this, just like Paul. We have been the people that condemned those for speaking the truth. Whenever we are challenged by people about our own actions, we tend to not like that very much. Some more than others, even within the churches, can get very defensive and even hostile when we're called out for our own sin. On the other side of it, we have all had stones cast at us by others. We have been the ones who have been looked down upon for our faith in Jesus. In my own life, I can think of several occasions where I was treated differently for my faith. It's honestly a small price to pay for being a faithful servant.

People in this world will hate you for your faith. It was foretold in the scriptures that we will be rejected just like Jesus was for speaking the truth. Do not be discouraged in these times. The further you dive into scripture and prayer, the more it makes sense, even for our suffering at the hands of unbelievers. Like Stephen before Paul, even if they take our lives, our souls are secure in Christ the Lord.

> How can you be different from the crowds and embrace the truth over resenting it?

JULY 24

Sinners for Strangers

But a Samaritan as he journeyed, came to where he was, and when he saw him, he had compassion. He went to him and bound up his wounds, pouring on oil and wine. then he set him on his own animal and brought him to an inn and took care of him.

—Luke 10:33–34

This passage speaks of a Jewish fellow who was robbed and beaten and left for dead. Keep in mind that Samaritans did not associate with Jews in those times. Now this man was passed by already by a priest and a Levite who wouldn't even bother with him, but as scripture says, the Samaritan had compassion. We have opportunities every day to show that kind of compassion to others. It may be as simple as an encouraging word to someone who might not expect it from you. Christ calls us to love our neighbor, and through evidence in scripture, everyone is our neighbor.

Today, while delivering at one of the stores I service, it was going like any other delivery. While I was loading my cart up with five-gallon bottles, an old man walking into the store began to shout and disrespect me because of where I had parked my truck. I park in the same spot every time. I did my best to keep my cool and not repay evil with evil, yet I was also feeling very frustrated as I continued my delivery. As I was getting empty bottles out of the return bin, another man came up to me and said, "Sir, don't listen to what that old man said. I appreciate what you do." Then a few minutes later, a lady who worked at the store inquired about what happened and told me that I didn't deserve that kind of treatment because I'm always nice and pleasant while working. I graciously thanked the both of them for their kind words. Now I don't know for sure if these two people were followers of Christ, but that's an example of how we ought to live. Be loving and encouraging to one another, especially complete strangers.

We're all sinners in this life. We've all fallen short of God's commands for us. When we carry ourselves in a way to build up others, we work toward a holier lifestyle. You may find yourself in my shoes as I was today needing encouragement, or you may find an opportunity to be that encouragement for someone else. When we interact with complete strangers, we have no idea what they may be going through. Be kind, be encouraging, and continue to love those neighbors of ours, as hard as it may be.

> How can you be a good Samaritan toward others in need?

JULY 25

Only One Truth

> So Jesus said to the Jews who had believed Him, "If you abide in my word, you are truly my disciples, and you will know the truth, and the truth will set you free."
>
> —John 8:31–32

In today's world, people use truth as a relative term. We hear phrases like "That's my truth" or "That's your truth." Well, here's another common phrase about those two. "That couldn't be further from the truth." We're in a culture that redefines certain words and phrases they don't agree with to make them sound better. To Christians, there is only one truth, and His name is Jesus. Jesus referred to Himself as the truth. If we're following anything but Him, we're following down the path of a lie.

Things in this world are not what they seem. We have people spreading lies posing as "their truth." The whole "believe what you need to believe" mentality is sending people down a path of destruction. The real truth actually tends to be silenced these days because of people getting offended. I heard a story about someone who came to hear a sermon at our church who posted on social media the next day, that they were attacked in church because of what was said in the sermon. Everything the preacher said was straight from the scriptures. Some people think because they disagree with the truth that they can just change it when it comes to biblical teaching. It's as if they are going back to Genesis 3 and believing the lie of the serpent: "Did God really say that?"

We are living in a time, now more than ever, where we need to constantly have our guard up. The unbelievers can be ruthless, and even in the churches, we must keep watch that those who wish to change the truth don't bring destruction from within. When we hold fast to the teachings of scripture, we are growing deeper and embracing the truth. If we look at the bigger picture of things, this life is so short compared to eternity. It's not that big of a price to pay to live a life of restraint with heaven on the horizon.

How can you hold the truth up?

JULY 26

Kinder Than a Believer

> Then they said to him, "What shall we do to you, that the sea may quiet down for us?" For the sea grew more and more tempestuous. He said to them, "Pick me up and hurl me into the sea; then the sea will quiet down for you, for I know it is because of me that this great tempest has come upon you." Nevertheless, the men rowed hard to get back to dry land, but they could not, for the sea grew more and more tempestuous against them."
>
> —Jonah 1:11–13

We all know what happens next, but these men originally didn't want to throw Jonah in the sea as they kept on rowing and tried to get to shore. These others on the ship with Jonah were, in fact, of all different religions. They were all crying out to their own gods to deliver them from this storm. Even though Jonah knew that this storm wasn't an ordinary storm, the others showed him compassion by not wanting to cast him overboard. If people of these other religions show more kindness than followers of Jesus, then what good are we doing for this world?

In this life, you will meet a lot of mean and nasty church people who proclaim to know Jesus on Sunday mornings, yet they treat people badly the other six days of the week. We are in church to give us the tools to minister to those on the outside. How are we living like Jesus if we can't even treat others with kindness? If people who worship false gods or follow other religions can do it, then we really have no excuse. We know the truth, and it's the only way to heaven, so we must be kind and be loving toward others, or they will never want to believe what we believe.

Christ didn't die on the cross and rise from the dead just for us to walk around acting like Pharisees. We read about these keepers of the law throughout the gospels who lived "holier than thou" lives yet still rejected Jesus and His ministry. You may encounter someone, and you are the only example of Jesus they've ever seen. That's a great responsibility and something not to take lightly. Let us be living examples of our faith all the time. It's not always an easy task, but it's what we must do to live out what we know.

> How can you show the true
> kindness of Jesus to the world?

JULY 27

Tear Off the Rearview

> Brothers, I do not consider that I have made it my own. But one thing I do: forgetting what lies behind and straining forward to what lies ahead, I press on toward the goal for the prize of the upward call of God in Christ Jesus.
>
> —Philippians 3:13–14

Moving forward is a hard thing for some of us. We can usually find daily reminders of our sins of the past. The further we get away from God, the harder it can be to come back. He's always waiting for us, but those desires we succumbed to in the past can be hard to break free from. God's grace is more than sufficient for us to break the chains of our pasts and move forward for a future with the Lord. We need to be in constant prayer and not put ourselves in situations that will tempt us to go back to our past lives.

When I think of someone with a terrible past, the apostle Paul is the first one that comes to mind. He wrote this scripture, in fact. The man persecuted followers of Christ and enjoyed doing it. What, other than the work of the Lord, could help him get over his past and move forward? Paul went on to write a lot of the New Testament and equip others to teach as he was doing after his conversion. Did Paul have regret about what he had done in his past life? I'm sure he did, but that didn't define his future in Christ.

Whenever you come to know Jesus, your past is irrelevant at that point. Think of the thief on the cross coming to know Christ in his final hours of life. What matters is that we take our future with Christ seriously. We need to adhere to His teachings and work toward a better future. We may have our struggles with reminders of the past and the temptation to return to it, but there's a much better future up ahead for staying true to the word and following Christ. Only through Him will your past sins no longer be a burden to you.

How can you escape the bonds of your past sins?

JULY 28

Forever a Loser

>And they marched up over the broad plain of the earth and surrounded the camp of the saints and the beloved city, but fire came down from Heaven and consumed them, and the devil who had deceived them was thrown into the lake of fire and sulfur where the beast and the false prophet were, and they will be tormented day and night forever and ever.
>
>—Revelation 20:9–10

There's always winners and losers in everything. I'm not a sports person by any means, but even I know that there can be only one winner of the Super Bowl. The truth is, God wins in the end, and the devil loses. Revelation is the only unfinished book in the Bible, meaning it never happened yet. If we know this to be true, then why are so many people siding with the losing team? The losers that know they're losing want to take down as many people as they can with them. The devil knows he's lost in the end, and the only thing he has left to do is to deceive enough of humanity to go down with him.

The problem with people today is that the losing side looks way more appealing than the winning side. Of course, that's only from an earthly standpoint. If we're looking at both sides from a biblical side, then it's pretty obvious what the truly more appealing side is. When sin entered the world, we were blinded. Our eyes may have been opened to way more, but we lost sight of the truth.

We have our own free will to make the choice to do right or wrong. The world is full of wrong choices that usually look more appealing than making the right choice. The right choice is always about restraint. If you come to a fork in the road on which choice you should make, you can pretty much count on the wrong choice being filled with all our earthly desires. Stick with the right choice and flee the temptation. Since God wins in the end, let's play for His team in all we do. Greater is the reward in heaven for those who stay true to the Lord.

How can you play for the winning team?

JULY 29

Stay on the Rails

My foot has held fast to His steps; I have kept
His way and have not turned aside.

—Job 23:11

Living life as follower of Jesus is never easy. There's one path to follow, and deviating from it would mean sinning. We're surrounded by temptation, and it's easy to feel overwhelmed with anything. When our lives get really tough, it's common to look for a worldly out to whatever we may be going through. In this passage, Job has been through a lot more than most people could ever deal with. Thankfully, his dedication to the Lord kept him on the right path. He knew what was right and wrong, and no matter what happened to him, he fixed his gaze upon the Lord and stuck to the righteous path.

I'm big into trains, model trains, or riding old railroads. As opposed to a car, a train can only go where the rails are. As long as it stays on the rails, it will go exactly where it needs to go. The rails for us are the path God laid out for us. Like Job, long before us, if we stay on the rails, we'll always avoid sin. Temptation may come our way, but if we stay on God's track, we won't succumb to it.

God laid out the rails in our lives. Are you willing to climb on that train and ride it to the end? It's a choice we have to make daily to stay on the rails and avoid any other path that would go against the Word of the Lord. Being a Christian, especially in today's world, is never easy, but it's so worth that life of restraint for an eternity in heaven with Jesus. All aboard!

How can you stay on God's path
no matter what happens?

TIMOTHY A. MILLS

JULY 30

Love Not Affirm

> Therefore my judgment is that we should not trouble those of the Gentiles who turn to God, but should write to them to abstain from the things polluted by idols, and from sexual immorality, and from what has been strangled, and from blood.
>
> —Acts 15:19–20

In biblical times, the Jews wanted to keep the Gentiles under the law of Moses. For someone who may have just received the good news, as a Gentile, the Old Testament ways were already passed thanks to Jesus. When someone becomes a believer, that's it. Not that there isn't work to be done to maintain their faith, but these old laws and traditions aren't necessary to follow Jesus. It's important for us to recognize a new believer's testimony and welcome them into the faith. We don't want to be the ones putting them down for their past or even their present if there's meaningless issues we don't agree with. Examples include appearances, career choices, or where someone lives. None of that matters. It's about obeying Christ and His commands.

The church has a really bad name sometimes for making up its own rules on who can and who can't come. Some folks are looked down on for whatever reason, and if they are not going against scripture, then who are we to judge what they do? The problem in today's society is that people are affirming over loving. The two are often confused. When we love people like Jesus calls us to, we are helping them out of whatever their life may be living and assisting them in living a more Christ-centered life. All the people Jesus healed who weren't believers were told the three famous little words by our

Savior: "Sin no more." Affirmation is saying, "Just be who you are and you can follow Jesus just fine." That couldn't be further from the truth. We are to be transformed by the gospel. We're not to just keep on living the same life and follow Jesus on the side or just think that He loves the way we are and we can stay that way.

It's sad in today's world that even churches are affirming sin. Some churches are saying that you can be whatever you want and live whatever life you choose and God loves you anyway. God loves all His children, but He doesn't want us to live a life that goes against His commands. If we truly know Jesus, then through the Holy Spirit in us do we get an unstoppable desire to follow Him. To quote one of my favorite preachers, Alistair Begg, "The Gospel is come as you are, it's not stay as you are." What a powerful statement in today's world. We are to be changed by the Gospel and let go of our worldly desires and temptations. It's a hard thing to do when there is great opposition out there, but we all need to stand firm for the truth. The truth of the Lord is the only truth there is.

> How can you love someone
> without affirming their sin?

JULY 31

Walk This Way

> Look carefully then how you walk, not as unwise but as wise, making the best use of the time, because the days are evil.
>
> —Ephesians 5:15–16

Walking through the world today as a believer is no easy task. In America, we don't have to deal with the same magnitude as far as persecution goes when it comes to other countries. Nonetheless, there is still evil about waiting to strike us down. When we walk unwisely as Christians, we are opening ourselves up to failure. The biggest failure being that we set a bad example of how a Christian should be. We need to seek the wisdom of the Lord each and every day and live as to set an example of what following Christ should be.

We don't want to be yoked with unbelievers, but we also must not live the life of a zealot just forcing our beliefs on others. Actions truly speak louder than words when it comes to following Christ. When we live differently and lead by example, we can use the time God has given us to be living examples of God's commands. We may fall short, but we must make that conscious decision every day to obey. I have an uncle who has always enforced the phrase "Clearly think, wisely choose." We must be able to think clearly to make the right choice. When we react out of anger or other emotions, we're not truly able to make the wisest choice.

Time is precious. We're never guaranteed tomorrow. If you knew you would be gone by morning, would it be well with your soul? Would you feel as though you followed Christ and set an example for the world to follow? Make good use of your time by choosing Christ every day. Let your actions speak for who you are as a believer. The tongue can be dangerous and can easily set a poor example for the Gospel. As I've always been told, we have two ears and one mouth. Therefore, we should be doing twice as much listening as talking. Listen for that heavenly wisdom to make the right choice today.

How can you clearly think so to wisely choose?

AUGUST 1

I'm Sorry

> Put on then, as God's chosen ones, holy and beloved, compassionate hearts, kindness, humility, meekness, and patience, bearing with one another and, if one has a complaint against another, forgiving each other; as the Lord has forgiven you, so you also must forgive.
>
> —Colossians 3:12–13

The phrase "I'm sorry" is probably one of the hardest things to say no matter what language. Not that it's hard to just say, but it's very hard to mean sometimes. It's often very hard just to recognize that you need to say sorry to someone. Compassionate hearts, kindness, humility, meekness, and especially patience are things that everyone lacks. We all need to strive to work toward those descriptions of ourselves. God has given us this command that we must diligently work toward those attributes.

Saying sorry isn't enough. Anyone can say that and not mean it. When parents tell their children to say sorry, they don't always explain why. Almost as if a child is off the hook just by saying sorry. What about asking for forgiveness? What about the one wronged doing the forgiving? These are the major backups to saying sorry. When we bear with one another, we are putting on the five attributes of this verse and handling complaints with one another in a godly way. It's not easy because sometimes we just want to be mad. We want revenge, and sometimes we want to be the ones to dish it out. Friends, take it from someone who has held onto so much anger for years. It's not how we're supposed to live.

No matter who it is, whether it's a spouse, a child, a coworker, or a friend, and especially if it's another brother or sister in the church, forgive and bear with one another through whatever the complaint may be. Some of us, including myself, have held onto things for years. We've let wickedness rule over us as to hold a grudge and not forgive. We're only hurting ourselves and damaging our relationship with the Lord by doing that. A self-indicted sentence for us to carry these burdens is a far greater punishment than what we should ever bring on ourselves. The Lord has given us the tools and freed us from these burdens. Let the Lord be your guide in any situation, especially these above verses.

> How can you bear with one another through a complaint without sinning?

AUGUST 2

Get Wise

Let the wise hear and increase in learning and the one who understands obtain guidance, to understand a proverb and saying, the words of the wise and their riddles.

—Proverbs 1:5–6

Wisdom is something most of the world lacks today. Our society is about doing whatever you want and not having to own up to the consequences. That's not how the biblical reality works. There are always consequences to sin. When we dive further into the Bible, we gain more wisdom through scripture. We need to be diligent in our learning and keep watch as to not fall into the temptations that the world tells us we don't need to worry about.

Everyone needs accountability. We all need those older and wiser folks to teach us more than what we already know. We need to humble ourselves to allow ourselves to be taught by others to gain more wisdom in scripture. I personally have several people in my life like that. Truthfully, we will never know it all when it comes to scripture, but we can make an honest attempt to learn as much as we can in this life.

Wherever you are in whatever stage of life you may be, don't be too proud to ever stop learning. God is so complex yet so simple that we need to be willing to develop understanding in our own lives for what we don't know. Here's you first tip on wisdom. Everything in scripture points to the cross. Live your life with a forever learning attitude.

How can you make gaining biblical wisdom a daily priority?

AUGUST 3

Surrender and Follow

> And as He passed by, he saw Levi the son of Alphaeus sitting at the tax booth, and He said to Him, "Follow Me." And he rose and followed Him.
>
> —Mark 2:14

When it comes to following Christ, there are a lot of things that we can't do. If we're truly following Jesus, then we need to leave things of our old life behind. We all will still fall short time and time again, but it's recognizing that we're in the wrong and going against scripture. Then we repent and take the measures to help us not do it again. There's always an earthly cost for following Christ. It may mean giving up relationships, old habits, or even in Levi's case, a career.

Levi, who we more commonly know as Matthew, was a tax collector. Now a Jewish tax collector collecting taxes from other Jews for the Roman occupation in Israel wasn't exactly a well-liked person. I'm sure back then no one would ever think Matthew would be chosen by the Messiah to be one of His closest followers. When Jesus picked Matthew and the other eleven, He didn't pick the clergy of the time. He didn't pick the students of other rabbis. He picked the imperfect common men and all their flaws. Excluding what Judas did, they all gave up their past lives, surrendered, and followed Him.

It's not always as simple as Matthew just getting up from the tax booth and throwing that life away. For most of us, it seems to be a lot harder than that. Jesus is calling all of us to follow Him. Even after the disciples followed Him, they were still imperfect and flawed people. God loves us no matter what, but His calling to us is to trust in Him for our burdens. Surrender those flaws at the cross. Obey His commands and dive deeper into His Word as to understand Him better every day. That's what surrender is about. Let go and follow Jesus.

How can you leave past life of sin behind and surrender to Christ?

AUGUST 4

A Better Way Not Found

> Then one of the twelve, whose name was Judas Iscariot, went to the chief priests and said, "What will you give me if I deliver Him over to you?" And they paid him thirty pieces of silver. And from that moment he sought an opportunity to betray Him.
>
> —Matthew 26:14–16

When Christ picked the twelve, He knew what Judas would eventually do. The prophecy had to be fulfilled that Christ would be betrayed by one of His closest followers. Imagine being handpicked by the Messiah to go on and change the world, but that's not good enough for you. Judas was in love with money more than Jesus. He thought he could find a better way to do things, but he was so wrong in the end. He had everything and threw it away for a worldly desire. It ended up costing him everything in the end.

Oftentimes, in today's world, we do exactly what Judas did. How shocking, I know. We betray Christ for things of the flesh more than we'd like to admit. When we are truly saved, we have it all. We have a peace like no other, and sometimes we don't even realize it. When we feel that we have a void in our life, we try to fill it with things like money, sex, drugs, alcohol, and the list goes on. We need to come to terms with the fact that we have everything we need through Jesus. He has even given us the fancy little guidebook known as the Bible to help us through.

Whatever you are going through, there is scripture to help. Jesus is all we need. Even if we're knocking on death's door, the soul is what matters most. These bodies of ours will eventually deteriorate and end up in the ground. What are we doing about our souls? Don't waste your time with things of this world that will never give you the peace Jesus can offer. Even if some of these things cause you temporary happiness, it's only a false hope on the way to destruction. Don't believe the lies of the world, and don't do what Judas did and betray Christ for worldly things.

> How can you tell if you are betraying Christ for the world?

AUGUST 5

Coming Home

> Let not your hearts be troubled. Believe in God; believe also in me. In my Father's house are many rooms. If it were not so, would I have told you that I go to prepare a place for you? And if I go and prepare a place for you, I will come again and will take you to myself, that where I am you may be also. And you know the way to where I am going.
>
> —John 14:1–4

One day, we'll all go home to the Lord in heaven. This world is truly not our home if we are believers in Christ. As the scripture says, He is preparing a place for us. Sometimes in this world, we do stray and have to turn around and come home. We've often ran from the faith in our lives. Whether we run from it because we want to indulge our own selfish desires or we feel too much shame, as though we are not worthy to come back to the faith, we can always come home to our Lord.

On this day, my family and I just returned home from a four-day trip to West Virginia to visit family. We had a wonderful time, but it was so good to come home, unpack, get our girls to bed, and finally relax in our own home. Even though we had a lot of fun visiting family and seeing the sites, it was great to come home and be back in our own beds. As Christians, we know that we need to return daily to our Father in heaven. No matter where we go or what we do, it's important that we are in prayer daily giving back to our Lord.

Wherever you are in life, sinner, come home. God is always waiting for us to return to Him. Jesus paid the price on the cross that we may have a relationship with the Father. Let us not take that for granted and be in constant prayer and worship of Him that we may not stray too far from our home in Christ.

How can you recognize when you need to come home?

AUGUST 6

It's Really That Simple

> From that time Jesus began to preach, saying, "Repent, for the kingdom of Heaven is at hand."
>
> —Matthew 4:17

People outside of the church have often made ridiculous excuses on why they can't be a part of it. Some would think that you need to have it all together to be in church. Some, deep down, may just feel unworthy and use any excuse in the book to be combative when it comes to being a part of the body of believers. The truth is, you don't need to be a Bible scholar or a preacher to come on board. This verse is the first step in becoming a believer. God will sort out the baggage as you dive deeper into the faith.

The church has a bad reputation sometimes for making up its own rules on who is worthy enough to be a part of it. I once heard the excuse from someone that he couldn't come to church because he had an earring. Well, I myself have earrings, along with tattoos and long hair. The body of believers I and my family belong to have never thought of me any different. The faith is what counts. When we take the initial step to believe, we then work toward obeying Christ's commands.

You never truly realize how close the kingdom of heaven is at hand. This world could be gone tomorrow, and all these struggles will be over. Let's live for God like that time is now. Let us repent of our sins and work toward a better foundation in Christ. Living for Him can have its challenges in a world that opposes Him, but the world He walked in opposed Him back then. He knows what it's like to be rejected. To have a message that some wouldn't want to hear. Life can be overwhelming and get the best of us sometimes, but one thing's for certain. An eternity with Christ is far greater than anything on this earth.

How can you repent of your sins daily?

AUGUST 7

Handpicked by the Lord

> For you are a people holy to the Lord your God. The Lord your God has chosen you to be a people for His treasured possession, out of all the peoples who are on the face of the earth.
>
> —Deuteronomy 7:6

This Old Testament verse was meant for the Jews in the ways of the old law of Moses. Flash forward to today, and it's something we can relate to as believers. When we have Christ in our hearts, we are treasured possessions of the Lord. We are won over to His side and cannot be taken away from Him. Not that the devil doesn't try because he sure loves to try and shake our faith in the King. We need to be thankful for our faith and stay close to the Lord. The Jews of the Old Testament were God's chosen people. When we look at the law fulfilled by Christ, we can all be God's chosen people when we accept Christ as our Lord and Savior.

I've often wondered throughout my life, What would my life have been like had I not been raised in a Christian home? Even though I had my struggles, my foundation in Christ that I had since I was very young brought me back to Him. I thank the Lord for the struggles He's brought me through what I couldn't handle on my own. He picked me from a young age to hear His message, and by His grace, I never lost sight of that. Even amid a life of sin and rebellion, I never forgot His promises.

When you take the step to accept Christ into your life, you are a chosen person for His greater glory. We're chosen to do His work and keep His commands. True salvation is being transformed by the Gospel and living it out. Mistakes will get made, but it's important that we repent of those mistakes and learn from them. God's grace is sufficient for us all. Live your life for Him as though you were truly handpicked by the King, because you are!

> How can you live a life as being
> handpicked by God?

AUGUST 8

Listen to the Music

Oh come, let us sing to the Lord; let us make a joyful noise to the rock of our salvation! Let us come into His presence with thanksgiving; let us make a joyful noise to Him with songs of praise!

—Psalm 95:1–2

Sometimes you just have to sing it out to the King! A big part of worship is music, no matter where you go to church at. I've always found that when I'm listening to worship music on my own or with our congregation that the Spirit can really move through music. Whether it be an old hymn or a newer contemporary worship song, it's all praise to our Lord. It's amazing what singing to God can do for your soul. When we sing with thanksgiving, as the verse says, we're offering our praise with gratitude.

In my church, I play bass guitar on the praise team. It's a privilege to be up there on Sunday mornings offering my talents and gifts that the Lord has given me. Some songs I prefer over others because I feel more connected to the Spirit with different songs. Some tunes can hit you just right, and you really feel the Lord's presence in worship. It's also important that when we play instruments or sing in a choir or even just participate in the congregation that we remember, it's not a performance. It's not about us glorifying ourselves but hiding ourselves behind the cross to give the Lord all our attention. May we see more of Him and less of us.

When you're on your own and have time to listen to music, I encourage you all to dive into some Christian music. It's a wonderful thing to help us get through a rough day or any day. Even singing by yourself to no music is still a way to praise our Lord. The music can be extremely uplifting and bring you closer to God in the process. Praise Him always.

How can you make Christian music a bigger priority?

AUGUST 9

Leave Your Sins Behind

What shall we say then? Are we to continue in sin that grace may abound? By no means! How can we who died to sin still live in it?

—Romans 6:1–2

When we've lived sinful lives before we came to Christ, those temptations can still tug at us to go back. Being in Christ means we are newly created. He has paid the price for our sins, and we need to live every day in thankfulness and watching that we don't return to where we used to be. Those sins and the sins of our futures have been paid for in blood, but we must not take advantage of the grace God has given us. If we are truly saved, why would we want to keep on sinning?

I've been a Christian my entire life. I was blessed to be raised in a Christian home, but I strayed away at point in my life. I was dealing with a broken family, and we moved two hours away from our home. My life fell apart pretty quick. I knew what the scriptures said, but my faith had never been tested up until that point. I found sins, pretty quickly, to try and fill these voids in my life. I knew what I was doing wasn't right, but I was a mess. Even after I was able to move back home, I still struggled. I continued down that wrong path for years. I didn't know how to get out of it. Fortunately, God's grace was shed on me through all of it. As the years rolled by, my faith increased, and I finally got the point where doing the wrong thing made me feel convicted every time. The right path is the only way to go.

Wherever you are in your faith, whether you're a solid believer or a struggling new convert, guard yourself. Keep watch that you don't fall into sinning again in the same old temptations that may have ensnared you for years. God will always be graceful to us, but we need to have a true desire to sin no more. We need to keep the mindset every day that our sins were paid for on an old rugged cross. Jesus paid it all for everyone.

How can you stop sinning?

AUGUST 10

The Right Tools for the Job

The craftsman strengthens the goldsmith, and he who smooths with the hammer him who strikes the anvil, saying of the soldering, "It is good," and they strengthen it with nails so that it cannot be moved.

—Isaiah 41:7

In any job that must be done, the right tools are always needed. Different tradesmen for different areas of work all have their own specific tools to get a job done. Being a believer in Christ requires the right tools. We have our faith, our Bibles, our churches, and we have each other to encourage and help strengthen one another to work toward the unification of the body of Christ. When we do anything with the wrong tools, we only frustrate ourselves and can potentially ruin what we're trying to accomplish.

I bet every one of us men here can say we've used a butter knife as a screwdriver that took a simple job way longer to do. All of us have screwdrivers, but why would we want to go down to our garage and get one? Sometimes, we need to go that extra distance to get the right tools to finish a job. In our faith, our scriptures are the right tools. We all have busy schedules, and time is something we usually don't have enough of. If we just try to coast through life being "good enough," what are we doing to grow? If we're not using scripture to help us ground ourselves deeper in our faith, then we need to consider using the right tool. Even in our churches. If we just attend a service, we are getting fed through the sermon, but why not get involved in a Sunday school or a small group? In those places, we have an even better open discussion environment to learn more.

Be the believer that you would want in your life. Our brothers and sisters in Christ are some of the best tools we could ever ask for when it comes to growing in our faith. There is always strength in numbers. (Trust me, I'm a union guy!) When we join together in praise and prayer and encourage one another, we're utilizing one of the greatest tools we have ever been given. Take the opportunity to pour into others as you are poured into as well.

> How can you utilize the right
> tools to grow in your faith?

AUGUST 11

Restoration Coming

I will restore to you the years that the swarming locust has eaten, the hopper, the destroyer, and the cutter, my great army, which I sent among you. You shall eat in plenty and be satisfied, and praise the name of the Lord your God, who has dealt wondrously with you. And my people shall never again be put to shame.

—Joel 2:25–26

When we look at the world through Christ-following eyes, we can see that it's not how it's supposed to be. Nor is it going to stay this way. Think of the things you deal with during everyday life that can cause you stress or put you through a trial. God has spoken that His promises are going to be fulfilled. We need to make the best of our time on earth and live life for Him. We've all been damaged by the side effects from sin, whether it's the generational sin or sins we've committed that leave us with earthly consequences. The Lord will restore us. Let us ever praise Him.

During the ages of twenty-five and twenty-six, my life was a wreck. I was chasing after things of this world that never gave true fulfillment. Even though I was left empty and brokenhearted, I still went right back to chasing those things again. The definition of insanity is doing the same thing over and over and expecting a different result. I struggled so badly thinking I could find my happiness and be restored. Friends, I'm here to tell you that nothing of this world could ever do that for you. Only through Jesus are we fully restored and have peace.

Everyone needs restored. A lot of people just don't realize how. Do you want peace in life? The answer is Jesus. Do you want to live a life of anger and dysfunction? Most certainly not, but too many people are caught up in it and don't know how to get out of it. There's only one way, and we need to grow closer to Jesus every day to walk a narrow path and live our lives for Him. Be restored in knowing Jesus.

How can you seek true restoration for your life?

AUGUST 12

Union in Christ

*I am the vine; you are the branches. Whoever abides
in Me and I in him, he it is that bears much fruit,
for apart from Me you can do nothing.*

—John 15:5

When we hear the word *union*, the simple definition is two or more things becoming one. Togetherness in the body of believers creates a stronger union for Christ. Higher numbers in the body of believers can always achieve more. When many believers come together in a church to bring support, a lot can happen. When a congregation prays together for the same thing, we're unifying ourselves toward a common goal. When people offer tithes to the church, we're using our money together to support the ministry. When we stand firm against opposition to the scriptures, we're in union with Christ.

Today was our annual union picnic. Us teamsters and our families all got to together for a wonderful time, all there with one strong connection. No matter which company those of us worked for, we're all brothers and sisters in the same union, paying our dues toward many different things. Those of us in our individual shops have contracts to negotiate for a better workplace, and it can be a disaster if our shop isn't united. We need to stand together in solidarity to be the union we want. The same is true for the union with Christ. When churches don't stand together against opposition, we only hurt ourselves.

Ultimately, God is in control and has a plan. Whatever is going to happen is up to His will. That being said, we need to live for

Him and pray, no matter what. Let us unify ourselves in this body of believers to grow closer to individual union with Christ. Walking with each other, as believers, in this crazy world is so much better than walking alone. We're one body in Christ. He is the vine, and we are the branches.

> How can you work toward union with Christ
> through union with other believers?

AUGUST 13

Getting in the Way

> For where jealousy and selfish ambition exist, there will be disorder and every vile practice.
>
> —James 3:16

Let's face it, we all get in the way. We get in the way constantly of what God wants for us, and then we learn the hard way that He was right all along. One major thing we can get in the way of is worship. Often, too many pastors and worship leaders can come off as making Sunday mornings a performance and not about worship. When any one of us who has that selfish ambition tries to further themselves and not the kingdom with worship, it is only distorting the reason why we're really there. When we humble our hearts for worship and look toward growing in Christ together, we are seeing Him through serving each other.

I have personally experienced this more with worship leaders. Church music directors can occasionally get too caught up in trying to make the music so perfect that they lose sight of why they are really there. Oftentimes, it becomes a performance for them. It becomes a chance for them to glorify themselves. In all honesty, who cares if someone plays a wrong note, sings a wrong lyric, or has a problem with an instrument? The Lord recognizes why we are there. When we are given those gifts and talents, such as music, it's important that we recognize where they came from—our Lord. We need to be reminded that it's never a performance no matter what we do up front in church. It always needs to be a reflection of the King.

Don't get in the way of God's glory. When you have an opportunity to be a part of worship, hide behind the cross. Let people see Jesus when they see you. We are vessels of the Holy Spirit, and we must live that way always, especially in church. When we really break down the Gospel message of what Christ did for us, we need true humility and selfless ambition to further His glory for our churches and those in the world we encounter.

How can you show less of yourself and more of Christ in worship?

AUGUST 14

Who We Were to Who We Are

> For we ourselves were once foolish, disobedient, led astray, slaves to various passions and pleasures, passing our days in malice and envy, hated by others and hating one another. But when the goodness and loving kindness of God our Savior appeared, He save us, not because of works done by us in righteousness, but according to His own mercy, by the washing of regeneration and renewal of the Holy Spirit, whom He poured out on us richly through Jesus Christ our Savior, so that being justified by His grace we might become heirs according to the hope of eternal life.
>
> —Titus 3:3–7

Wow, is that a lot! One thing I really held on to in these verses is that we see the three parts of the trinity working together in our lives. When we look at what we were before Christ, it needs to be nothing like what we are now. Through the Father, Son, and Holy Spirit, may we become the men and women who we're called to be. I'm reminded of the old hymn, "Jesus paid it all, all to Him I owe, sin had left a crimson stain, He washed it white as snow." The sins of our old lives leave many battle scars all over us, but in Jesus we are cleaned up well.

When we look at the first part of the verses talking about our old lives, can you relate to any of that? I'll be the first to admit, each one of those things I lived for in my old life. It's even easy for us to be tempted to go back there when something negative happens to us. Do not be fooled by the enemy. If what you had there wasn't fulfilling before you met Christ, it's most certainly not going to be fulfilling after. When those negative moments interrupt our lives, we need to remember that we can't get through it with our own works. Only through Jesus's mercy and love can overcome.

This is definitely a passage to highlight in your Bible. Be reminded of this daily. Your old life is nothing anymore. Even if you are still facing consequences to your sins, that does not define you. What defines you is your faith in the Lord. Cling to Him and know that He is enough. Nothing in this world could ever give you the fulfillment you have living in the Spirit. Times may get tough, and it's definitely a life of restraint, but it's worth every second that we stay faithful.

> How can you hold on to who you are in Christ over who you were without Him?

AUGUST 15

Reaching for the King

> Answer me quickly, O Lord! My spirit
> fails! Hide not your face from me,
> lest I be like those who go down to the pit.
>
> —Psalm 143:7

When David wrote this one, he was losing hope. He had exhausted all options and only needed the Lord. How often do we do that? We're reaching our breaking points where we know that we've got ourselves in a mess, and the only way we can get out of the situation is through our Lord. In a world like today, it's not uncommon to be so overwhelmed that we're just in dire need of surrender, even us believers!

In my younger years, I may have been the subject of this verse on more than one occasion. I was living a reckless life while still attending church on Sundays. I was so hardened that the sermons and the lessons just weren't getting through to me. I didn't have the desire to follow the Lord that I do now. Many times came and went where I would put myself in bad situations and came crying out to God to get me out of it. He got me where I am today, undeservingly, but only through His grace.

I think when we stick to His commands and follow Him daily, we may still get overwhelmed at times, but we don't have those feelings of despair like the entire world is crashing down on us. If we continue to stay close to Him, we don't have the worries of the world. Times may get hard, but God's grace never fails. His love for us never changes. Stay in prayer and in the Word to ground yourself in Christ so you may not be shaken by the storms of this world.

How can you be at peace whatever comes your way?

AUGUST 16

Denying out of Fear

So everyone who acknowledges me before men, I also will acknowledge before my Father who is in Heaven, but whoever denies me before men, I also will deny before my Father who is in Heaven.

—Matthew 10:32–33

When we think of denying Christ, probably the first thing that would come to one's mind is Peter's denial three times as Christ was being led away. In today's world, it's not uncommon to deny Christ through our actions. Often, we are tempted to go along with the crowd. We might choose not to go against the grain if we are afraid of being rejected by those around us. This is a prime example of us trying to please the world instead of doing what is right in the eyes of the Lord. How we treat others is probably the top thing that we can do differently than the world.

When I was a young rebellious teenager, I recall a situation at a video game store. Another customer was there trading in some music albums and other things. After he left, the clerk at the register began to make fun of him for some of the things he traded in. He continued this behavior, and when he realized that I could hear him, he apologized to me. These words still echo in my memory as I replied, "I don't know him." I think back to that day and realize that I could have made a difference. I could have come to the other customer's defense, even though I didn't know him. I could have been a light for Christ that day, and I rejected the opportunity out of fear. I didn't have the courage to stand up for what was right.

Thinking back to that situation years later, it's always been a reminder that one of the simplest we can do to not deny Christ is to treat others with love. We can find opportunities every day to stand up for Christ and the truth He's given us. When we all get to heaven eventually, we certainly do not want to be denied in front of the Father. We all may fall short and struggle, but we always have the chance to get right with Christ here on earth.

> How can you weed out ways in your life
> that may be denying Christ?

AUGUST 17

So Easy a Child Can Do It

> Truly, I say to you, whoever does not receive the kingdom of God like a child shall not enter it.
>
> —Mark 10:15

Sometimes children can understand things way better than adults. They can see things in black and white. The gospel message is included in that. To break down the message in the simplest form, Christ was born like a normal human. He ministered to people, He died on the cross, He rose from the grave, and He's coming back! Live for Him until that day. Children can grasp that pretty easily. Adults sometimes have to think too much about it. We've been poisoned by the world to try and question every last detail, yet it doesn't really matter in the long run. Repent, believe, and live the life the Lord calls you to live, obeying His commands.

It's always a joy to see what we call "a moment with young disciples" in our church. It's the part of the service where the children are called up front and given a lesson by our director of children and family ministries. Hearing those precious little ones interact with the lesson and answer the questions correctly is always a privilege. These little ones get it. It's really that simple and doesn't need to be so complex. The message is clear about what Jesus has done for us that our little members of the congregation already have it figured out.

When we as adults have gone through trying times, we can often be discouraged and start overthinking the message. The enemy preys on things like this where He can instill doubt in us. Reject him immediately and cling to the Lord. Keep focusing on a childlike faith. No matter what age we are, we are all children of the King!

How can you keep faith as simple as a child can?

TIMOTHY A. MILLS

AUGUST 18

Lies to Divide

> Now the Spirit expressly says that in later times some will depart from the faith by devoting themselves to deceitful spirits and teachings of demons, through the insincerity of liars whose consciences are seared, who forbid marriage and require abstinence from foods that God created to be received with thanksgiving by those who believe and know the truth.
>
> —1 Timothy 4:1–3

Those later times? We're in them. Does any of this sound familiar to you? Are you experiencing these kinds of people in your own church? It's not uncommon anymore. We find that these kinds of people have already departed from their faith, and sometimes they don't even know it. They are believing the lies so much that they think they are progressing the faith, but they are really just distorting it more. These are the kinds of folks that like to look at certain scriptures and ask the same question as the serpent, "Did God really say that?"

No matter what church you belong to, you will always find division. Sometimes it's just a difference of opinion, but other times, it can be a more serious division because some want to change scripture. I personally know people who have left our church because they wanted to change certain scriptures and expected everyone to just go along with it. When anyone is trying to push an agenda or put anything above the Gospel message, they are basically saying the Gospel isn't enough. They limit what God can do. God can do everything.

It's a shame that there is so much division in churches, but in some ways, it can resolve in a better way. When these dividers are stood against and eventually leave the church, you gain strength in keeping the church focused on the right direction. Pray for these people, but do not follow them down the same path. Continue to grow deeper in the truth. Stand up for the Word. When the world caves to certain ideologies, that does not mean that the church should follow in the same path. We are to be different. We are to live for the King.

How can you figure out who is dividing the body of believers?

AUGUST 19

Reaching for the Broken

> Beloved, never avenge yourselves, but leave it to the wrath of God, for it is written, "Vengeance is mine, I will repay, says the Lord." To the contrary, "if your enemy is hungry, feed him; if he is thirsty, give him something to drink; for by so doing you will heap burning coals on his head." Do not be overcome by evil, but overcome with good.
>
> —Romans 12:19–21

Well, we've come to another part in the book of things we wished God never said. However, He did, and we must follow His command. The truth is, we all struggle with this. We all have a problem when it comes to considering ourselves a victim in any situation and wanting the person who wronged us to pay dearly. I'm sure many of us have wanted them to pay with our own hands. Friends, reject that idea. The Lord will have His day with those who have persecuted us.

My wife and I were dealing with a situation involving a family member who turned her back on us. This is a person who we were always there for and also there for her son. Things had happened, and as much as we tried to love her and be there for her, we were suddenly the enemies. We pray for her daily and her son, and at any point in time, we would be there for her if she needed us. Some people can't stand it when we obey this command. They can get even more mad when we don't retaliate. Truthfully, I think it leaves their heads spinning when someone can still be so kind and loving toward some who may have persecuted them.

Remember this, friends. At any point during the crucifixion, Jesus could have stopped it all. He could have slaughtered all those who were involved. He could have come down from the cross and said, "I'm done with this" and wiped out the entire earth. But no, He led the perfect example of this command. You think you have it hard being nice to someone? Think of the cross. We are all going to struggle with this because of our own sin, but we can still make a conscious effort to treat those people far better than they treat us. Devote it to prayer to help you with this. It's a big one we all need to get better at.

How can you treat your enemies better than the way they treat you?

AUGUST 20

When the Seasoned Saints Go Home

> But we do not want you to be uninformed, brothers, about those who are asleep, that you may not grieve as others do who have no hope. For since we believe that Jesus died and rose again, even so, through Jesus, God will bring with him those who have fallen asleep.
>
> —1 Thessalonians 4:13–14

Grief is something we all know is inevitable, but we know we are going to have to face it at some point with the loss of a loved one. Fortunately for us, we have a peace given to us by our Lord when we deal with loss. When a loved one who knew Jesus passes on, they are truly alive and well through Him. We may miss them and be hurting in their absence, but they are walking with Jesus, free of any pain or sorrow.

This morning, at our outdoor church service, our pastor announced that one of our "seasoned saints," as we refer to those elderly folks in our church, had passed away. She was in her nineties and was still attending a Bible study with our church hosted on Zoom every Wednesday from the nursing home she was at. Ms. Bert was a very faithful woman of God. She taught me and also my mother in Sunday school and was a huge blessing to our church for decades. There were many tears this morning after we sang "How Great Thou Art." She is now with our Lord, and even though she is dearly missed, there is an overwhelming sense of peace in knowing where her faith was—in Jesus.

Friends, we will all go through grief in our church families. Loss on earth is inevitable, but eternal life awaits us in heaven. We can rejoice in knowing that our loved ones are no longer suffering. They are in eternal peace. Those of us left below are to live for Christ and await our day that we meet Him in glory.

How can you be at peace over the
loss of a fellow believer?

AUGUST 21

Above Reproach

> We who are strong have an obligation to bear with the failings of the weak, and not to please ourselves. Let each of us please his neighbor for his good, to build him up. For Christ did not please Himself, but as it is written, "The reproaches of those who reproached you fell on me."
>
> —Romans 15:1–3

It's easy to go through life trying to please ourselves. We search for things that give us enjoyment, but overall, we will never be completely pleased by things of this world. Try as we might, we will always want for me. There is only one way to be completely fulfilled, and that's through Jesus. When we live selfless lives and carry each other's burdens, we are setting examples of what Christ did for us. He didn't come to earth to please himself and live a comfortable life. He came to live a perfect life, only to be given up to the hands of men who lead Him to a cross.

Serving is an opportunity we all have a chance to do every day. It doesn't even have to be anything organized through a church. God calls us to build others up. We can do simple things each day for others. An encouraging word can go a really long way for some people, especially a complete stranger that you know nothing about. Take time to pray for God to give you these opportunities to live out these verses.

These commands are crucial in a world like today. Far too many people are so short-tempered and filled with wickedness. When we love as Christ loved and live in the manner He commands us, we have so much better opportunities to reach someone in the darkness and lead them to the one who can give them true hope. We can't change people. Only God can do that. But it's our responsibility to share that good news and lead by example.

How can you build others up through Christ?

AUGUST 22

Born Again

*Jesus answered him, "Truly, truly,
I say to you, unless one is born again he
cannot see the kingdom of God."*

—John 3:3

We've all heard the term *born again*. To really comprehend this can be somewhat difficult yet so simple. Being born again is accepting Christ as your Savior and Lord and accepting His forgiveness of our sins. The old life is now gone. We are truly a new creation in Christ. This, friends, is the only true way into heaven. Jesus holds the key, and He's not keeping it from us. He's standing there holding it out for us, and all we have to do is accept it. That can be very hard for some people, but why? Do the earthly fears set in? Are the side effects of sin so strong that someone couldn't possibly believe the love Jesus has for them? What about other faiths that say differently? Many distractions try to get in our way, but the narrow path is still in sight.

Do you often hear when someone passes away that "they're in a better place"? Typically a cliché statement from a relative who doesn't know Jesus along with the deceased, who didn't either. How could we even offer comfort to someone like that knowing, by scripture, that their deceased relative is truly not in a better place at all? I think at that point, the best comfort we can give someone is to just listen while they grieve. If we stand with them in their sorrow and earn a right to be heard, then we may be able to share the good news with them. That's truly a sign of God making good out of bad.

Live out being born again. Don't go back to your old life. Certainly, share this news with others. The more people that hear the message, the more God may work in their hearts. People don't often instantly believe, but when the seeds are planted, God can do the rest. Jesus paid much too high of a price for us to just stay in the world. Live out your faith daily. Search for the lost, and may God use you to bring them His hope.

How can you live a born-again life?

AUGUST 23

Unlikely Heroes

And Joshua the son of Nun sent two men secretly from Shittim as spies, saying, "Go, view the land, especially Jericho." And they went and came into the house of prostitute whose name was Rahab and lodged there. And it was told to the king of Jericho, "Behold, men of Israel have come here tonight to search out the land." Then the king of Jericho sent to Rahab, saying, "Bring out the men who have come to you, who entered your house, for they have come to search out all the land." But the woman had taken the two men and hidden them. And she said, "True, the men came to me, but I did not know where they were from."

—Joshua 2:1–4

The story continues with the downfall of Jericho as Joshua and the Israelites marched around it, by the Lord's command, and it crashed to the ground. Rahab's home was spared because of her obedience in helping the spies search the city. Let's think about this for a second. When did you ever hear of a prostitute doing work for the Lord? This may be the only time. Rahab might have had a rough life by her own choices, but she took the opportunity that was given to her. Is your past so bad that you can't serve the Lord? I would think not.

Let's look at today's world and the excuses people give. No matter who you were, it's who you are in the moment you respond to God's calling that really matters. God can choose anyone. He doesn't discriminate in a negative or positive way. Whoever He chooses will make good work for His glory. Many people have lived terrible lives of sin up until God called them, and then they left it all behind.

Whoever you are and whatever you've done, God may be calling you today. You may be the one to do something great for Him. Some of us might have never had anything to do with God up until now, but He can still use us. We're all unlikely heroes in a way for whatever He may call us to do. Open your hearts and be mindful that you may be called at any moment for something to further God's kingdom.

How can you accept a calling from God regardless of your past?

AUGUST 24

Don't Lose Sight

And Peter answered Him, "Lord, if it is you, command me to come to you on the water." He said, "Come." So Peter got out of the boat and walked on the water and came to Jesus. But when he saw the wind, he was afraid, and beginning to sink he cried out, "Lord, save me." Jesus immediately reached out His hand and took hold of him, saying to him, "O you of little faith, why did you doubt?" And when they got into the boat, the wind ceased. And those in the boat worshipped Him, saying, "Truly you are the Son of God."

—Matthew 14:28–33

Doubt can slip in on us very easily. Sometimes it's hard to fathom the miracles of Jesus and what He is truly capable of doing. Our focus must never be off Him, no matter what we do. Often, the daily distractions can lead us away from maintaining our faith. We must make the Lord our biggest priority. Never lose sight of what God wants for us. Even in our busy schedules, it's not hard to take time out of our days to commit to prayer. We should always give the Lord our time.

Another distraction can be our own selfish desires, even in church. When we're in a leadership role in our churches, it's important to never forget why we are there. It's a common thing for our own faith to struggle when all we are doing is constantly pouring into others. When we are leading worship in a musical sense, we are worshipping just as much as the congregation. We should never make it a performance and turn the focus to us. We cannot be caught up in ourselves or why we are really there. All involved and all attending worship are all ultimately there to worship.

God is always faithful, even when we don't always get the answers we want. The path to follow Him has always been narrow. We must walk that tight rope all our days as to not fall off in the distractions. May we always hide behind the cross so our sight will always be on Him in everything we do.

How can you keep your sight on the Lord always?

AUGUST 25

What's Most Important

He sent and had John beheaded in the prison, and his head was brought on a platter and given to the girl, and she brought it to her mother. And his disciples came and took the body and buried it, and they went and told Jesus.

—Matthew 14:10–12

Not a very pretty picture if we're all imagining how John the Baptist went out. John paved the way for Jesus. He was one of the most dedicated followers who knew his place and his purpose for furthering God's kingdom. I'm sure we all wonder, though, why he wasn't there through it all. Why didn't he get to see Christ's death, burial, and resurrection? We may never know the exact reason, but John had all he needed. Sometimes, we don't know why things happen to us, but it's often been said, "God gives His toughest battles to His strongest soldiers."

Look at our world today and see that some people who reject God live a life of comfort, and some of the followers of Jesus live what would seem to be very troubled lives. What's most important to remember is that Christ is enough. It doesn't matter what trouble we go through or what the world may think of us. We truly have it all. Even when these earthly bodies fade and we greet death one day, the soul will never be broken. Our souls belong to Jesus. This life can throw whatever it wants at us. Our souls are secured.

Remember, friends, anything you may be going through, even if it's knocking on death's door, Christ is enough. He's always been enough even when we don't realize it. We need not worry about the trivial things of this world. One day we'll all join Him in glory, and none of this will matter anymore.

How can you focus on Christ's teachings as the most important thing in your life?

AUGUST 26

Old-Fashioned

> They will perish, but you will remain; they will all wear out like a garment. You will change them like a rob, and they will pass away, but you are the same, and your years have no end. The children of your servants shall dwell secure; their offspring shall be established before you.
>
> —Psalm 102:26–28

If you haven't figured it out by now, God never changes. His plans have always been the same, His nature remains the same, and His love certainly never ceases for us. His Word, of course, doesn't change either. If we know all these things, then why does it seem so often that people are trying to change His word? Why do people want the message to be something it's not? Some folks think that because time progresses and the views of the world change, somehow God will change His mind on things. No matter what the way of the world is today, if God gave us commands, we are still to follow them.

I've often heard things like "the Bible is old-fashioned" or "out of date." Even things like "get with the times" or "this is the new reality," come out every now and then. Friends, these are nothing but lies of the enemy. We cannot have faith in God, yet something in our lives is still not enough. We can't hold onto things that we think are unfair or unjust. If you want to look at something really unfair and unjust, look at Jesus. He paid it all when it should have been every one of us on that cross for our sins. Don't have a chip on your shoulder about something in this world contrary to scripture. God can take care of it if we let Him.

The Bible must remain constant through all of time. Every one of us will be dead and buried one day. What are we leaving behind for the next generation? We shouldn't be out there perverting the gospel to a bunch of young folks getting them on board with a lie. We need to be strong and encourage others to know that no matter what, God will always be the same. We need not worry about some of these hardships of this world when it's already been taken care of by Jesus himself. Things may change with churches or organized worship, but the message is always the same.

How can you teach those that think that the Bible needs to change?

AUGUST 27

To Know True Love

Beloved, let us love one another, for love is from God, and whoever loves has been born of God and knows God. Anyone who does not love does not know God because God is love. In this the love of God was made manifest among us, that God sent his only Son into the world, so that we might live through Him.

—1 John 4:7–9

Love is such an overused word, especially for those who have never known true love. The true love that we accept in Christ Jesus is something that some folks haven't truly accepted yet. The word *love* is thrown out for just about anything these days. We love certain foods, movies, music, and hobbies, but do we really know what love is? Love came in the form of a man who went to a cross to die for our sins. Jesus showed us what true love is all about.

It's oftentimes puzzling to me when I hear unbelievers talk about love. They, of course, are only going by what the world's standard of love is, but if they don't know Jesus, then how could they even fathom what love is? When you have a husband and wife who don't know Jesus, could they ever truly love each other? Marriage is hard enough, but it's even harder when Jesus isn't at the center of it.

Friends, love is something so special. The true love the Father has for us to send His only son to take our place on the cross is something that can be very hard to wrap our brains around, yet it's so simple. Love is simple in the long run. Love one another as Christ loves you. Get to know true love by getting to know Jesus better every day.

How can we know true love through Jesus?

AUGUST 28

Persecution Unfolds

About that time Herod the king laid violent hands on some who belonged to the church. He killed James the brother of John with the sword, and when he saw that it please the Jews, he proceeded to arrest Peter also. This was during the days of Unleavened Bread.

—Acts 12:1–3

    Those twelve apostles of Christ did not have easy lives. Most of them were martyred for their faith. James, the brother of John, was the first to go. Being apostles didn't give these guys a life of ease on earth. John the beloved was the only one not to die in the way of a martyr. These chosen men lived out their faith and greeted death as one step closer to Jesus.

    Persecution is inevitable for anyone who believes in Jesus. In some form or another, we are all going to face it. If we flash forward to today in America, we probably don't have to worry about being killed for our faith, but we will surely be treated differently because of it. When we don't go along with the crowd, people wonder why. Some folks may even turn hostile on us because we are not partaking in some of the same things they are. For example, many years ago, I was invited to a bachelor party by someone who was a member in a wedding party. I didn't know anyone involved except the one who invited me. When it comes to worldly bachelor parties, some men choose to go to an "adults only" kind of place. Catch my drift? Well, after hearing that's where this was going to be, I respectfully declined. I informed the one who invited me that I do not go to places like that. Not once did I ever judge him or criticize him for going there, but I knew as a Christian, I couldn't do that because of my faith. I was rejected and called self-righteous and that I thought I was better than the other people going. It all comes down to people not liking you when you go against what they do. Stand firm, friends, because God's way is far better than giving into the world.

When you face that persecution, just remember, it's all been foretold. We can lose in this life and still win for eternity in the next when we have Jesus. This life is so temporary that even if we are martyred for our faith, we only gain a life of eternity with Jesus. Live for Him and preach His message to all that will hear. It's said that the apostle Andrew preached for three days while he was being crucified for his faith. Even in our own death, may others be won over to Christ.

> How can you be at peace when you are persecuted for following Jesus?

AUGUST 29

Out of the Spotlight

> Beware of practicing your righteousness before other people in order to be seen by them, tor then you will have no reward from your Father who is in Heaven.
>
> —Matthew 6:1

In a world today where everyone wants to get ahead or be recognized for whatever good they have done, we as Christians must stay out of the spotlight and keep the focus on Christ. We hear the Bible tell a lot about idol worship, but do we ever stop and think that we might be idolizing ourselves? When we try to put ourselves in the spotlight for what we are doing, we are only giving God less credit. He sure doesn't deserve that. It's a constant self-analysis of our actions that we must be aware of.

Did you ever see pictures of someone on social media who gave money to a homeless person but had to post a picture of themselves doing it? That's a prime example of what the scripture is saying. The motives behind kindness or giving or even worship are not always in the right mindset. If those things are done in the name of ourselves, then who are we really glorifying? Ourselves! We're not glorifying God by showing off what we have done for others. There may be a time and place to share those moments with others, but we must be mindful of why we are telling others about what we have done.

If your mindset in doing things for others isn't fixed on God, I'd encourage you to rethink why else you would do these acts of kindness and so on. All our actions need to be focused on Christ and sharing His message with others. We must not be too proud or arrogant in the things we do for others. When we are serving, the world needs to see Jesus. We are just vessels of the Holy Spirit to do His work and not our own. Be humble enough to give credit where credit is due.

How can you put Jesus before yourself when serving others?

TIMOTHY A. MILLS

AUGUST 30

I Love to Tell the Story

> These twelve Jesus sent out, instructing them, "Go nowhere among the Gentiles and enter no town of the Samaritans, but go rather to the lost sheep of the house of Israel. And proclaim as you go, saying, the Kingdom of Heaven is at hand. Heal the sick, raise the dead, cleanse lepers, cast out demons. You received without paying; give without pay."
>
> —Matthew 10:5–8

To tell the old, old story of Jesus and His love. Oh, what it must have been like to be one of the twelve on this mission. Hearing from Jesus himself what to tell the world. I'm sure these disciples had their doubts and concerns about going out into the world to preach the Messiah's message, but they did it, nevertheless. They all loved their rabbi (I'm sure even Judas may have initially, and they went out and preached His word to the world).

Do we love to tell the old story? Are we on fire for Christ in our everyday lives? It's something we may need to examine in our own lives. We are fast-forwarding from then to now, but the commands are still the same. Jesus may not be in the flesh telling us what to do, but we still need to obey His commands and go out to reach the lost. We need to be passionate about our faith. We need to be diligent in learning how to be better in our faith. When we go out and preach His word, we must do it in a way where we present the Gospel message for what it is and be joyful in doing so.

It's easy to let your faith get on the back burner. Never lose sight of Jesus and His message to us. We should be more excited and committed to proclaiming His word to the unbelievers. The spark might not be all there for us right now, but there will come better days for us in our faith where sharing the message with others becomes more natural, and we are more joyful in doing so. Reach for those around you who are lost and preach His word to all who will hear.

How can you be more passionate about the message of Christ?

AUGUST 31

Stage Fright

Equipping the Called

"Come, I will send you to Pharaoh that you may bring my people, the children of Israel, out of Egypt." But Moses said to God, "Who am I that I should go to Pharaoh and bring the children of Israel out of Egypt?" He said, "But I will be with you, and this shall be the sign for you, that I have sent you: when you have brought the people out of Egypt, you shall serve God on this mountain."

—Exodus 3:10–12

Good old Moses, whom we all know, wasn't completely on board with God's plan at first. Moses needed that reassurance from the Lord on the mission at hand. It's easy to think that we can't do something on our own because we can't. Only through God can we achieve the goals He sets out for us. When we are called to do something by Him, He is going to equip us with what we need to get it done. God may not be coming to you in a burning bush audibly telling you what to do, but He sure has a message for you. Can you discern His plans for you through scripture?

Have you ever heard the phrase "God never gives us more than we can handle"? That, friends, is not true at all. We can handle nothing without God. Moses, so many years ago, was not going to go to Pharaoh and make him release the Israelites on his own accord. Moses needed to be equipped by the Lord, and the Lord was going to make it happen through him. We need to be humble enough to know that all these things come from the Lord. We have no power as humans. That all comes from God.

God may have a mission in mind for you right now. It may be something as big as moving to another country as a missionary or just serving in your own church. Whatever it may be, He will give us the tools and the courage we need to go on this mission for Him. When God sends us on a mission, He is always faithful. We need to be faithful to Him to accomplish the goal. We must trust in God always that He knows what He's doing.

How can you discern God's mission for your life?

SEPTEMBER 1

All You Need Is Love

> If I speak in the tongues of men and of angels, but have not love, I am a noisy gong or a clanging cymbal.
>
> —1 Corinthians 13:1

Love is something the good old church folk often lose sight of. How often do you hear stories of people who walked away from the faith altogether because someone in the church treated them in a very unloving way? It's something most people will tell you when it comes to why they don't go to church or don't believe at all for that matter. Someone not very grounded in the faith could easily be turned off and walk away because of someone else's actions. There is always a chance to love greater as a Christian.

Whenever we have our family prayer every night, the last thing said before amen is "Help us to remember how much we love each other and how much we love You." We have to constantly remind ourselves that when we don't act in love, no one is going to take our Christian faith seriously. If we treat others without love and claim to love and know Jesus, are we really living out our faith?

Remember, friends, love is what Jesus is all about. He has a whole list of commands we must obey, but He also offers His grace when we fall short. We need to be the same as others in all we do. We need to be loving when we have to tell someone about the path they may be going down. They don't always want to hear it, but they will be way more receptive if we come at them with love over criticism. Be mindful of sharing the love of Christ balanced with the law of Christ.

How can you be more loving to those in need?

SEPTEMBER 2

Those Who Won't Heed

> And if anyone's name was not found written in the book of life, he was thrown into the lake of fire.
>
> —Revelation 20:15

We don't talk about hell enough in the church. It's easy to just want to go to church to get a feel-good feeling and only focus on the love and nothing else. The fact is, many will face this fate in the end. This is not something that should be used to scare people into believing in God, but on the other hand, it should scare you to think of this. Not knowing God is the worst thing you could possibly do in your life. We are not getting out of this world alive, so where are we going when we're gone?

I have heard of people leaving the church over things like this being preached. Sometimes, pastors can get labeled as doomsday preachers if they refer to anything to do with hell. We cannot just write this off. It's a reality that needs to be brought up. People must know the serious consequences of not following God. Like all scripture, these in Revelation describing the punishment in the end for those who chose to reject God need to be taken very seriously. In the end, we will all be judged, and there's no fooling God of who has followed Him and who hasn't.

Like all things in scripture, presentation must be done in love. We shouldn't be standing on a street corner screaming at passersby that they are all going to hell, like some do, and there's nothing they can do about it. We should be sharing the good news in love that others may not face this terrible fate. We often warn people of other things or paths in life that they may be facing. Why wouldn't we want to warn them about a decision that will affect their eternity? Even though everyone ultimately makes their own choice on which destination they will end up at after death, we need to be pointing people to make the right choice. Choose Jesus and spend an eternity with Him.

> How can you present hell to
> others in a loving way?

SEPTEMBER 3

Pass the Buck

The man said, "The woman whom you gave to be with me, she gave me fruit of the tree, and I ate." Then the Lord God said to the woman, "What is this that you have done?" The woman said, "The serpent deceived me, and I ate."

—Genesis 3:12–13

Here we have the "the fall of man" where it all went wrong. Not only did Adam and Eve eat the fruit from the tree, which God commanded them not to do, they now are trying to take the blame off themselves. Ultimately, they are blaming God for what happened. Adam is saying it's the woman's fault because God sent her, and Eve is blaming the serpent for her decision to eat the fruit. It all comes down to our own actions. We need to hold ourselves accountable and realize that even if we are tempted, we are still making the choice if we give into temptation and end up in sin.

How many times have you heard people use the phrase "the devil made me do it"? It's as if people think they no longer have control over their own actions and need to blame it on something. For us believers, we have the Holy Spirit within us, and we need to be even more cautious with temptation as to stay away as far as possible. Adam and Eve questioned God. They didn't fully trust God's plans for them. Are we fully trusting in God? Are we questioning His plans for our lives? It's okay to wonder, but do not make it an obsession where the seed of doubt may be planted and start to grow.

Accepting blame for ourselves is a hard task, but it's a lot easier to accept your own blame and try to do better than to hold on to being what you think is right. It can become a life sentence that we lay down for ourselves on refusing to be free from simply admitting we were wrong about something. Throughout my life, I've heard many people say they can't do something in life because of what someone else did to them, like their upbringing. We all have to hold ourselves accountable to our own actions, so we may fulfill our freedom in Christ, accept His grace, and move on with a better understanding of how to serve Him.

> How can you accept blame from
> a biblical standpoint?

SEPTEMBER 4

Get with the Good Habits

For this reason I remind you to fan into flame the gift of God, which is in you through the laying on of my hands, for God gave us a spirit not of fear but of power and love and self-control.

—2 Timothy 1:6–7

As believers, we truly have a gift from God. We should be at peace with anything that comes our way. However, it's very easy to get caught up in the world with our daily routines, busy schedules, and maybe even some bad habits that can distract us from focusing on the Lord and His faithfulness. We often enter different seasons in life that may be harder than others, but we need to be reminded that God is still in control, and He has a plan for us regardless of how we may think or feel at the current moment.

Not many people look forward to the end of summer. Trust me, I'm one of them. I've never looked forward to the season of autumn my entire life. For the first time, though, this year I became very excited for the new season. Our oldest daughter is going into her second year of preschool. Our youngest daughter was starting "Mom and Me" with my wife, and we came to find out that we are expecting our third child! Church is booming, our oldest daughter is in the Cherub Choir, my wife is singing with the Chancel Choir, and I am starting another season with our praise team at church. A lot is happening! We find ourselves being committed to our church and ultimately our faith in God even more these days. Our goal was to be at church more than just on Sundays and to strive for our family unity and go deeper in our faith in Christ. These good habits we are keeping can keep us very busy, but they are very rewarding in the long run.

TIMOTHY A. MILLS

When you are going all in at your church, it doesn't leave much time for some of our old bad habits. We can definitely get caught up in the busy times and get burned out, but when we keep ourselves busy with our faith, it really doesn't leave much time for those things of the past to sneak up on us. Good habits of being in the word, being in church, and being surrounded by other believers can work wonders for our spiritual well-being. I would encourage all who read this to make time in their own lives to get in these good habits.

How can you keep good habits to fan the flame of your faith?

SEPTEMBER 5

Nine to Five

Let the thief no longer steal, but rather let him labor, doing honest work with his own hands, so that he may have something to share with anyone in need.

—Ephesians 4:28

Most of us have our career paths. Some of us need to get our acts together when it comes to working. When we work, we need to remember that we are working for the Lord. Work ethic should be standardized around our faith. No matter what career path we are on or what job we may end up in, we must still let our faith shine through by our actions, even in the secular workplace. Making enough money to support a family and even more to be able to give back is a wonderful blessing to have.

I've met some people throughout life who just refuse to keep a job. They work for a while, quit or get fired, and then take forever to find another dead-end job and the cycle repeats. Laziness doesn't work with our faith. We all think of our careers as work, but work is a big part of what our faith is about. After we have accepted Christ into our hearts, we must work to maintain our relationship with Him. We must be in the Word, in prayer, and in a body of believers. Granted, that doesn't get us into heaven by our own doing, but with our faith, we should have a strong desire to work for the Lord.

Whenever you are irritated at work and don't feel like giving it your all, think again. Be reminded that you work for the Lord. You work for a greater purpose. Work hard in all areas of life, and ultimately, you will have a way better outcome. As the scripture says, when we work hard and earn, we may have more to give to help get others back on their feet. Money can be very dangerous and also addictive to some people who just want more and more. Be reminded of the good things you can do with your earnings to serve God better.

How can you work hard knowing you ultimately work for the Lord?

SEPTEMBER 6

One with the Son

Jesus said to them, "If God were your Father, you would love me, for I came from God and I am here. I came not of my own accord, but He sent me. Why do you not understand what I say? It is because you cannot bear to hear my word."

—John 8:42–43

I'm sure if you ask people if they believe in God, most would say yes. Even though some don't want to admit it, pretty much everyone believes in God to some extent. Most people have no problems telling you that. When it starts to get messy and very personal, it is when you ask someone if they know Jesus. You can't possibly know God without knowing His Son. So many people can get very hostile at the name of Jesus when in reality, they really don't know much about Him. For those of us that do know Him, we are eternally grateful for His life on earth and what He's done for us.

Why is it that people get so mad? Well, scripture did foretell us of that happening, but what could make someone so resentful and hostile when it comes to Jesus? We had a great debt of sin that created in our own selfish desires, and He took the punishment away from us and put it on Himself. When we recognize what Christ did, we know that we should have been up there on that cross dying for our own sins. If we are choosing to believe in God, we can't do it without Jesus.

It can be very frustrating witnessing to people who say they believe in God but won't accept Jesus. We must approach with caution, but even more importantly, love. We want people to see what Jesus is all about, and a good way is through our own actions. A lot of people in the end will profess to know God, but they never paid any mind to His Son. That's the focal point of God. Accept Jesus as being God or it's all for nothing.

How can you recognize Christ
every day in your life?

SEPTEMBER 7

The Lord's Desire

> With what shall I come before the Lord, and bow myself before God on high? Shall I come before Him with burnt offerings, with calves a year old? Will the Lord be pleased with thousands of rams, with ten thousands of rivers of oil? Shall I give my firstborn for my transgression, the fruit of my body for the sin of my soul? He has told you, O man, what is good; and what does the Lord require of you but to do justice, and to love kindness, and to walk humbly with your God.
>
> —Micah 6:6–8

There's a big difference between works and faith. The two must go hand in hand, but the Lord doesn't require of us to do all this offering of worldly things. He wants us to obey. In the words of Keith Green, "To obey is better than sacrifice." In the Old Testament, sacrifices were made constantly because of the sins of the people. They weren't enough. Jesus had to come down and be the perfect sacrifice for all of us. So with no more sacrifices, what is left but to obey?

Often, too many people don't want to believe or be involved with the church because they feel like there's too much they need to do. On the contrary, there's no special works, chants, or ultra-religious acts that we need to do. We need to get to know Jesus so we know how to obey His commands. This is really what separates the Christian faith from religion. Religion is man's attempt to earn his salvation. Christianity is Christ saying, "You can't do it on your own, so I'll do it for you." None of these religions have a deity that did all the work, and we just have to accept it. It's really quite simple.

We don't need to be all religious to follow Jesus. We just need to obey. Man has drawn out the faith and made it way more complicated than it has to be. I believe that's why the church has given itself a bad name. When we take the faith into our own hands and add or subtract things, we are getting a very different result. We need the truth God has given us in His Son, Jesus.

How can you obey over offer?

SEPTEMBER 8

Fear to Flee

> The Lord has taken away the judgments against you; He has cleared away your enemies. The King of Israel, the Lord, is in your midst; you shall never again fear evil.
>
> —Zephaniah 3:15

Is it easy to fear in today's world? Absolutely. There are many things that cause us to fear. We get anxiety very easily sometimes over things in everyday life. Evil lurks about all around this earth to distract us from the Lord. We must be grounded in His Word, discern His plans for us, and steer clear of those evil things that can easily pull us away from what the Lord wants for us. As scripture says, the day will come when evil will no longer be a factor. Evil won't exist anymore in the end. In the meantime, we need to cling to the Lord each and every day.

So what do we fear? Do we have fears at work? At home? Even in church because of some division that can happen? We are going to experience fear of something to a certain degree throughout our lives. It's important to remember that whatever fear you may have, God is way bigger than that. God is more than willing and able to take these fears away. Let not your fears consume you, but consume His Word to not be shaken by fear.

This life is so temporary. Things that we fear today might not even matter tomorrow, let alone in the end. God is faithful, and He has it all worked out for us. We must use our time on earth wisely to get to know Him better and await the day of His return. Think about whatever fears you may have and lift them up to Him in prayer. You are not defined by fear. You are defined by your faith in the Lord.

How can you have peace over fear?

SEPTEMBER 9

The Successor's Clause

> And they still went on and talked, behold, chariots of fire and horses of fire separated the two of them. And Elijah went up by a whirlwind into Heaven. And Elisha saw it and he cried, "My Father, my Father! The chariots of Israel and its horsemen!" And he saw him no more. Then he took hold of his own clothes and tore the in two pieces.
>
> —2 Kings 2:11–12

It's probably unlikely that the Lord will send down a chariot to carry someone up to heaven before death. However, we don't live forever. When we are in a leadership role or we have great respect and admiration for someone that is, we need to recognize that someone else is going to need to be trained up to succeed them in that role. Oftentimes, it doesn't work out the way we want. Sometimes people take over a leadership role in a way that is not pleasing to the Lord. We must be faith conscious of who we put in our church leadership and even who we vote for in elections.

Elisha needed to continue the ministry of Elijah. As his successor, if he didn't obey God and stay on the same path, then the line of that ministry would be lost until a new successor was called. In that time, though, if Elisha wasn't continuing the Lord's work that He started in Elijah, then how many people might not have heard the Lord's teachings? It's a good reminder for ourselves that if we assume a leadership role of a very prospering ministry, we must discern what the Lord wants us to do. We must be humble enough to learn from our predecessors, good and bad, and trust in the Lord to lead us.

Ministry can get distorted by the world over time. If the scriptures are the true Word of God and never change, then why should our ministry change over time? We can always discuss ways to do things differently or even better than our predecessors, but we must never look changing scriptures to meet the times. The scriptures will always be relevant no matter what year it is. Obey God and go deeper into His Word. Stay on that narrow path to guide your ministry in a way that's pleasing to God.

How can you be a good successor of a ministry?

SEPTEMBER 10

Standing on the Promises

> For it is better to suffer for doing good, if that should be God's will, than for doing evil.
>
> —1 Peter 3:17

How often are we faced with the choice of doing what is right in the eyes of the Lord or doing what is easy in the eyes of the world? If we really look deeper into this verse, we find that we are standing at these crossroads multiple times every day. The world is about doing things as easy as possible. Too many people live in the mindset of "If it feels good, do it." We might hear, "No one will know about it, so just do it" for whatever the situation may be. As believers, we know these excuses don't work with God. He has commanded us to do what is right, and He knows when we make the wrong choices. Fortunately for us, there is grace, but our desires need to be fixed on Him.

Evil is waiting around every corner to trip us into sinning. If we go on living a sinful life knowing what is right, then what good are we for God? We can also be too pleasing to the world for that fear of persecution. I think at some point, everyone has looked for the approval of other people, but when our faith goes to the wayside for their sake, then is that really a person that needs to be held in high regard in your life? Doing what is right can be far from easy, but the more we ground ourselves in our faith, the easier it gets to steer clear of these temptations of the world.

It's a fact that people will persecute us to some degree for our faith. When we suffer insults and opposition from others, it may be hard to deal with or hurt our feelings, but have peace in the Word knowing what God says about it. His servants have a far greater reward in heaven for standing firm against those who persecute us. You may lose people from your life because of your faith, or you may be ridiculed for your beliefs. Pay no mind to it and press on toward Christ. Let Him guide you through the hurt. He truly knows more than anyone what it's like to be persecuted and feel physical and mental hurt. Trust in Him!

How can you have peace even in persecution?

SEPTEMBER 11

A Simple Life

> Better is a handful of quietness than two hands full of toil and a striving after wind.
>
> —Ecclesiastes 4:6

Is your life simple or far too complex? That may be a question you have to think about, and that's quite all right. When we live our lives in service to the Lord, life gets way simpler. When we have the guidebook in our hands, the scriptures tell us everything we need to know. We don't have to waste time with worry and make our lives more complicated. It's not always an easy thing to do, but the more we keep it simple with our faith in the Lord, the easier our lives can get. When we stretch ourselves too thin in so many different directions, it's easy to get burned out.

I listen to a lot of different kinds of music. One of my favorite songs is called "A Simple Life" by Ricky Skaggs. He sings about all these things that make up living a simple life, and the first line of the chorus is "And my favorite book was wrote about a man that died to save my soul." What a wonderful reminder to us all to keep Jesus first for living that simple life. When we have that quietness as the verse says and steer clear of the toils of this world, only through Jesus will life get even more simple.

We all have problems, whether it be with family, work, or even in our church. Complications may come around, but what are we to worry about when we have Jesus? We may still get stressed, still feel hurt, or even be confused or agonizing over a situation, but let's be reminded of what Jesus has done for us. This is all the more reason to be in the Word daily. You never know what God has in store for you. Keep life simple and praise the Lord for what He continues to do in your life.

How can you keep your life simple?

SEPTEMBER 12

Symptom of Being Human

> Then the Lord said, "Behold, the man has become like one of us in knowing good and evil. Now lest he reach out his hand and take also of the tree of life and eat, and live forever."
>
> —Genesis 3:22

Congratulations! You're going to die. Fortunately, you're not alone. We are all going to die one day, and this is the reason why. Adam and Eve had two significant trees in the garden of Eden. One they could eat, from which was the tree of life, and the other which they couldn't eat, from which was the tree of the knowledge of good and evil. Thanks to them, we all will pass away on earth. It's just a common fact in today's world that we are all going to die eventually. Not too many people realize that we were meant to live forever. Fortunately, there is hope.

Do you ever attend funerals where everyone is so heartbroken and so upset that they can barely function? My wife and I had a former friend who lost her grandmother who was in her nineties when she passed away. This former friend of ours, who did not know the Lord, was so broken up about this that she couldn't function right for that first year and beyond over the loss. Those who don't know the Lord have no hope after death. Even when they lose loved ones who are believers, they personally do not know the hope their loved one had and is now in paradise with Christ. Death is only the beginning of eternity, and we know through the scriptures that we will be raised from the dead with Christ to live forever with Him in eternity.

It's easy to get caught up in thinking about the end of our earthly lives. That's just a symptom of being human as a result of the sin Adam and Eve committed. We need to show symptoms of our faith and focus on what we need to do before death comes so we will be ready for the life that awaits us. Choosing Christ is our only option to live forever in heaven with Him. Do not be afraid or worry about death but rejoice in knowing where your soul is sealed.

How can you be content with death?

SEPTEMBER 13

Stopping in Your Tracks

> Be still, and know that I am God. I will be exalted among the nations, I will be exalted in the earth.
>
> —Psalm 46:10

Sometimes in life, when situations arise, we try to fix them ourselves. We often obsess over why something isn't going right or working the way we want it to. It may seem like something that without fail should go a certain way, and we stress ourselves out when it doesn't. This is a perfect time to follow the command of this verse. In these cases, we need to step back and just let God be God. We need to surrender what control we think we have to Him and let Him work it out for His glory. Even if it's not the way we imagined, it's going to work out way better in the long run.

What are some of the things we may stress about? Well, work is probably a big one, but on an even more intimate level, what about our marriages? How about our kids and our families? Any sort of relationship can come to a point when it falls apart. No matter what it is, God is still in control. When we truly surrender to Him, He has the greater plan. I often think of things in my own life where I wanted to do it myself, and in the end, God's way was best. When we bought our first home, we were trying to do it our way and get what we thought we needed. There were so many struggles in our home until we turned back to the Lord, made church a priority, and ended up moving only three minutes down the road from our church. We had to surrender and give up some of our own selfish desires to let God do His work in our lives.

Wherever you may be in life in whatever situation, remember that God is God, and you are you. You can't do better than He can. I've tried. It doesn't work out. Let Him write your story. You just be the pages.

How can you step back and let God be in control?

SEPTEMBER 14

Knocking on Heaven's Door

> Behold, I stand at the door and knock. If anyone
> hears my voice and opens the door, I will come in
> to him and eat with him, and he with me.
>
> —Revelation 3:20

While we're here on earth, our only real important task is to let Christ into our life. Everything else will fall into place from there. As the verse says, He is there knocking, waiting for you to let Him in. We have a whole lifetime to do it, but why wait? If one would wait and never allow Christ in, it would be too late in the end. We would be the ones knocking on the door, but no answer would come after we reach death.

Sin can be so enticing that we think we just don't need to let Christ in. Most things that are truly bad for us, we often don't want to let go of because they rarely look unappealing. Most people in the world today who don't know Christ don't see a reason to let Him in. If you feel like you have it all, then why live a life of restraint? This is where the lies of the devil start to infiltrate the minds of unbelievers and try to disrupt the believers' relationship with God. No matter what your life is like, you need Jesus.

When Christ comes to your door, what will you do? Will you reject Him, will you keep Him waiting, or will you throw that door open and embrace Him? Christ is knocking at our door daily. We always need to have room for Him in whatever we do. Think of your daily routine. Is Christ involved in everything? You may need to analyze yourself on a regular basis to recognize how you might struggle with this. Leave that door wide open for the Lord. Let Him be in your life always.

How can you keep the door to your life open for Jesus?

SEPTEMBER 15

Right Turned Wrong

According to the number of the days in which you spied out the land, forty days, a year for each day, you shall bear your iniquity forty years, and you shall know my displeasure. I, the Lord, have spoken. Surely this will I do to all this wicked congregation who are gathered together against me: in this wilderness they shall come to a full end, and there they shall die.

—Numbers 14:34–35

Are we ever ungrateful for what the Lord has done for us? All the time. Truly, we can never be grateful enough or ever come close to paying Him back for all the blessings we have. Why then do we often choose to go back to the life He brought us out from? Whatever sins we lived in that brought us temporary false comfort are no match for what the Lord has in store for us. We need to trust in Him and let His plans unfold for our lives. If God brought us out of a life of sin with minimal consequences, then who are we to say He won't give us over to those sins again if choose to go back to them?

When the Israelites were brought out of Egypt by the Lord, I can almost picture them being on a high for a while. Once that high wore off, they became impatient. They were ungrateful and already forgetting God's mercy upon them in Egypt. Their promised land was now going to be unattainable to those who grumbled against the Lord. They made it so far, and they ruined it in their ungratefulness. Does that sound familiar in your own life?

Whatever kind of life you had before Christ came into your life, stay away from it. God wants to have a loving relationship with you. Don't reject Him out of impatience. His plans are always the best, even if we don't always like His timing of things. We always need to be reminded to step back and trust in Him to help us through whatever valley we may be walking through. This life is nothing compared to eternity. Don't be upset or impatient with God over things of this world that truly don't matter in the end.

How can you recognize when you are being ungrateful to the Lord?

SEPTEMBER 16

Unqualified Messengers

> Thus says the Lord GOD, Woe to the foolish prophets who follow their own spirit, and have seen nothing!
>
> —Ezekiel 13:3

When we go to worship or seek counseling from other believers, are we always getting the right message? I know in our church, we have excellent gifted leaders who make it their life's mission to grow closer to the Lord and understand His Word more every day. That's not always the case for other churches. Unfortunately, some church leaders don't have the right motives when it comes to their positions as spiritual leaders. Some are in it for themselves. Some are in it for money. Some actually want to play God. These are the unqualified messengers we need to keep watch for. The biggest question is, how do you know? How do you spot a false prophet?

Our relationship with God must be up close and personal. Our faith will not stand if it's riding on the coattails of someone else. If our faith is not our own, then it's just contingent on what someone else is doing. That's not how it works. The more we grow closer to God, pursuing that love relationship with Him, the more we come into the understanding of what He wants to tell us. Many people, even in the church, can lead us astray. You will eventually come across someone who will preach false doctrine or try to take you down a road that is wrong from a biblical perspective. When we are not grounded in our faith and able to discern God's true message for us, then we could potentially be led astray by anything.

You don't need to be a pastor to be knowledgeable of God's commands. You don't need a doctorate in biblical studies to be able to discern God's Word. While those things may be extremely helpful and help you to be more knowledgeable of our Lord, anyone can take time to invest in knowing God. Even a union truck driver with a Bible like myself has the opportunity to grow closer to the Lord and understand what He is calling me to be. Do not be discouraged because of where you are in your faith. Humility will help you to know there is always room to grow. It comes down to our individual faith to discern whether a church leader or any spiritual leader is giving you the right information or the wrong information.

How can you truly discern right from wrong biblical information?

SEPTEMBER 17

The Upper Story

His brothers also came and fell down before him and said, "Behold, we are your servants." But Joseph also said to them, "Do not fear, for am I in the place of God? As for you, you meant evil against me, but God meant it for good, to bring it about that many people should be kept alive, as they are today. so do not fear, I will provide for you and your little ones." Thus he comforted them and spoke kindly to them.

—Genesis 50:18–21

When I read this passage, all I can think is, *Wow, God!* The story of Joseph is rather sad if you look it at with a worldly lens, but it is an amazing testimony of God's plans unfolding even if things look grim. Joseph had a rough life for a while. He was betrayed by his brothers and sold into slavery. He starts to get a little relief in Egypt when he is made head servant by his master, Potiphar, but that's cut all too short when Potiphar's wife tries to seduce Joseph. Joseph flees because he knows that would go against what God would want. However, Potiphar's wife lies to get him to think Joseph did lay down with her. He's then thrown in prison. Seems pretty grim to anyone who reads it. To the world, this is unjust and honestly makes no sense, but then there's the factor that made it all work for good—God.

In your own life, remember that we can always see the lower story going on. That's our own world. What we need to be reminded of is the upper story, God's story for us, that isn't always instantly revealed to us. You may find yourself in these situations where the lower story is very consuming. Life might not be where you want it to be, and it can be a struggle. Be reminded that God has a story to tell through His Son, Jesus, and we're all the main characters in our own way.

Wherever you are going in life, be mindful that you may end up in a situation like Joseph. You may end up being betrayed. You may end up getting falsely accused of something. No matter what is happening, remember that God's story isn't over for you yet. Joseph ended up ruling over Egypt with Pharaoh, and his brothers even bowed before him long after they betrayed him. God's story is always better than our own even if we can't see it right away. Be patient, hold fast, and pray. God is writing your story without you even knowing it. He will write it for His glory, and His plans will unfold in your life.

> How can you distinguish lower story from upper story?

SEPTEMBER 18

Sojourning

Jesus answered, "My kingdom is not of this world. If my kingdom were of this world, my servants would have been fighting, that I might not be delivered over to the Jews. But my kingdom is not from the world."

—John 18:36

Sojourning means temporarily or permanently residing some place that is not necessarily their home or where they come from. Jesus was sojourning on earth when He was ministering to the world. We ourselves need to be reminded that the world is not our home. As believers, our home is in the kingdom with Jesus. We only temporarily reside here, awaiting our day in glory with the King. For that time being, what are we to do? When we accept Christ and become a new creation, we start to see the world lose its luster. Things of this world become far less appealing than they used to because there is so much better in store with Christ. We just need to make good use of that time.

When we recognize that we are all sojourners with Christ, we also realize that some people don't look at it like that. The ultimate good use of our time in this world would be to live out our faith and encourage others to walk down the path of Christ as well. Many people think this world is their home. They believe this is it. When you are gone, you're just in the ground and done. That is far from the truth. We are just traveling through this world for a little while in the long run.

As you sojourn through this world, remember that the trials and the hard times you face are just as temporary as this world is.

This is not the end goal. Look toward the prize in Christ and live for Him. Live for the next life in heaven. While there may be things of enjoyment in this life or things that bring us satisfaction, nothing can compare to that of knowing Christ. As we draw near to Him, may we look less at things of this world for our fulfillment. It can be somewhat discouraging to think that we may be on the outs with this world, but be comforted in knowing that Christ was too. He was also despised and rejected. He went down this path before us and for us. We belong with Him.

How can you be comforted knowing this life is so temporary?

SEPTEMBER 19

Knowing about God versus Knowing God

But now that you have come to know God, how can you turn back again to the weak and worthless elementary principles of the world, whose slaves you want to be once more?

—Galatians 4:9

Anyone in the world will tell you they know about God. Even the devil knows about God. No matter what religion of the world someone may practice, most will tell you about some knowledge they have of God. All religions talk about God, but only the truth talks about Jesus. To truly know God is to truly know Jesus. When we truly know God as opposed to just knowing about Him, we develop a deeper understanding in how to live a holier life. We develop the stronger desire to follow Him.

Now that we know the Lord better, what shall we do? When we accept Christ as our Savior, He must also be accepted as our Lord too. Accepting just the Savior part is admitting we need to be saved, but the Lord part is where we tend to struggle with. Christ needs to be the Lord over our life. Whatever we do, it must align with His commands. When we as Christians may screw up and go back to our old life for whatever reason, we start to feel bad about it. That's called conviction, and that just means our spiritual pulse is alive and well. Even if we did sin, we know not to go down that road again as to disobey God's commandments.

How do we get to know God better? Consider staying in the Word more often for starters. The Bible is the number one selling book of all time, and it's the guidebook we need to know God even better. When we take time out of our days to read the scriptures and dive further into the Word, we are opening our hearts and our minds to know God even better. Keep watch over yourself that you may not be too influenced by this world. Stay close to your body of believers as the coals burn brighter together. The Lord knows you inside and out. Get to know Him personally more and more every day.

How can you truly get to know God?

SEPTEMBER 20

Words of Law and Love

> He said to them, "Take to heart all the words by which I am warning you today, that you may command them to your children, that they may be careful to do all the words of the law. For it is no empty word for you, but your very life, and by this word you shall live long in the land that you are going over the Jordan to possess."
>
> —Deuteronomy 32:46–47

When we hear the scriptures, are we really taking them seriously? It's easy to slack in a world like today that has no problem going against scripture. When we teach our children or anyone younger than us the Word of the Lord, we are passing on that fire that burns for God. Scripture may not always be easy to follow, but we must make a conscious effort to take God's Word to heart and obey His commands for us. We have the guidebook to a better life. Let's use our Bibles every day to know Him better.

Have you ever known someone to weaponize scripture and only use certain passages to use against others while there are other passages that they are failing at? We've all encountered those zealots in our lives. When we come at people with the scriptures, we must be alongside them in love. Only through love will the scriptures be passed down through the generations. If we look at our world today, every generation is at risk for the fire of Christ getting dimmer, but as long as it's burning in a few hearts, wonders can be accomplished. It's a good reminder to be better examples in our faith leading those in love.

Do you take your Bible everywhere with you? A lot of folks at least have the Bible app on their phones. I personally love having that book with me wherever I go. There's just something special about turning through the pages of the sacred texts that makes me feel closer to the Lord. Be reminded that the words of law are all about love. The commands given are not holding us back or restricting us but holding us to a standard that keeps us free from the bonds of sin. The Word will always be there as a tool to guide you closer to the Lord.

> How can you take the Word everywhere with you and lead people to it?

SEPTEMBER 21

See for Yourself

Now these Jews were more noble than those in Thessalonica; they received the word with all eagerness, examining the Scriptures daily to see if these things were so.

—Acts 17:11

When Paul and Silas were in Thessalonica, things weren't going very well for them. The Jews there refused to believe and started up a mob against them. On the contrary, when they were in Berea, the Jews there not only heard the Word from Paul and Silas, but they also did their own research in the scriptures and opened their hearts and minds to seeing it for themselves. Faith must be our own. Even if we are in church, hearing sermons, and attending Sunday school, it's up to us to strengthen our faith by staying in the Word. We don't want to be stagnant in what we know but grow even more understanding of what we don't know.

How many people do you know who just refuse to believe the Gospel message? I'm sure there are a lot. How many of these people do you think did their research in the scriptures and still don't believe? I bet that number is very small. Like the Jews in Thessalonica, we find the same kinds of folks in today's world. So many people don't want to believe based on what they know but have no desire to understand what they don't know. The answers are all in the scriptures, and the more we open our hearts, the more that will be revealed to us.

When you witness to others, remind them that what you are telling them is coming straight from scripture. Be mindful of your words as you witness to others as to not pass on information that is not in the scriptures. A lot of people who don't believe don't want to believe. They won't even consider anything out of scripture, and I personally believe that's because they don't want to be wrong. They don't want to be left with doubt of not believing. Lee Strobel is a good example of someone who set out to prove the whole faith wrong, so he did his research, got into the Word, and interviewed people. At the end of it all, he could do nothing to prove it wrong and became a huge voice for Christ in our world today. As you've heard me say many times. We have the guidebook. Let's be open to using it daily.

> How can you reference to the
> Word for any occasion?

SEPTEMBER 22

Point of No Return?

> Then after he had taken the morsel, Satan entered into him. Jesus said to him, "What you are going to do, do quickly."
>
> —John 13:27

This one is going to be filled with questions I don't have all the answers for, but I would encourage you all to seek further counsel on this subject. The hard question is, while we are on earth, is there ever a point where we can't come back to God? Have we ever gone far enough away from Him that the enemy now has ahold of us and won't let go? When I read this passage over and over again, I think Judas made his decisions to go so far, but at this point, Satan took over. Judas surrendered control to the enemy and betrayed our Lord. After it was all over, scripture tells us that Judas changed his mind when he saw Jesus condemned to death. By then, it was too late to take back what he had done. I believe at this point, Satan left him to his own grief, but was that grief enough to turn him back to God?

Demon possession is something we often don't think about, but that doesn't mean it's not happening today as it has in biblical times. Just as God doesn't force someone to believe and serve Him, I believe the enemy doesn't either. Influences come from both sides. God gave us our own free will to choose. He loves us so much that He gives us a choice. Just as we grow to know God through scripture and attend church and learn more about Him every chance we get, we can also unknowingly do the same thing with the enemy. The lies of this world continue to grow, and the enemy's followers grow in number.

The devil has lost in the end, but we don't have to lose with him. Before it's too late, we must get right with the Lord. We must be willing to repent and be sealed in God's love. That doesn't mean there won't be harassment from the enemy while on earth, but earth is nothing compared to an eternity with God in heaven. Don't wait. Choose whom you will serve. God will always be greater.

How can you avoid serving the enemy?

SEPTEMBER 23

Behind the Scenes

For those who serve well as deacons gain a good
standing for themselves and also great confidence
in the faith that is in Christ Jesus.

—1 Timothy 3:13

A church takes many people to trust in the Lord and work together to make it run. The head pastor of a church can't do everything, nor should everything fall on them. The officers in a church help make the church function and work together as one body in Christ to lead the church closer to Him. The deacons are some of those behind-the-scenes folks that serve in the congregation doing just about anything. God calls them and others to serve in His house to further the ministry.

In my Saturday morning men's group, we were going over a section in our workbook about having a tender heart and being able to hear God when He's setting out a mission or opportunity in front of us. When we tune our hearts to hear Him, the clearer it becomes when He's calling us. Sometimes people are often asked to serve in a certain way, and a lot of times they may say, "I need to pray about it first." While praying for guidance to a decision is always encouraged in the faith, sometimes it's best to jump on the opportunity when asked to serve. We can miss an opportunity to serve the King when we hesitate. That same day, I got a call from one of the members of the nominating committee asking me if I would be interested in becoming a deacon for a three-year term. I was just about speechless, but I made sure to give a loud resounding yes!

No matter what God is calling you to do, be open to it. You never know what or when He might have in store for you, but it's important that you listen for the call. Don't miss out on an opportunity to give back to Him. We sometimes tend to doubt ourselves when it comes to this, but that's all the more reason to trust the Lord. When He wants us to serve, He will equip us with what we need for His plans.

How can you hear God's calling for your life?

SEPTEMBER 24

Rewind and Replay

Come, let us return to the Lord; for He has torn us, that He may heal us; He has struck us down, and He will bind us up.

—Hosea 6:1

Sometimes in life, we get to certain points where we are hitting a dead end. We've lived lives of sin that have gotten us nowhere, and the only direction to go is back to the Lord. If we consider the temptations of the world, there are many. Different people are tempted by different things. When we indulge these temptations, we may think we are in control, but we are only getting further from the Lord. It's times like these where we really need to rewind and replay. We don't always get the chance to replay, so we better jump on the opportunity before it's too late.

When you are a believer and you stray, you will never be content. Even if we are not living the way we should, we still have some degree of conviction. When we truly accepted Christ into our lives, the Holy Spirit lives in us. We may not always listen to Him, but His voice is still in our lives. When we don't listen for some period, sometimes we start to face even harder trials in our lives. The Lord will often let us mess our lives up so much that only He can restore us. If we listen in the first place, we don't always have to go the wrong road of pain and suffering and then realize we need to turn back to Him.

There is always a risk that we sin so much that it costs us our lives. Sometimes there are no second chances. I personally don't want to be standing at the pearly gates trying to plead my case if I went out in a sinful blast. If God gives you a second chance, then what are you going to do about it? We are all sinners. We need to accept that and also accept that we need a Savior. When Jesus is the head of our lives, we have to maintain that desire to serve Him and obey His commands. Do not be deceived by the things of this world. The Lord has the ultimate plan for us, and salvation is the top priority to Him. Make that the top priority for your life.

> How can you replay when given
> a second chance from God?

SEPTEMBER 25

Who We Belong To

Whoever is of God hears the words of God. The reason why you do not hear them is that you are not of God.

—John 8:47

Hearing the Word of God is a true gift of being a believer. We gain understanding in the scriptures and discernment in making decisions. Do you ever feel like you're just dead in the water on these things and don't know what to do? It may be time to get back to who you belong to. As believers in Christ, we have had our hearts softened to accept Him into our lives. It's an ongoing lifelong process from then on out to truly hear the Word of God. Scripture is everything when it comes to being a Christian. As you've heard me say many times throughout this book, we have the true guidebook in our Bibles.

If you feel like you have strayed and can't hear God, then what should you do? Sometimes we need to do that "cleaning house" process in our lives and rid ourselves of distractions. If we are going through addictions, we need to seek the proper help for those. Further straying from the Lord usually involves us filling our lives with more things of this world. Whenever we decide to come back to Him, we have to get rid of a lot of those things to hear His message and comprehend what we can once again.

The Lord reveals a lot to us. We just don't always see it because we have the blinders on. The distractions get in our way and cloud our judgment. The Lord is always calling to us, and He wants us to hear Him. There's work, through Him, on our part that needs to be done to maintain that relationship with Him. The Lord loves us all and wants us have a relationship with Him. He wants us with Him in glory forever and doesn't want to see a single soul lost to hell. He's giving you the opportunity every day to hear His word. Trust in Him and cast your burdens at the cross so you will not be clouded in your understanding.

How can you truly belong to God?

SEPTEMBER 26

Failure to Communicate

Behold, the days are coming, declares the Lord God, when I will send a famine on the land—not a famine of bread, nor a thirst for water, but of hearing the words of the Lord. They shall wander from sea to sea, and from north to east; they shall run to and fro, to seek the word of the Lord, but they shall not find it.

—Amos 8:11–12

When we don't hold the Lord as our first priority, it's hard to hear what He has to say. The failure to communicate is not on His part but on ours. When we run too far from Him, it's hard to hear what He has to say. If we are close to Him, seeking an intimate love relationship with Him every day, it becomes clearer what He has to say to us and where He is leading our lives. Think of an airplane or a ship without a captain. We would be dead in the air or the water. The same is true for our spiritual lives. This world can sure be rough, so why go through it alone, especially when we can know our Creator personally?

I'm sure you have met many different people in life like I have. Have you ever been around a chronic complainer that plays the victim in every situation? I've tried to point these types of people to the Lord, but they usually give the excuse that for some reason or another, the Lord doesn't do anything for them. When you have a hard life or situations that can be hard to deal with but you don't take the necessary steps to fix these problems, then why should anyone else listen to you complain? Sometimes the same is true for the Lord. He can always intervene at any point in time, but He wants true surrender. He wants us to give it all to Him. He's the ultimate problem solver, but you must be willing to turn to Him. Not just to ask for help but to live for Him daily.

Don't get to the point in your life where God seems so far away. It's easy to get there with the temptations of this world. As you've heard me say before, sin is never unappealing. When you are caught up in sin, your relationship with God can go downhill pretty fast. He's always there for us, but we need to live for Him. When we enter sinful lifestyles, how can we expect to hear what He is telling us? Through the good and the bad in your life, stay faithful to the Lord. It's easier said than done, but trust me, it's worth it.

> How can you hear what God
> is telling you today?

SEPTEMBER 27

The Way of the Lord

Many are the plans in the mind of a man, but it
is the purpose of the Lord that will stand.

—Proverbs 19:21

It's no surprise that we all have plans. How many times a day do we talk about our plans or keep a tight schedule or create deadlines for ourselves? It's almost crazy to imagine how much we think we are in control. These plans we have might not always be the Lord's plans for us. When we fill our minds with our own ideas or plans, are we leaving much room for God's plans? We always need to step back and take time to listen to what He wants for our lives. No matter what kinds of plans we come up with, the Lord's plans are far greater than our own.

Over the course of my life, I've had many plans of my own. I can't think of the amount of times they have changed. If my plans weren't centered around God's plans, then they weren't necessarily good for me. A lot of times, I did get to see that the plans I had that God cancelled was because he was protecting me. The trouble I would have gotten into had He not intervened I can clearly see now. When He became first in my life is when things really started to work out. It's not always instant, but His plans were slowly revealed to me, and I truly found His ways to be more superior in my life than anything I could have come up with.

Whenever you have an idea or a plan, just remember that if it's not glorifying to God, then it's probably not good for your life. If you still try to pursue it, then I pray God intervenes in your life like He has done for me. It's easy to have worldly wants, and we get so caught up in ourselves that we are missing out on something that He has in store for us that will be so much better. Pray for God to reveal His plans for your life and trust in Him that He always knows what's best.

How can you embrace God's plans for your life and not your own?

SEPTEMBER 28

Revealing Reading

The unfolding of your words gives light; it imparts understanding to the simple.

—Psalm 119:130

God's Word that we have at our fingertips in this country is a true privilege to have. We have our Bibles and even the Bible apps on our phone. We are free in this country to be in the Word of the Lord, so why aren't we doing it more often? The only way to truly get to know the Lord is through His Word. His message in those sixty-six books is a lot to learn, but it will never be truly revealed to us if we don't read it. God reveals things about Himself in the Word. Even if you have read the same scripture over and over, you can always learn something more. Scripture today means far more to me than it did years ago because I make the effort to understand it more. Scripture is always relevant, but it gets even more relevant on a personal level when we can relate to it.

How many people do you know who don't believe in God but won't turn to the scriptures to see if they're wrong? You also find people who say, "I've read the Bible and still don't believe." If you truly want to know how real God is, read His scriptures with a humble heart and let Him guide you. The more I read, the more I understand, and the more I do not understand. I just keep reading because what I think I don't know may be revealed to me, and what I think I know might actually need a different perspective.

If you hope to learn anything, you must study it and figure out how it works. The same is no different in our faith. If we want to understand God's plans, ways, and purposes, and how that relates to our lives, we need to be in the Word. We need to read scripture daily. You never know what God could be revealing to you when you read His Word. I pray you learn something from it soon.

> How can God reveal Himself to
> you through His Word?

SEPTEMBER 29

Prepare for Battle

Finally, be strong in the Lord and in the strength of His might. Put on the whole armor of God, that you may be able to stand against the schemes of the devil. For we do not wrestle against flesh and blood, but against the rulers, against the authorities, against the cosmic powers over this present darkness, against the spiritual forces of evil in the heavenly places.

—Ephesians 6:10–12

If you haven't heard straight from the Lord, life will not be easy. When we really look into the magnitude of what we are dealing with in the spiritual realm every day, we are truly in a battle. What should we do? Stand there and do nothing? That's a pretty good way to be overtaken in the battle. We are called to fight. The full armor of God has been given to us that we may defend our faith and fight for what's right.

We recently got to watch the movie *Nefarious* with our church leaders. The premise is that a death row inmate, possessed by a demon, is being interviewed by a psychiatrist. After talking with the psychiatrist for quite some time, the demon-possessed man says, "Are you ready for round two?"

The psychiatrist replies, "I didn't know this was a fight."

The demon-possessed man comes back with "That's why you're losing!"

Take a closer look at our world today, using the Bible as your guide, and see how many people are losing to the spiritual forces of evil. Most of these people, I'm sure, have no idea that they are losing just like this psychiatrist in the movie I mentioned. If someone doesn't know they are losing, then they wouldn't think that they need to be fighting back.

We are given a gift from God with our salvation. The enemy knows he's lost us to the Lord but will do whatever he can to torment and tempt us in this life. Let me tell you, folks. God is much stronger than that. We have the Holy Spirit in us to intercede for us and protect us. We must put on that armor every day and be ready for battle as it can come out of nowhere. The Lord is faithful. Stay faithful to Him in all you do.

> How can you put on the full
> armor of God every day?

SEPTEMBER 30

What Do We Stand For?

> Only let your manner of life be worthy of the gospel of Christ, so that whether I come and see you or am absent, I may hear of you that you are standing firm in one spirit, with one mind striving side by side for the faith of the gospel, and not frightened in anything by your opponents. This a clear sign to them of their destruction, but of your salvation, and that from God.
>
> —Philippians 1:27–28

One thing certain in life is how God is always for us even if we don't deserve it. Even when we sin and fall short of His commands, we never fall short of His grace because He loves us so much. Keep in mind that with all of that, we should have a growing desire to live for Him and be in fellowship with other believers. When we are standing firm in one spirit, we have nothing to fear. No matter what our adversaries may throw at us, we have the power of the Holy Spirit within us. When we show God's love as opposed to retaliating in anger, that is part of what sets us apart from the rest of the world.

Today was our community's homecoming parade. It was a wonderful time to see the folks of the community marching down the boulevard in their different groups. It went from sports to music to different clubs and such. Seeing all these kids joined together for each of their respective groups got me thinking about when us believers get together. As the kids marched, they were all joined as one supporting their sport or music. As believers, we need to be doing that with our faith. We need to be joined together as one body of believers to make an unstoppable force in this dark world today.

When we don't put God first, then how do we know what we really stand for? Only one thing can be at the head of our lives. If that isn't God, then maybe it's time to reevaluate our priorities. We only get there by prayer and being in the Word and in fellowship with other believers. It may be a hard adjustment, but it's something very necessary for a successful relationship with God. My family has personally had to make changes, even where we lived, for our relationship with God to get to number one in our lives. It's not always easy, and sometimes we struggle, but that's where we all need to strive to be. Taking a stand for the King every day.

How can you tell what you stand for?

OCTOBER 1

Light of the Son

> Long ago, at many times and in many ways, God spoke to our fathers by the prophets, but in these last days He has spoken to us by His Son, whom He appointed the heir of all things through whom also He created the world.
>
> —Hebrews 1:1–2

Most people believe in God. Ask around and find out. How many people, though, believe in Jesus as the only way to get there? God is such a loosely used name throughout all beliefs of this world, but there is only one way to get to know our true Father God. Being a follower of Jesus is what sets us apart from all those that simply say, "I believe in God." The religious aspect is just believing in God and hoping you're "good enough" to get into heaven. The relationship aspect is that we need a personal relationship with Jesus because we can't get into heaven on our own.

I have met so many people who are very passionate about God being real. I've heard some refer to themselves as "spiritual." I don't know if that just makes them feel better about their thoughts, but "spiritual" isn't enough. Jesus is more than enough. When the spiritual people think they are living a good life and earning their way into heaven, they are missing the bigger picture. The grace of Christ through His bloodshed on the cross paid the price so all those "good enough" people can accept Him and be in eternity with Him forever.

When we share the message with anyone, it all has to come down to the cross. The sins we commit separate us from God, and that's why we need Jesus. No one could ever earn their way to the

Father by their own works. Jesus did that for us. That's an act of love we could never be "good enough" for or even grateful enough for. Even if we can never pay back the love that we've received, let us strive for a greater desire every day to live for Christ.

> How can you put the Son at
> the head of your life?

OCTOBER 2

Lawbreaker Jailbreak

> For whoever keeps the whole law but fails in one point has become guilty of all of it.
>
> —James 2:10

No pressure there. Congrats, you failed! I know this one is starting out to be not very comforting, but believe me, there is hope. When we don't acknowledge sin in our lives, then it can become less important to recognize why we need a Savior. As we have talked about in the past, Adam and Eve's sin against God separated us from Him. It only took one screwup in the garden of Eden to change the course of humanity. Just one. This is why we need a Savior. The sin had to be paid for, and the price was death. Thankfully for us, Jesus took our place and conquered death.

We often hear people make excuses or try to justify their own sin. We hear things like "I've been good enough" or "No one will know" and so on. The truth is, we can never be good enough, and God always knows what's going on. This is pass or fail, and we have all failed. Examine your own life and just think of all the times you have sinned, even just today. Just go down the list yourself and see how many things you have done wrong. We all need God's mercy in our lives for those things we fall short at.

There is hope in Jesus. The price has been paid, and grace has been extended to each and every one of us. Give yourself grace as well so that God's grace may restore you and you don't hold yourself in regret. We will never be good enough for God. He just loves us so much anyway that He doesn't want to lose any of us regardless. Don't focus on perfecting yourself. Focus on how perfect Jesus is.

How can you truly know the need for a Savior?

OCTOBER 3

What Kind of Life

> Peace I leave with you; my peace I give to you. Not
> as the world gives do I give to you. Let not your
> hearts be troubled, neither let them be afraid.
>
> —John 14:27

I'm gonna use the *S* word—*stress*! Stress is something everyone has. It's unavoidable. Your perspective and way you deal with it is what counts. That being said, it's not just how we deal with it, but it's who deals with it. The only true stress reliever in a broken world is Jesus. People get so overwhelmed with stress and do not always deal with it in a constructive way. When we have Jesus, we have a peace that can get us through no matter the situation. The situation that's causing us stress might not even change, but through our faith in God, we have a better perspective to see the bigger picture in any situation.

While I was at work today out on route, I overheard a conversation between two individuals at a store I was delivering to. One had said something about being stressed, and the other replied, "If you aren't stressed in today's world, something must be wrong with you." I thought, what kind of life is that? What kind of life would you be living if you were always stressed about something? I wonder if these people talking even knew the power that God has to take their stress away. When we hear unbelievers saying such things, it's even more important as Christians that we should show the world how we can be set apart from all of that. Our peace we receive through Christ should be reflected in our actions.

As Christians, we all face trials of many kinds. We're not immune from bad things happening to us. When we consider this verse, let's live it out. Let's continue to seek Christ every day and cast these burdens on Him who lovingly carries them for us. When people want to know what kind of life I have, I want them to see Jesus. If the world thinks that's what's wrong with me for not getting stressed too easily, then so be it.

How can you be relieved of stress through Jesus?

OCTOBER 4

Answer the Call

Thus says the Lord who made the earth, the Lord who formed it to establish it, the Lord is His name. Call to me and I will answer you, and will tell you great and hidden things that you have not known.

—Jeremiah 33:2–3

The further we grow in our faith, the more God will reveal to us over time. When we trust in Him and live a life pleasing to Him, the more we will understand what He wants to reveal to us through scripture or prayer or even through other believers. God will always answer in His perfect timing when we call upon Him. It's time for us to answer His calling when He calls us to do something for Him.

While I was out on my route on this day, I made a little detour to the Home Depot I serve which I normally do last. As soon as I got out of the truck, I was in conversation with a complete stranger. He began to speak about my journey in life and looking at things from a different perspective. He talked about strength and getting through life. I found it a perfect opportunity to witness to him when I said, "I carry my Bible with me everywhere."

His reply was "That's not enough." At first, I thought, *There's no way this guy is a believer*. Until he followed up with this: "Carrying your Bible isn't enough. The Word needs to be in you, and you are carried by the Holy Spirit." This man was no unbeliever. It turns out that he knew scripture very well and was teaching me even more. He was from Romania and grew up in communism where Christianity is very suppressed. This man answered God's call just to talk to me today, and we both weren't originally planning on being there at that time. The Lord works in those perfect ways to put us where we need to be for His glory. It was so comforting to meet someone like him that was on fire for the Lord.

Whenever God calls, we need to answer. When we call Him for our needs, we want Him to answer us. We often get very impatient when we don't get what we want immediately. Sometimes, like me today, we don't even realize when He's calling. I could have just gone about my day or just brushed off the conversation with this brother in the faith today, but I could feel God holding me there to listen to what this guy had to say. We don't always get it right, but when we do, it's impossible to not see God's hands at work in and around us.

How can you answer God's call today?

OCTOBER 5

Daily Reminders

> Then Gideon built an altar there to the Lord and call it, "The Lord Is Peace." To this day it still stands at Ophrah, which belongs to the Abiezrites.
>
> —Judges 6:24

Every day there are things that remind us of our Lord. When we take a quick look at His creation, we can be quickly reminded of God's presence in our world today. Sometimes we can even create our own reminders of thanks and reverence to Him. Gideon built this altar to Him as a reminder of His peace. Gideon had his own doubts about what God was doing, but the Lord was slowly revealing His plans to him. I'm sure in those times, many people who saw that altar were reminded of God's presence.

I have my own reminder that I carry with me everywhere. It may be a controversial topic in the church, but one of my tattoos is like that altar for me. I have a cross on the inside of my left arm. The cross is breaking chains, and it has three simple words around it: I AM FREE. I got it done in 2009, and its core meaning has never changed. But over time, it has developed new meanings to me about God's promises. We can never have too many reminders as God brings us to milestones in our faith.

Some reminders, like His creation, are for everyone, but we often have those personal reminders that are only between us and God. The path to walking in a holy lifestyle is very narrow and very hard to walk sometimes. Personally, I need those reminders just as much as anyone to avoid falling off the path. I know myself. If I fall, I'm going to fall hard and fast. We all need to fight to stay on that path, and those little reminders God places in the world can be a huge reminder to keep on going toward Him.

How can you find those little reminders of the Lord every day?

OCTOBER 6

Becoming Like Christ

> Be imitators of me, as I am of Christ.
>
> —1 Corinthians 11:1

Such a simple yet profound verse. The apostle Paul had his conversion and devoted his life to ministering the good word of the Gospel to the nations. Most of the New Testament is written by him. The New Testament overall is a good start. To become more like Christ, we must understand His message. Going through the four Gospels is the first place to look. As we are introduced to Jesus and read His ministry unfolding, we see His true purpose. He came here with sacrificial love for us that He paid the price for us. Now that we know that, what else are we to do? It's time to look deeper into the Word. Let the scriptures teach you about holy living.

A lot of people believe in God, as we've talked about before. How many people are truly focused on becoming like Christ? It's a daily upkeep in our lives to continue getting to know Jesus. We will always fall short, but our desire needs to be fixed on Him. Most of us have our own opinions of Jesus, but unless you are diving into the Word and attending church, you have no idea of the magnitude of Jesus.

You will struggle at this. I promise. Fear not, because you are not alone. Every single day we are not doing enough for God. We can never repay Him for what He's done for us, but we can choose Him every day to make things right. Get to know and be more like His Son, Jesus. Only then will you truly be able to know how to walk that straight and narrow path. Let's go through scripture together to grow in our knowledge of Christ.

How can you be like Christ?

OCTOBER 7

Where Are You, God?

> Now when Jesus came, He found that Lazarus had already been in the tomb four days. Bethany was near Jerusalem, about two miles off, and many of the Jews had come to Martha and Mary to console them concerning their brother.
>
> —John 11:17–19

I believe this one's title is a frequently asked question of believers and unbelievers alike. When we consider this passage, Lazarus was very ill, and Jesus knew about it. When He first got the news, He didn't jump up and run to get to Lazarus and heal him. Jesus waited two more days before He went to see Lazarus and his sisters. By that time, Lazarus was gone. You have to imagine what Mary and Martha were going through, knowing Jesus could have saved their brother but chose not to come immediately.

How many times in our lives do we not get what we want and think God is no longer listening to us? We are human. It's easy to get impatient with God, but His timing is always perfect. As Christians, we need to have faith that regardless of what is happening in our lives, God is still in control. If He seems silent, believe me, He is still up to something way better for us in the long run. As for unbelievers who pose this question in time of tragedy, maybe it's time they start living a life for God and getting to know Him instead of just treating Him like an insurance policy to bail them out when they get into trouble.

Now back to Mary and Martha. When Jesus arrived, Martha said to Him, "Lord, if you had been here my brother would not have died, but even now I know that whatever you ask from God, God will give you" (verse 22). Martha and Mary were starting to see that it didn't matter that Lazarus died. They still had the faith that even if Jesus wasn't there, He was still going to take care of them. Sure enough, He calls Lazarus, and right out of that tomb he comes. That's the faith we need to strive for. We need to believe, for certain, that no matter what happens, God is working things for His glory. It's not always easy, but faith is always a work in progress. We don't have to wonder where God is. Even if we can't always hear what He is saying, He is truly listening to us and will always have everything under control. Believe, friends.

<blockquote style="text-align:center">How can you have the faith to know where God is?</blockquote>

OCTOBER 8

Comfortable Prison

> Why is the Lord bringing us into this land, to fall by the sword? Our wives and our little ones will become a prey. Would it not be better for us to go back to Egypt?
>
> —Numbers 14:3

We often find ourselves clinging to bad situations for whatever reason. I would say most of the time, it's probably because we are afraid of change. We get complacent in a situation that isn't necessarily good for us. Even if life could be much better in the long run, we don't always want to put in the effort and faith it takes to make those changes in our lives. We need, more than ever, to trust in God and allow Him to take the reins of our lives. Even if we don't always fully understand what He is doing, we must have faith to know that He is still in control. When we are going through these changes, we have to be careful not to go back to where we were just for the sake of being comfortable. Change is always necessary throughout life. Let God help you with changes in your own life.

The Israelites got pretty ungrateful at this point in their story. They have already been brought out of their slavery in Egypt. God had them standing at the gates to the promised land, but they were afraid. After seeing some of the people already living there, they rebelled. It's crazy to think that after the trials they faced in Egypt, they would want to go back there as opposed to trusting in the Lord. This is exactly what we do sometimes. I'm sure you can think of a time where the grass was greener right where you were at before God put you on a path out of there.

Don't get caught up in that comfortable prison that you have put yourself in. As you have heard me say before, sin is never unappealing. If you have a lot of things of this world that go against God's teachings, you may have an easy life on earth, but it wouldn't be honoring to God. That holy change is crucial for spiritual growth and a healthier relationship with the Lord. Don't be afraid, even when things seem dim, to keep that faith and trust in our Almighty God. When He puts us on a path, it may seem difficult, but believe me, He's got a plan for your life. Be grateful for His doings and trust in Him.

How can you trust in God that He has something better for you?

OCTOBER 9

Final Shot at Redemption

Then Samson called to the Lord and said, "O Lord God, please remember me and please strengthen me only this once, O God, that I may be avenged on the Philistines for my two eyes." And Samson grasped the two middle pillars on which the house rested and he leaned his weight against them, his right hand on the one and his left hand on the other. And Samson said, "Let me die with the Philistines." Then he bowed with all his strength and the house fell upon the lords and upon all the people who were in it. So the dead whom he killed at his death were more than those whom he had killed during his life."

—Judges 16:28–30

Samson wasn't just an ordinary human being. Before he was conceived, the angel of the Lord appeared to his mother with a message that Samson would save Israel from the hands of the Philistines. Now if we look at Samson's life, one would think there was no way this ungrateful, defiant man could do anything for the Lord. He broke all the rules. He married a Philistine girl, got divorced, hooked up with a prostitute, and then got himself in big trouble with Delilah. Delilah, another Philistine woman, seduced Samson into giving away his secret of his strength—his hair must not be cut. This looks like a real man of God, right? Let's not just look at Samson but what the Lord is capable of in even the darkest situations.

You or someone you know might be this person. When we know the Lord, we shouldn't be indulging in any of those things Samson was involved with. The pure defiance to disobey God and go after things of this world can easily overtake our mindset. Even so, for those of us who have fell pretty far from our faith in the past, that doesn't mean God isn't still at work in our lives or using us for His glory. Those darkest moments in our lives can be used by Him and for Him to shed His light even in our suffering and defiance.

At the end of Samson's life, he was blinded and put in prison, but the Lord used him one last time. Samson truly got his redemption in the end as he died with the Philistines. He may not have followed God's commands, but God used Him one final time to destroy more Philistines than he ever did. When we look back on our lives, even when we disobeyed, we can sometimes see that God was still using us all along. We have that grace to learn from our mistakes more than anyone.

How can you still be used by God even in your own defiance?

OCTOBER 10

In Case You Didn't Know

> And we know that the Son Of God has come and has given us understanding, so that we may know Him who is true; and we are in Him who is true, in His Son Jesus Christ. He is the true God and eternal life.
>
> —1 John 5:20

Here comes my repetitiveness again. Everything has to point to Jesus or it's all for nothing. Sure, the Bible has great rules for anyone to follow—don't kill, don't steal—but if it wasn't for Jesus, it would be about us earning our way to our salvation. Jesus is what separates every other belief from Christianity. In every major and minor religion out there, it's all about self and works. It's about living a life that earns your way into the afterlife. When we look at our faith, we can go back to the garden of Eden and plainly see that just one sin separated us from God. Just one! We have all sinned many times since then. Have you sinned today? Maybe we sometimes don't even realize it. That's where Jesus comes in.

Examine the major religions and see that it's all about man and his attempt to earn his way into salvation. Let's take Buddhism, for example. The cycle of death and rebirth must continue until one has lived a life "good enough" to attain enlightenment. Many others are like this. Hinduism also believes in a similar stance on reincarnation. The more we indulge in scripture and grow closer to God, the more we find this to be the greatest love story of all time. We could never do it on our own, so God did it for us. He did it through His Son, Jesus, taking on all the sins of the world, past, present, and future. When Jesus bowed His head and took His last breath on the cross, He cried out, "IT IS FINISHED!" It truly was and still is finished.

So in case you didn't know, everything we believe in comes down to Jesus. Only through Him do we gain our knowledge in the faith and understanding God's promises. We have a bright hope and beautiful future with Him if we choose to accept it. The more you get to know Him, the more you truly feel God's love. Choose Christ every day.

How can you feel your faith coming together through Christ?

OCTOBER 11

When You Know, You Know

> This is now the second letter that I am writing to you, beloved. In both of them I am stirring up your sincere mind by way of reminder, that you should remember the predictions of the holy prophets and the commandment of the Lord and Savior through your apostles, knowing this first of all, that scoffers will come in the last days with scoffing, following their own sinful desires.
>
> —2 Peter 3:1–3

How many things in this world can we be certain of? When it comes down to it, the only things we can be certain of are from God. We may think we have things figured out or plans for our future, but one thing we can be certain of is we aren't guaranteed tomorrow. When we look at our world today, we may see a very dark place, but we can also be rest assured that these things have been foretold. These scoffers the passage talks about can be seen everywhere. How many people do you know continue to follow their own sinful desires? You yourself may find that even you are following sinful desires. When folks won't repent of their sins and move closer to God, it's already been foretold.

In our world today, the church is censored, and they are trying to silence us. Some of you older folks probably remember a time when the ten commandments were still posted on the walls of public schools. The world tries to move further away from God and get Him out of anything public. They try to take any mention, let alone recognition, of the Lord away from the public eye. Ever heard of the term *separation of church and state*?

This verse should be a charge to all of us to decipher the believers from the unbelievers. We are not off the hook just yet. The unbelievers still have a chance to change. We need to be the ones spreading the light through the world from the Holy Spirit that lives in us. Do not be discouraged by those of this world that mock our Lord and won't repent of their sins. Share the message with those who will hear. Don't worry about those who won't hear. It's far too easy to get frustrated with those who won't believe. Do not fall into despair but move on and share with others that will hear. We are to plant the seeds, and God will do the rest, even if it involves His judgment upon them. Be transformed by the Gospel and live your life according to His commandments.

How can you gain peace through prophecy?

OCTOBER 12

Long Line of Losers

> It happened, late one afternoon, when David arose from his couch and was walking on the roof of the king's house, that he saw from the roof a woman bathing; and the woman was very beautiful. And David sent and inquired about the woman. And one said, "Is not this Bathsheba, the daughter of Eliam, the wife of Uriah the Hittite?" So David sent messengers and took her, and she came to him, and he lay with her. (Now she had been purifying herself from her uncleanliness.) Then she returned to her house. And the woman conceived, and she sent and told David, "I am pregnant."
>
> —2 Samuel 11:2–5

Oh, David, what have you done? When we look at David's life, we see that he was called by God to do His works. At a young age, he was anointed to be king. Some would have said, "I'm sure he was destined to be a righteous man for God's kingdom." Well, as we can see here, David got caught up in his own sinful desires. Can you imagine, a man of God, caught up in a sin like this? David was someone who the Spirit of the Lord "rushed upon" when he was called to be king. How could someone like this ever fall into a trap of sin? We often find ourselves in the same battle, and sometimes, we reject what God wants and lose. Now that doesn't mean we are out of the game.

If you are like me, you tend to be a critic of yourself more than anyone else. Personally, when I have sinned and even continued to sin, I have felt severe regret and shame. The further I slipped away from the faith, the more I thought it would be impossible to come back to God. I was just another believer in a long line of losers who failed. Fortunately for David, for many of us, and for me in my walk of faith, God still uses those who have disobeyed. No matter what the circumstances are, we have God's grace through Christ. Our sins are forgiven, and we don't have to have the shame and guilt that prevents us from repenting and moving on.

When you feel like you have done something to make God not love you, consider David. He was a murderous adulterer who knew God and knew that he was sinning against the Lord and chose to do it anyway. Don't let your mistakes make you think God loves you any less. Repent, learn from it, and move on.

How can you be reminded of God's love for you even when you sin?

OCTOBER 13

Better Is the Day

> And all these, though commended through their faith, did not receive what was promised, since God had provided something better for us, that apart from us they should not be made perfect.
>
> —Hebrews 11:39–40

It all comes down to faith. Having it, believing it, and living it out in a dark world. I would encourage all of you to read all of chapter 11 and see some of the heroes of the Old Testament mentioned in their actions of faith. Some of the people Paul writes about in Hebrews didn't have it so lucky in this life. Some didn't make it to old age and had a life of being an outcast, even being tortured or killed. Even so, it comes down to God's plans. If this life doesn't turn out the way we would like it to by our faith, we have an eternity in heaven with our Lord. That is far greater than anything this earth has to offer.

If we look back on our lives now, no matter what age, we all had plans at some point that didn't go the way we thought they would. For those of us with faith with our Lord, we can mostly see that He had something better for us all along. The things I longed for, some in recent past, have changed drastically, and I have seen the hands of our Lord at work in my life that worked it out all for the better. When those situations aren't brought to what we want them to be and flipped upside down, a lot of times, we come to realize God was molding us into something better. Thanks be to Him for knowing our lives better than our own.

So in this life, don't grow weary of keeping the faith through trials. There will be much better days coming your way. It might not even be in this life, but it will come when we are in eternity with Him. Stand firm on His promises, even if it takes you to the grave, and what awaits you will make this life look like nothing. Easier said than done, I know. I, too, am learning this more and more every day. Surround yourself with the body of believers, stay in His word, and most importantly, keep the faith in Him.

> How can you have faith knowing this life may fail you?

OCTOBER 14

Promises After We're Gone

And the Lord said to Him, "This is the land of which I swore to Abraham; to Isaac, and to Jacob, I will give it to your offspring. I have let you see it with your eyes, but you shall not go over there." So Moses the servant of the Lord died there in the land of Moab, according to the Word of the Lord, and He buried him in the valley in the land of Moab opposite Bethpeor; but no one knows the place of his burial to this day."

—Deuteronomy 34:4–6

When we pray, we are not always going to see results. Sometimes, they happen long after we are gone. In Moses's case, the Israelites rebelled against God after they were out of Egypt, and the Lord declared that none of them would enter the promised land. However, their descendants would make it into that land. Sometimes in our lives, the things we pray for or work toward involving others come to fruition after we are gone. As tough of a thought it may be, we don't need to see the results. Our faithfulness in prayer for someone else may get them the results, and we aren't always around to see it.

You see it in movies and read about it in books where someone's dying prayer for another's salvation is said, and then they don't live to see the one's faith journey that they were praying for. This is just one example of the point I am getting at. In our family, I am one of the youngest of the cousins because my mother is the youngest of six. One of my older cousins had no children, and our grandmother prayed for years for her to have a child. She went through a divorce with her first husband and remarried several years later. By that time, our grandmother had passed away. Almost three years after she was gone, my cousin gave birth to her daughter. Our grandmother never lived to see that and meet the little one. God just may have taken her prayers into account that eventually blessed my cousin with her little one.

We don't always have to be around to see the result. Think of the disciples of Christ, if you will, who thought He would return in their lifetime. They knew the result, especially the apostle John, but didn't live long enough to see it. What matters most is the faith we put in God. It's not a necessity for us to see His plans unfold. Remain faithful in Him in all we do and continue in prayer for those loved ones of ours. Our prayers can continue to the next generation. Our Lord is faithful, and no matter what the outcome of our prayers are, and whether we get to see it or not, we need to continue in prayer to Him daily. We want God's glory to increase and not our own.

> How can you be faithful to God in prayer
> knowing you may never see the results?

OCTOBER 15

The Right Stuff

A scoffer does not like to be reproved; he will not go to the wise.

—Proverbs 15:12

Do you ever notice the folks that constantly bad-mouth our faith will never go to a church leader to ask the questions of their doubts? Most people who talk badly about Christianity have no idea what it's all about. Some have been hurt by the church, and instead of either looking for another church or confronting church leadership, they just abandon the faith altogether, holding a grudge against God and condemning the entire church. People like this are usually part of a group or have people in their lives that will affirm their feelings about the faith and go along with their opinions.

It happens far too often, where we seek advice but we don't accept it if it's not what we want to hear. We may go through several church leaders, asking the same questions until we get the answer we want. If you are a Christian and you ask a question about the way you may be living and you don't get the answer you want, that's usually a good thing. Sinful desires are things that can easily consume us and draw us further away from God. Go to these leaders in church who will tell you the answers to living a holy life and be humble enough to accept the answers if they are backed up by scripture.

Most people just don't like to be told they are wrong. In our world today, it's almost sickening how people drive themselves to the point of insanity when they can't be right about something. As Christians, we need to be far different from that. We are called to live in humility, knowing that we don't know it all. Fortunately, God does know it all, and we don't have to. Stick to the right ways of Him, and never be afraid to seek the right biblical counsel for the things we do not know.

> How can you be more at peace knowing
> that you don't have to know it all?

OCTOBER 16

The Cost

> When Jesus heard this, He said to him, "One thing you still lack. Sell all that you have and distribute to the poor, and you will have treasure in Heaven; and come, follow me." But when he heard these things, he became very sad, for he was extremely rich. Jesus, seeing that he had become sad, said, "How difficult it is for those who have wealth to enter the kingdom of God! For it is easier for a camel to go through the eye of a needle than for a rich person to enter the Kingdom of God."
>
> —Luke 18:22–25

Jesus gave us a lot of commandments when He was on this earth. We don't get to pick and choose which ones to follow, but we must make a conscious effort to follow them all. This wealthy fellow was so attached to his money that he didn't want to let that go for our Lord. Money isn't the only thing that can hold us back. Greed, in general, for anything not of the Lord's will is going to hold us back every time if we don't let it go. The cost of following Jesus is never easy when it comes to opposition of this world, but it's a life of restraint that we must always work at.

There are always things in our lives that are going to distract us from following the Lord to our fullest potential. We need to recognize these things and make the proper adjustments in our lives to obey Him. It comes easier to some than others, but it takes discernment to truly identify what those things are that we are holding on to. There is a far greater reward in heaven for trading those things of this world to follow Jesus better.

We are all a work in progress with these verses. As we consider this passage, we may find that we are like that rich young ruler who was holding on too tight to something of this world. We may need to examine our lives daily to better adjust to what God expects of us. There are far greater treasures in heaven than what this world has to offer. I may sound like a broken record, but this life really is short compared to eternity. Don't fill it with trivial things that don't matter in the long run. Even those things that bring us enjoyment now are nothing compared to what we will receive in heaven when we pass away from this life. As much as I would like to see a camel go through the eye of a needle, I think I would rather get to heaven before he does it!

> How can you figure out what you might be holding onto in this world?

OCTOBER 17

What a Beautiful Name It Is

> And whoever speaks a word against the Son of Man will be forgiven, but whoever speaks against the Holy Spirit will not be forgiven, either in this age or in the age to come.
>
> —Matthew 12:32

The name of Jesus is the sweetest name of all. As believers, we know that He is the focal point of our faith. The one who gave it all for our sins because He loves us so much. So why is it, in our world, that no other deity out of any religion is slandered and shamed as much as Christ? In some other religions, if you slander the name of a god or prophet, that could cost you your life. Those other religions rule with an iron fist against anyone who opposes them. Has the world just become so desensitized that the name of Jesus means nothing to them?

I often get far too angry when I hear people slandering our Lord. We hear it everywhere these days. It's become common talk in public and in the workplace. His name is even slandered on television shows and movies. I stop to think, how could anyone say one bad thing about Jesus? I think if people actually knew what He was about, they would have to be ashamed of themselves. I have to be reminded of this verse that if He can forgive them for speaking words against Him, then how could I not be more forgiving about this subject?

Remember to keep His name sacred. For those that don't, be patient with them. As a Christian, it's hard to not cringe when you hear His name taken in vain, but can you imagine Christ forgiving those who were nailing Him to the cross? He sure did it regardless. This is just one of the many reminders of forgiveness that we need. Jesus laid out the path for us to follow, and as narrow as it is, we must choose Him every day.

How can you keep the name of the Lord sacred?

OCTOBER 18

When Lives Are Changed

> When Jesus saw him lying there and knew that he had already been there a long time, He said to him, "Do you want to be healed?" The sick man answered him, "Sir, I have no one to put me into the pool when the water is stirred up, and while I am going another steps down before me." Jesus said to him, "Get up, take up your bed, and walk." And at once the man was healed, and he took up his bed and walked.
>
> —John 5:6–9

When people meet Jesus, lives surely are changed. When this man, who had been paralyzed for thirty-eight years, sat by the pool that day, he never thought that would be the last day he was there waiting to be healed. Just like that man, we, too, can be healed by Jesus in ways we could never imagine. Jesus didn't just heal him of an earthly ailment. He healed him of a far greater infection—his own sin. We may have our own physical or medical struggles on earth, but the real prize is being forgiven for our own sin that we may rise from the grave with Christ and be in eternity with Him.

When we accept Christ into our hearts, it isn't always the same result as the man by the pool. While he was given something he had always longed for, we aren't always as thankful. It may be a process to grow further in thankfulness to Christ. Some people accept Him and don't feel any different for quite a while. That's why we need to be in the Word and surrounded by the body of believers. It's easy to be on a high or feel not too different when we come to Christ, but that gives us all the more reason to keep that fire burning from day 1 so we don't slip back into our old ways.

Whether you had a conversion like the man at the pool or you feel like nothing really spectacular happened when you converted, there is something happening within you. The Holy Spirit now lives in you, and if you don't realize it yet, you will grow with the proper cultivation of the seeds planted in you. Continue seeking Him and growing closer to Him by being deeper in the Word and in fellowship with those growing with you. As believers, we are all in this together.

How can you truly be healed by Jesus?

OCTOBER 19

Ain't That America?

> Live as people who are free, not using your freedom as a cover-up for evil, but living as servants of God. Honor everyone. Love the brotherhood. Fear God. Honor the emperor.
>
> —1 Peter 2:16–17

Freedom is such a big part of our patriotic culture in America. From "Let Freedom Ring" to "Freebird," being an American is a constant celebration of freedom. That's not enough, though. The true freedom we all need more than that is through Christ. Through Christ, we are free from our own sin. There's nothing wrong with being patriotic, and we should be thankful for this great nation, but we need to remember where it ultimately comes from. That being said, too much freedom can also be a problem. When we have too much of a free rein over what we can do, things can get tricky. We are often permitted by society to do whatever we want, but that's not always right in the eyes of the Lord.

Too much freedom can actually become a form of bondage. When we exercise too many freedoms at once, we can get burned out very easily. The bigger problem with too much freedom is that we sometimes can take advantage of our freedom, which almost turns into a license to sin. We do not want that. Living in our freedom in Christ requires restraint on our part. Christ has already forgiven us for the sins we haven't even committed yet. Why would we want to go on sinning when He paid the price with His precious blood on that cross for us? We need to be grateful for His offering of Himself for us and not take that for granted.

Christ isn't asking us to walk on eggshells or be so worried about sinning that we starve ourselves of living. He wants us to live and enjoy life following Him. A truly free life comes from accepting His commands for what they are and making a conscious effort to follow Him daily. No matter how bad our lives can get from oppression (or in some countries, people are jailed for their faith), we can rest assured that we are freer than anyone since we know Jesus.

> How can you be free in restraint
> of things of this world?

OCTOBER 20

From Riches to Rags

> When many days had passed, the Jews plotted to kill him, but their plot became known to Saul. They were watching the gates day and night in order to kill him, but his disciples took him by night and let him down through an opening in the wall lowering him in a basket.
>
> —Acts 9:23–25

When we think we can't give up what we do in our normal everyday lives to glorify God, all we have to do is look at the apostle Paul. Most people that we try to witness to will sometimes use an excuse along the lines of "I'm not Jesus. I can't live a perfect life." The truth is, we could never live a life like Jesus. Thankfully, we get to see the conversion of the apostle Paul who lived a life opposing Jesus's teachings and His followers. If we look earlier in Acts, we can read about the stoning of Stephen. Paul was pleased at the killing of a follower of Jesus. This is the ultimate story of repentance where a vile and sinful human being became free of all hate and malice and chose to follow Jesus.

Do you know anyone who might fit this category of Paul's old life? Even the most horrible human beings have a chance to turn around and follow Jesus. Some people do have a conversion that is a complete 180-degree turn from their old life to become grounded solely in Christ. Do not ever doubt what God can do. When the Lord came to Ananias and told him to go to this man (Paul), he had his doubts because of all he heard about him. Nevertheless, the Lord had bigger plans, and Ananias followed His commands.

So, fellow believers, be patient with those around you who don't know Christ. One day, those kinds of people may be teaching you things about the Lord! It doesn't always work out that way, but the Lord already has it in mind who He will choose to serve Him. It may be someone who we are least likely to suspect. Paul had the life according to earthly standards, but he didn't have the life Christ promised for him. He left it all to follow Him. Trust in the Lord and know that He will use whoever He wants to use at any time to do His will.

> How can you be patient with
> those who oppose Christ?

OCTOBER 21

Not Doing Enough

Jesus Christ is the same yesterday and today and forever. Do not be led away by diverse and strange teachings, for it is good for the heart to be strengthened by grace, not by foods, which have not benefited those devoted to them.

—Hebrews 13:8–9

Do you ever feel like the upkeep of our faith is unattainable? Maybe it's getting you burned out, or your mindset is off on certain days over others. Being consistent in our faith is something we must constantly work toward every day. We must have the desire and be willing to close the gap between our church lives, home lives, and work lives to be more consistent in behaving like a believer all the time. As our scripture tells us, Jesus never changes, and that's what we need to strive for every day. We need to be unchanged by this world.

This morning, in my men's group, this subject was brought up. Are we always doing things focused on the Lord? I brought up that when I'm driving at work, I may be listening to a worship song followed by an AC/DC song. Sometimes it does feel like I'm not putting in enough effort in my faith just by something simple like that. It's a hard thing in a world today to be in constant fellowship with the Lord. Daily distractions come from left and right. We have our homes, work, and other activities that may take our focus off the Lord. What do we do from here? I think anytime we feel that nudge that we may not be giving the Lord enough time, it is a good thing. It means the Holy Spirit is working to lead us in the right direction. If we are not feeling that tug from the Holy

Spirit, it may be time for us to take a few steps back and examine our relationship with God.

Congratulations to us on knowing that we will never live the life Jesus lived. We can only keep trying to be better every day to follow His commands. We are all in this constant battle together as believers in working to live Christ-centered lives. We are going to fail at times, but we can always mend our relationship with God and accept His grace. The Lord knows your heart and knows when you are trying. Even if you struggle with this, He will always be there for you.

How can you work toward living a more consistent spiritual life?

OCTOBER 22

Every Generation

And all that generation also were gathered to their fathers. And there arose another generation after them who did not know the Lord or the work that He had done for Israel. And the people of Israel did what was evil in the sight of the Lord and served the Baals. And they abandoned the Lord, the God of their fathers, who had brought them out of the land of Egypt. They went after other god, from among the gods of the peoples who were around them, and bowed down to them. And they provoked the Lord to anger.

—Judges 2:10–12

Here we go again, Israel. When Joshua and his elders eventually passed away, the new generation of Israel rose up. As the scripture says, "They did not know the Lord." I think that mainly means that they lost sight of His promises because of their own greed and not being taught right through the previous generations. They got comfortable and forgot how the Lord took care of their fathers in bringing them out of Egypt and providing for them in the wilderness. The Lord allowed them to see the error of their ways, but they continued to rebel. When He raised up judges to intercede for them, they rebelled after each judge had passed. One would think they were never going to get it right.

Every generation that comes has its own chance to follow the Lord or rebel. To quote the late great Ronald Regan, "Freedom is never more than one generation away from extinction." The same is true for teaching the younger generations about our faith. I have met many Christian folks out there and experienced it in my own family where one generation was so faithful to the Lord while the next couldn't care less. Whether we have children or not, we as Christians have a responsibility to share the message with everyone, especially the younger generations. It only takes one generation to rebel that could set a course for the future of the family, but it also can be one generation that brings the future of the family to revival.

Consider it a great honor that you have Christ in your life. As believers, we know it isn't going to be easy, but it's worth everything to know Jesus. The rest of the world needs to know about Him, especially our children, grandchildren, and so forth. Lead them in the direction of the Lord and rely on God to ground them in their faith so they will be continuing the teachings with their own children one day. The greatest gift you could ever give your children is the message of Jesus.

> How can you teach the next
> generation about Christ?

OCTOBER 23

Learn, Grow, and Commit

> Teach me, O Lord, the way of your statues; and I will keep it to the end. Give me understanding, that I may keep your law and observe it with my whole heart. Lead me in the path of your commandments, for I delight in it, Incline my heart to your testimonies, and not to selfish gain!
>
> —Psalm 119:33–36

We don't become biblical scholars or 100 percent obedient to God overnight. Like anything else worth doing in life, faith takes work. We have to learn more about God. We have to learn about His teachings and how we follow them. It's a lifelong learning process that we will work at until the day we die. I think it's important to realize that we will never be able to learn everything. Some might get discouraged and think, *Then what's the use if we could never learn it all?* Don't let that stop you from learning as much as you can about our Lord.

When we become in Christ, we have a small seed that has been planted. As we cultivate our faith, it's time for the seed to grow. We want to be in the Word every day, watering that seed with scripture to grow closer to God. This also entails going to church, and not just on Sundays. While church services are a great way to go, everyone is going to need more than just that. There are many opportunities to grow through other church activities as well. There are group studies, church officers, volunteer groups, and so on. Consider how one of these could cultivate your spiritual growth even more.

To truly follow Christ is to commit following Christ and obeying His commands. Commitment is something we all dread for one reason or another, but this commitment is what separates you from life and death. When we commit to Christ, we are able to conquer death as He did. We will rise from the grave with Christ and join Him and the Father in heaven. We always need to commit to Him, even when we feel burned out or don't really feel like it. Commitment to Christ needs to be our main focus as believers before anything else. Everything else will branch down from there.

How can you recognize the best ways to learn, grow, and commit?

OCTOBER 24

When We Disobey

And the Lord appointed a great fish to swallow up Jonah. And Jonah was in the belly of the fish three days and three nights.

—Jonah 1:17

Consequences of disobeying God are something that some of us don't think about as much as we should. God forgives us when we disobey, but that doesn't mean it's always a no consequence result for us. Sometimes there are lifelong consequences as a result of sinful disobedience. What's important for us to know is what God expects of us. He made the line between obeying and disobedience, and the more we seek Him, the clearer it becomes where that line is.

Let's take Jonah for example. Now we all know the story of the fish. Most unbelievers can tell you that story. We know the ending, however. Imagine what Jonah must have felt being in the belly of the fish. Those three days and nights must have felt like three years for him. He was completely hopeless thinking this was his consequence to sin, dying in the belly of this fish. Imagine the feeling of gratitude he had when that fish spit him out.

There are many second chances God gives like this one. We can probably think of many times in our life when we received a second chance. We need to be mindful that in some cases, there are no second chances given. Jonah got one, but we might not. That's why we should make every attempt to obey God in all we do. Blatant disobedience could end up costing us a lot. This is not to scare anyone into believing but to teach you that there is a much greater reward and a better life ahead for obeying our Lord.

How can you see disobedience and second chances in your life?

OCTOBER 25

Who Gets the Credit?

> Behold, I have given you authority to tread on serpents and scorpions, and over all the power of the enemy, and nothing shall hurt you. Nevertheless, do not rejoice in this, that the spirits are subject to you, but rejoice that your names are written in Heaven.
>
> —Luke 10:19–20

This one is a big strive for humility. In our world, when something gets accomplished by someone, it's easy for them to take all the credit. Unbelievers usually have the mindset that they control their own destinies and anything that they work for is all because of their own efforts. As Jesus tells the seventy-two in this passage, rejoice that your names are in heaven. He is where the authority comes from, and His works are done through us.

As believers, we all have lives outside church with our own responsibilities. Our careers are some of the biggest things we deal with. When we work hard, we get rewarded or promoted to a higher status within our companies. Regardless of the work we put in, which is important, it's ultimately God that gets us where we are. Think of someone who vouches for you and refers you to a job. You might have the qualifications and the right résumé for the job, but in these cases, who you know might be the reason you get hired.

Let us not be too proud or too boastful of these accomplishments. When we think we are the ones in control and making plans or working hard toward our own goals, be mindful of our Creator who has the ultimate control over every situation. The credit should always be given to Him for every great thing or advancement in our own lives. When we humble ourselves and put the glory on Him, we are giving credit where credit is due. It's always because of God.

How can you give God all the credit for
the accomplishments in your life?

OCTOBER 26

Simple Signs

"Behold I will stand before you there on the rock at Horeb, and you shall strike the rock, and water shall come out of it, and the people will drink." And Moses did so, in the sight of the elders of Israel. And he called the name of the place Massah and Meribah, because of the quarreling of the people of Israel, and because they tested the Lord by saying, "Is the Lord among us or not?"

—Exodus 17:6–7

Sometimes we just need those simple signs from God to calm us down in our frustrations. Life can get very hard, but it's even harder without God. When the Israelites were wandering in the desert, they became very thirsty, which made them very irritable. They even went as low as to question whether God was with them at all. We might not drink from the water in the rock, but as each day goes by, there is living evidence all around of God being with us.

There was a time years ago that I felt so lost and so far from God that I didn't doubt His existence, but I just couldn't fathom what He was doing. I prayed for a sign, over and over, yet I didn't see or feel anything. Consistently, I still prayed. Looking back to those dark days in my life, I realized His existence and involvement in my life was there all along. I never lost faith in prayer, and even though nothing happened, so to speak, something was happening. I was still putting my faith in Him even though I felt like He wasn't doing anything. He was right there all along.

The water in the rock was the reminder for the Israelites that God was still with them the whole time. Just like when they were in Egypt, He never left them to their despair there either. You will find your version of the water in the rock if you tune your heart to hear the Lord and seek Him. Simple signs are everywhere. Be reminded and comforted of how much He loves you. Even when you feel distant from Him, He's always there with you.

> How can you see simple signs
> from the Lord in your life?

OCTOBER 27

Know Your Limits

Peter said to Him, "Lord, I am ready to go with you both to prison and to death." Jesus said, "I tell you, Peter, the rooster will not crow this day, until you deny three times that you know me."

—Luke 22:33–34

Sometimes in our lives, I'm pretty sure it's safe to say for all of us that we can definitely get ahead of ourselves. Our hearts may be in the right place initially, but we can often strive for ambitions too great for us to handle at the present time. While ambition is a good thing, especially when it comes to doing the work of the Lord, we need to recognize our own limits. We can't do anything without the guidance of the Lord. Peter was a man we could all learn a lot from. He had the right ambition, but even he didn't know his limits. The Lord revealed those imperfections to him.

When I used to do youth work, we would go on a mission trip every summer. It was often a spiritual high when coming home from a trip. It was like one was ready to take on the world and do God's will nonstop. Slowly, the high would wear off, and it was very easy to slip back into old ways. Countless years went by where I would do just that. I would be so on fire for the Lord and then turn right back to my own sinful nature. I was relying on myself to sustain my faith, which could never work. I was missing the foundation with Him that I truly needed.

Do not be too arrogant as to tell the Lord what you will and won't do. Peter thought that at this point in his life and was severely mistaken. Now God's grace was sufficient enough for Peter, just as it is for you, but don't rely on your own works to sustain your relationship with God. Only through Him will your spiritual life be nurtured. When we rely on the Lord for our strength, we realize how weak we are. That is all the more reason why we need a Savior.

How can you know your limits?

OCTOBER 28

What He Came to Do

For the Son of Man came to seek and to save the lost.

—Luke 19:10

No matter what we read in scripture, it all has to point to Jesus. The whole Old Testament is building up to His birth, and the whole New Testament is what we do now that He came and went. The most beautiful name, yet to some He is the most hated. Scripture is fulfilled either way. When we have questions or doubts about Him, it's important to remember what He came here to do. The lost get found through Him, the sick get healed, the sinner has a way home.

The Jews of that time never would have thought the Messiah they knew of would come in the form of Jesus. They were looking for a warrior to slay the Romans and take out all their adversaries. They could not have fathomed someone like Jesus coming down and doing what He did. He ate with the sinners and the tax collectors and wasn't the holier-than-thou type like the Pharisees were. The people needed a Savior to love them enough to die for their own sin.

Everyone needs that same Savior today to die for their sins. It should have been us up on that cross paying the price, but Christ took care of that for us. We were all lost to sin until He did what He did. May we be ever thankful for Christ coming to seek and save us lost souls who surely didn't deserve His grace. Let's live it out in thankfulness to Him every day.

How can you truly understand what Jesus came to do?

OCTOBER 29

What We Really Need

> She said to them, "Do not call me Naomi; call me Mara, for the Almighty has dealt very bitterly with me. I went away full, and the Lord has brought me back empty. Why call me Naomi, when the Lord has testified against me and the Almighty has brought calamity upon me?"
>
> —Ruth 1:20–21

The little book of Ruth has a lot we can learn from in a big foreshadow to the cross of Christ. Ruth and Naomi were both widows, and Naomi was Ruth's mother-in-law. Naomi ended up being widowed and losing both her sons. Ruth was the wife of one of her sons. Ruth cared for Naomi, yet she remained bitter against the Lord. Ruth, however, remained loyal to Naomi and ultimately faithful in the Lord. We see that she eventually meets Boaz, who redeems her in a way out of his own faithfulness to the Lord. Ruth could have been just as bitter as Naomi, but pleasing the Lord and staying faithful to Him was a much better option.

Today we had a funeral service for my wife's grandfather, who passed away this week. Many people attended, and family from all over came to say their goodbyes. At the end of the service, the immediate family got a moment of privacy with him to say goodbye. My wife's grandmother prayed the most wonderful prayer a newly made widow could pray. Even in the sadness, the focus was toward the Lord in what He had done in her husband's life. What a testimony that was to see the work of the Lord still working in the broken heart of a recent widow.

We all grieve at things like this, but ultimately, we need to still be faithful to God. It's far too easy to be like Naomi and just blame God in certain situations. We need to be reminded that no matter what loss we may face on earth, He is still enough. God's grace and peace is sufficient for all of us. When we believe in the message of Christ, we know the ultimate destination in the end for us. The journey may be hard walking a narrow path, but the kingdom of heaven is at hand. Be in thankfulness to the Lord, knowing that you don't ever have to go through something like this alone. God is still good and still with us even in the sorrows.

> How can you remain faithful
> to the Lord in grief?

OCTOBER 30

The Magnitude of Faith

> And His disciples said to Him, "You see the crowd pressing around you, and yet you say, 'Who touched me?'" And He looked around to see who had done it. But the woman, knowing what had happened to her, came in fear and trembling and fell down before Him and told Him the whole truth. And He said to her, "Daughter, your faith has made you well; go in peace, and be healed of your disease."
>
> —Mark 5:31–34

For this woman He was speaking to had a bleeding disorder. She suffered for many years. In the Jewish culture of that time and the laws of Moses, she was considered unclean. She was shunned by her own people. They must have thought, *The audacity of this woman to show up in public surrounded by people that she could've made unclean just by touching them.* That is why she just wanted to touch Jesus's outer garment to be healed and not make Him unclean. In her heart, she had the faith and had nothing left to lose. She believed 100 percent that she would be healed, and our Lord fulfilled.

Where do we stand with our faith today? Do we have the faith of this woman when it comes to our problems in life? It's a hard question, I know. I think it's easy to get in the mindset of knowing God can do something but not knowing if He will. That's just where faith has to take over. We might not always know God's plans, and it sure doesn't always work out for us the way it worked out for this woman. Regardless of whether things work out the way we want to or not, the point is that our faith in God should still be consistent. If we are in the sunshine or the storm, He is still with us.

Some of us have had our faith tested more than others. When we are grounded in the foundation of Christ, nothing will shake us. It's easy to get mad about things or grieve and wonder what God is doing. There is a big difference between those things and doubting God's existence altogether. All the main heroes in the Bible had their struggles in trusting what God is doing, but they knew He was still always there. He's always there with us today. May your faith not be shaken by things of this world that will all eventually pass away.

How can you see the magnitude
of your own faith?

OCTOBER 31

Dissension in the Ranks

I appeal to you, brothers, by the name of our Lord Jesus Christ, that all of you agree, and that there be no divisions among you, but that you be united in the same mind and the same judgment. For it has been reported that there is quarreling among you, my brothers.

—1 Corinthians 1:10–11

That old church in Corinth sure can be related to today on many levels. Quarreling in churches is something that is far too common these days. As Paul writes in the first verse of this passage, we must be united in the same mind and judgment. Ultimately, we need to all be fixed on Christ. If everyone is in that kind of focus, there should be no room for disagreements. It's important that we try to work out whatever differences we have, or we may just be holding up our church body from advancing further into what Christ wants for us as a whole.

Today's world has lots of things to disagree on. As some churches have fallen to worldly things, scriptures are being ignored. One of the biggest problems of church unity comes from some folks who want to take things in scripture and blatantly disregard them. There are things that are nonnegotiable in scripture. No matter what year it is or how the times change, His Word is forever the same. I'm sure, like me, you have seen entire denominations divide over disagreements. When you have a side that wants to follow the scriptures and the other side doesn't, it's time we be the light and speak truth into the lives of those who oppose the Word.

It's safe to say that most divisions in churches all comes back to the same question Eve was posed with in the garden of Eden: "Did

God really say that?" We all need to be careful with that one. When we are quarreling over things that don't really matter, we need to ask ourselves if that's how Christ would handle things. How could we be any different from this evil world if we are acting in the same manner of hate inside the church? We must pray and continue to promote unity in the body of believers all the time.

How can you promote unity in your church?

NOVEMBER 1

The Golden Rule

> So whatever you wish that others would do to you, do also to them, for this is the Law and the Prophets.
>
> —Matthew 7:12

The good old golden rule we've all been told. Even among unbelievers, a lot of people always say, "Treat others the way you want to be treated." What sets us apart from those unbelievers is that having the Holy Spirit in us equips us to treat others far better than they deserve when we feel they have wronged us. It becomes far easier for us as believers to treat others the way we want to be treated when we have that love of Christ in our lives.

We as Christians need to keep in mind that even when we are not treated right, we still have to treat others right. Today, while doing delivery to a chocolate shop, I went about my normal business, and the manager was there. I kindly asked him if I could rotate the water bottles for him before I left. He, not wanting to inconvenience me, reluctantly accepted. After I was done, he offered me some free chocolate to take home. I gladly accepted that! It was a simple thing I did for the customer, and it was recognized. Now that wasn't why I did my part, but sometimes we do get rewarded. On the other hand, I can recall a time years ago in a grocery store parking lot where another man had car troubles and asked if I could jump the battery on his car. After that did not work, he asked to use my phone to call his wife. I let him make the phone call, and his wife was coming to pick him up. I got absolutely nothing for that, not even a thank you! Was I bitter about it? Did I make a nasty remark or retaliate? Not at all! Some people don't always recognize our efforts, but that doesn't mean the Lord forgets things like that.

When we treat those people like we want to be treated, the Lord sees that. Even if some people don't come back and treat us the way we are treating them, we are still seen in the eyes of the Lord as sticking to His commands. It's not always easy, especially when dealing with those not so loveable folks, but our Heavenly Father sees us. We are made to live for Him, not other people.

> How can you treat others the way
> you want to be treated?

NOVEMBER 2

Lost and Found

The Lord is not slow to fulfill His promise as some count slowness, but is patient toward you, not wishing that any should perish, but that all should reach repentance.

—2 Peter 3:9

The Lord has given us a gift in His Son, Jesus. We have one job, and all we have to do is accept the Son. As we consider this verse, it's black and white that the Lord does not want to lose one of us to being unrepentant at the edge of death. Why is it then that so many people in this world are lost? Not all wish to accept Christ and think they can find a better way. If repentance doesn't come their way, a bitter fate will they have to endure. We as Christians need to be presenting the message in a loving way as much as we can to reach those that are lost and help them to be found in Christ.

I want to look at a particular subject involving this verse that I think we all go through. In our churches, our body of believers, sometimes people leave. People get mad or lose faith, and their faith journey may go very dark for a while, if not for the rest of their lives. Those members of our body that leave are still members. For those of us active in the body, we need to be patient with these folks and be willing to reach out and keep tabs on them in respectful loving ways. When I was on leadership in my first youth group, the leader always wrote kids off when they left the group for whatever reason. He always used to say something like they wanted to live their own life, or they wanted live in sin. To these kids, this was the only form of church they had, and they were pushed away. I always picture the Amish shunning someone when I think of that old group. I often think of how many kids ditched their faith and walked a different path because no one cared that they left that group.

If you're a body of believers, do your part for all. It's easy to serve those within the church, but what about those struggling members you don't always see? These are the ones having faith issues. The ones who might not make it to repentance. Just as the Lord doesn't want to see them perish, we should not either. Sometimes God is calling us to be a vessel of light with Him shining through us to pull others out of the darkness.

How can you help the lost to
be found in Christ?

NOVEMBER 3

Kill a Word

> There is one whose rash words are like sword thrusts,
> but the tongue of the wise brings healing.
>
> —Proverbs 12:18

Rash words are something we hear every day. Take a walk in public and you will hear some very foul things said from those passersby. In my job, I am in the public every day. I can recall a lot of times where these rash words were said to me. However, I am not completely innocent, and I can think of times where I said things that were very unkind and even more un-Christlike to other people. In our sinful nature, we want to just scream obscenities back at someone who was cruel to us. That's the easy way out, friends. To be wise, we must use our words to bring healing. This world sure does need a lot of it.

You probably remember the old saying you heard growing up. "Sticks and stones will break my bones, but words will never hurt me." That's just simply not true. Words can hurt far more than physical pain. With physical pain, it eventually heals. You may be left with a scar or two, but that little reminder of a physical pain isn't nearly as consuming as mental scars from those who have said cruel things to us. The advantage we have as Christians is Christ's example of forgiveness. Think of Christ being handed over to the Romans for the crucifixion. The crowds screamed for Him to be crucified. He was ridiculed and mocked by these Roman soldiers. On the road to Calvary, he was insulted and belittled. In all of this, not once did he retort an unkind word. What He did say was more powerful than any retaliatory comment: "Father, forgive them, for they know not what they do."

If only those sword thrusts the verse refers to could be turned around to kill these nasty words altogether. As Christians, we desperately want to see hate turned into love, though not everyone will do that. We can only control our own actions. When those hurtful and hateful words are thrown at us like we don't matter to someone, just remember, we matter to the Lord. We matter so much to Him that He allowed His Son to be led to the cross to take the punishment of sin for us. Desire to do what is right in His eyes. Use your words carefully, and do not speak unkindly of those, even those who may be persecuting those. Love your enemies and seek the Lord in these times of trials.

How can you watch your words?

NOVEMBER 4

Employed by the Lord

> For we are His workmanship, created in Christ Jesus for Good works, which God prepared beforehand, that we should walk in them.
>
> —Ephesians 2:10

You've heard the saying "You had one job!" Truth is, we do have one job. It's working for the Lord. This may be one job as a whole, but there are many assignments. There are many commands to follow. Believe it or not, there is a deadline. Before you are dead, you need to know Jesus. God has laid out the schedule for us. We don't know when it ends, but we know the tasks at hand to get the job done. Good thing for us, He doesn't fire us just because we messed up on something. We are never going to hit every goal in the faith, but it's important to remember as we work for the Lord to keep His commands and give ourselves grace when we miss the mark.

Aren't you so glad God is not like some of the past employers you may have had? For almost exactly two years, I worked for a trucking company that was pretty thankless and also ruthless when it came to the way employees were treated. One night, one of my coworkers got into an argument over something unimportant. He ended up shoving me. There were really no hard feelings about it, but the company used that as an excuse to fire the both of us. There was no grace at all. In the long run, it was a blessing in disguise for both of us.

When we work for the Lord, we are working for the greatest cause in history. We are created by God and for God to do His will. He doesn't need us to do His work to get Him further, but He wants us to do His work to get ourselves closer to Him. Be mindful in everything you do and how that reflects working for the Lord. God is always faithful, and He wants us to willingly desire Him and to do His commands.

> How can you work for the Lord in all you do
> and accept His grace when you fail?

NOVEMBER 5

Dark to Light

Sing praises to the Lord, O you His saints, and give thanks to His holy name. For His anger is but for a moment, and His favor is for a lifetime. Weeping may tarry for the night, but joy comes with the morning.

—Psalm 30:4–5

We have all lived in darkness for a period in our lives. It may have been a quick occasion, a season, or even years, but we have all been there where we have not carried out our faith as we should have. As the passage tells us, God's anger doesn't last very long, and truly, His joy is just around the corner if we want it. We just have to make the choice to receive it. God gives us the choice to live in the light or stay in the darkness. He made patience, so He sure doesn't have a problem with kicking back and waiting for you to choose Him. He will always help you step by step to get back to Him.

This time of year is always rough for me. We changed the clocks back, and it gets darker way earlier now. I was diagnosed with clinical depression at a young age, and I have always been more affected by this time of year. Fortunately for me, I don't have to worry or be defined by that condition. Through the night, I may be more anxious, I may be more depressed, but I know He is faithful. I could not imagine going through this condition without the Lord guiding me every step of the way. Depression is a common thing people struggle with, but this is the only way to deal with it. When it comes to that and other conditions, the darkness may feel like it's closing in, but the light of the Holy Spirit is shining out of you.

Jesus Himself experienced that darkness on the road to Calvary. He knew what it was like to feel the darkness closing in more than any of us, but He also knew that Easter morning was coming. The suffering didn't last forever, and He was fully restored as He walked out of the tomb. As we get to know Jesus more, we can see that every problem we ever have, He can relate to. It doesn't stay dark forever. The light of the Father, Son, and Holy Spirit is always there to shine through in the end.

How can you see the light in the darkness?

NOVEMBER 6

The Old Redemption Story

> In Him we have redemption through His blood, the forgiveness of our trespasses, according to the rives of His grace, which He lavished upon us, in all wisdom and insight making known to us the mystery of His will, according to His purpose, which He set forth in Christ.
>
> —Ephesians 1:7–9

If there was ever a story of true redemption, it would be Christ redeeming us through His bloodshed on the cross. The death, burial, and resurrection of Jesus is where we all were redeemed for our sins. Do we ever realize the magnitude of that? Do we really take in every lash of the whip He took for us or every hit the nails took as they were being pounded into His hands and feet? It's not a pretty picture in your mind now, is it? We don't often want to think of it because anyone would feel guilty knowing someone else took the brunt for them. We must always remember what it took to redeem us.

Being somewhat of a writer, I feel as though I am always writing stories in my head. They could be about any subject, really. The one thing they all have in common is that good wins over evil. No matter what, there is going to be redemption involved with those character's hardships. Some movies where innocent people are killed off always made me come up with redemption stories for those not so fortunate characters. That's what God does for us. He is up there writing our story. He's giving us those second chances we don't deserve, rewriting our direction in life, and redeeming us in ways we never dreamed.

TIMOTHY A. MILLS

For what God has done for us with His Son, Jesus, that alone should be enough for us, right? To some, that doesn't feel enough. They want things of this world for their redemption, and that is never going to happen. Things of this world can only give a temporary solution or basically a high. Jesus is here to stay. His purpose for us is permanent redemption. His way leads us to freedom. Do not be so caught up in anything of this world to think it can offer you a better deal than what Jesus can do.

How can you be redeemed by Christ?

NOVEMBER 7

If We Are the Body

As for the one who is weak in faith, welcome him, but not to quarrel over opinions.

—Romans 14:1

If you have someone coming into your church who's new and has that weak faith, you have a great responsibility. It's not just the pastors or the church leadership who welcome someone new. It's everybody's job. As the body of Christ, we always need to reach to those folks who are lost or new to the faith to bring them closer into what we have. A lot of people who go to church for the first time in a while or ever have a lot of the same negative experiences. Not one person took time to reach out to them. We need to be willing to step out and bring them in.

Now what happens next? If a new believer is going to start sharing their story with you, the last thing you need to do is condemn them for what they did wrong. It's most likely that they already know how wrong they have been. That's probably why they came to church to begin with. We don't ever want to hurt someone before they even had a chance to get to know the church because they may never come back. There are always going to be disagreements over opinions, but be graceful to those who may be getting out of a sinful life. Their story isn't over yet. This is why the body needs to be patient and loving toward these people as their journey into the faith has just begun.

So going from here, just remember to keep the love going toward these people. There will be a time to get things out in the air of different beliefs, and those beliefs that may be unbiblical will be brought to light in that person's life. That's not something we should worry about until that person knows they are in a safe environment to be open to the church about themselves. Let's not forget that no matter how hard we try, we can't change people. That's God's job. We must commit to loving all and letting God do His job of molding them. Continue to pray for those in your church who may be new to the faith. Take time to reach out to a new church member.

How can you be welcoming to new church folks?

NOVEMBER 8

Hearing God Speak

> Jesus said to them again, "Peace be with you. As the Father has sent me, even so I am sending you."
>
> —John 20:21

The Lord is always sending us. Now I am not going to discuss whether God audibly speaks to us or not. That's a discussion far greater than the knowledge I have. I will say, however, that sometimes we get those feelings of the Spirit coming over us that we just know exactly what we should do. The Father sent Jesus to us to pave the way and teach us. We are not off the hook at just that. We have a great responsibility and spiritual duty to be sent out to share His message with those who don't know Him.

Today, while I was at one of my stops that was quitting service, I was there to pick up all their empty bottles and a rack. The office sent someone out with a forklift to assist me in loading it all on the truck. We worked together to complete the task, and an overwhelming feeling came over me as I climbed back into the truck. I knew right then that I could not leave without sharing the message of Jesus with this guy. I felt the Spirit tugging at me to speak truth into his life. He was quiet but also receptive as I asked him questions about his life and then shared the good news of Jesus with him. We shook hands, and I told him I would be praying for him. Now I only know the surface of this guy's life, but I kept thinking that the Spirit led me to him to share the light with him for a reason. That may have been exactly what he needed to hear at that very moment in his life. God's timing is never off.

Every Sunday in our benediction, our pastor always says, "You go nowhere by accident. Wherever you go, God is sending you there." How true is that? God sent me there today not just because it was on my route for the day but to be a light in just one person's life today. Believe me, He can send you places you never dreamed of to share the message to this dark world.

How can you respond to a call from the Spirit?

NOVEMBER 9

Old-School Believer

> For whatever was written in former days was written for our instruction, that through endurance and through the encouragement of the Scriptures we might have hope. May the God of endurance and encouragement grant you to live in such harmony with one another, in accord with Christ Jesus, that together you may with one voice glorify the God and Father of our Lord Jesus Christ.
>
> —Romans 15:4–6

You have heard me say it many times. We have the guidebook. Those precious words in the Bible truly give us the hope we need. When we understand those words and discern what God is telling us, we grow even more deeply rooted in Him. The instructions we are given are not to be taken lightly. We are going to fail every day at trying to keep His commands. The important thing we need to recognize is that no matter what scriptures we follow better than others, we can't just change scripture or water it down to meet our needs. When we struggle to keep the commands, we can't just say we don't have to follow certain ones because we don't want to.

Let's flash forward to today's world. How many people do you know who try to change scripture to live an unbiblical lifestyle? I'm sure you know a lot. There is a huge difference between struggling to keep the scriptures and trying to change them altogether. Those who want to change scripture to keep on living their sinful lifestyle are basically saying that even God can't change the way that they are. If that's your way of thinking, then what hope do you really have? No matter what kind of sinful life you are living, God can change you and redeem you.

Maybe I'm just an old-school believer, but I believe we need to make conscious efforts every day to understand, follow, and live out scripture. We must discern scripture every day and ask the Lord to help us correct those errors we have. No matter where you are in life, if your hope is in the Lord, He can change you. He can mold you into His perfect creation. Put your trust in Him and allow Him to work in your life.

How can you keep the scriptures the same?

NOVEMBER 10

The Trees

A healthy tree cannot bear bad fruit, nor can a diseased tree bear good fruit. Every tree that does not bear good fruit is cut down and thrown into the fire. Thus you will recognize them by their fruits.

—Matthew 7:18–20

Just like the trees, those who don't bear the fruits in their lives aren't going to make it in the long run. For me personally, I want to spot other believers in the world before they just come out and say they are Christian. I want to see results. Actions truly speak louder than words. On the other side, I want people to know that I am a believer by my actions. Did you ever meet someone who may have been cussing up a storm and speaking in other coarse ways and they tell you they are a Christian? Doesn't seem like there is much evidence for that.

Years ago, I knew a man who claimed to be a believer. He was very knowledgeable about God. He bore no fruit in his own life though. He didn't go to church; he used very foul language constantly, including taking the Lord's name in vain; and he had relations with women outside of marriage on a regular basis. This doesn't mean that someone may have learned something spiritual from what he may have said, but what kind of witness is that overall? Is that the light of Christ being shone and the heart of man that's growing in his relationship with the Lord? Certainly not. That's a lacking of desire to let go of things in this world and grow closer to the Lord.

When we bear those good fruits, the world notices. Believer or not, it's easy to spot someone who is a true believer today. Those going against the grain of the world are everywhere. Striving daily to obey Christ's commands and grow closer to Him is our mission. That is how they will know us by our fruits. Our faith isn't based on words. It's based on action in the world every single day.

How can you tell if you are bearing good or bad fruit?

NOVEMBER 11

Coming Back Around

And the Lord restored the fortunes of Job, when he had prayed for his friends. And the Lord gave Job twice as much as he had before.

—Job 42:10

Everyone in their life has been where Job was. Job, however, never faltered in his faith in God. He may have wondered why all these bad things were happening to him, but he never lost his foundation that was built upon all he knew about the Lord. Sometimes in life, whenever we go through trials, it's hard to see the end of. I'm sure Job was really wondering when things were going to end. He had almost nothing left that could be taken away from him, and the Lord swooped in and restored everything.

On this day, we got to celebrate with our uncle on my wife's side in his wedding to his wonderful new bride. Because of complications from COVID-19 in late 2021, his wife of almost thirty-three years, our aunt, passed away. He was devastated all around. Over the next year and a half, he was in bad shape and actually went through a very bad mental breakdown. He and I talk almost every day out on the road, and it has been a blessing to see how far the Lord has brought him since then. His new bride, our new aunt, is a wonderful lady who loves the Lord just like he does. All that sorrow and waiting that he went through is now revealing the bigger picture.

Remember, nothing on earth lasts forever, good or bad. One day, there will be no more bad at all for those of us found in Christ. The Lord always comes back around in these times of trouble. It is important for us to stay hopeful in the Lord and keep our trust in Him no matter what we are going through. It's too easy to lose faith in bad situations. Don't take the easy way out. Be patient with the Lord and His timing. In a situation like this, He will reveal His greater plan in the end. We just have to hang in there for a rough journey sometimes.

> How can you patiently wait on the Lord's plans to unfold?

NOVEMBER 12

Leaving Matters out of Your Own Hands

> He said to his men, "The Lord forbid that I should do this thing to my lord, the Lord's anointed, to put out my hand against him, seeing he is the Lord's anointed."
>
> —1 Samuel 24:6

Before you read the rest of this, I'd like to invite you to read the whole chapter. It's worth diving into this whole story to encompass today's message. To start, you'll notice in these verses there is Lord with a capital *L* and lord with a lowercase *l*. The capital is referring to God, and the lowercase is referring to King Saul. Now King Saul was anointed by God to be the king, but he rebelled, and David was up and coming as the next king. Saul set out to kill David, but in this situation, David had his opportunity to kill Saul, and he didn't take it. He knew, as verse 6 says, the Lord would forbid him from doing such a thing. We go on to read further in the book that he spared his life again, and when Saul eventually died, David did not find this to be good news at all. Talk about restraint and forgiveness!

In our lives today, how many times do we want justice to be done? We end up lusting for blood when it comes to our enemies. It may not be that extreme, but our sinful nature longs for revenge sometimes. In this case, everything worked out for David in the end. Saul didn't succeed at killing him, and David did succeed at becoming king. Now we can't see the future in our lives, but imagine being wronged by someone so bad you think there's no point of return or no other way to go than to get back at someone. When we calm down in our anger and wait without any action other than prayer and staying close to the Lord, sometimes we find that the situation never really mattered, and the Lord got us where we needed to be anyway.

A lot of times in life, faith requires action. We need to move and go and act on something immediately, or we might miss an opportunity to follow the Lord's direction. In situations like this, sometimes waiting is exactly what we need to do. We never want to sin in anger, and even if the situation we are going through leads us to a point where we think we can control the outcome, just remember that what God would want us to do is far greater than what we want to do according to our earthly standards. I can't stress enough how important this is for our spiritual lives. We need to wait upon the Lord and make sure we are obeying Him always.

How can you wait in a situation like this?

NOVEMBER 13

Before Your Beginning

Before I formed you in the womb I knew you, and before you were born I consecrated you; I appointed you a prophet to the nations.

—Jeremiah 1:5

When we are born, we always look at that as our beginning of life. When it comes to the Lord, we were thought of long before we ever emerged from our mothers' womb. Our story has already been written. God already had us in mind before the world knew our names. We are all God's beautiful creations that He has perfectly put together. Life is often not taken as serious as it should be. Our lives are a gift from the Lord, and we should be celebrating by living our lives for Him.

Today is actually my birthday. In my younger years, I didn't value my life as much. I did a lot of things that weren't directed toward following Christ back then. Life sure was hard at some points, and dealing with a vindictive case of depression, I never imagined I'd be around this long. My whole problem was that I didn't look at my life with the value that the Lord looks at me. We need to remember how precious we are in the eyes of the Lord. From those little babies in the womb to the eldest of folks we know, we are all God's children.

Getting older isn't something we always like to think about, but it's also a privilege denied to many. My mother-in-law lost two of her brothers within five months of each other back in the mid-nineties. Don't ever take your life for granted. God has a plan for you. He knows you, and He loves you very much. Every year that goes by is even more of a chance we have to get to know God and grow deeper in our faith with Him. We need to be grateful for where He has brought us in life and be hopeful for where He is taking us. Every season of life, no matter what age, is gift from God.

How can you keep growing in your faith no matter what age?

NOVEMBER 14

Pour in to Pour Out

> Keep your heart with all vigilance, for
> from it flow the springs of life.
>
> —Proverbs 4:23

The world tells us to follow whatever our heart's desire may be. The Bible tells us quite the opposite. We are to guard our hearts. Many have been deceived by the desires of the heart. We need to always be careful of what we are taking in because it will be reflected in what we put out. We want those springs of life to flow from our hearts as opposed to the hate and malice of this world. Our hearts should ultimately reflect our love for Christ and should be shown through our actions in this life.

When I was involved in tree work years ago, we took down a lot of trees. Some of them would be shred through a wood chipper. If the right trees were all cut down to just the logs with no branches or leaves, you practically use the wood chips as mulch. Sometimes it just came out that clean. The brush and leaves would just be dumped aside. In our lives, when we do the proper trimming of those things that aren't good for us and keep our hearts from taking in the desires of this world, what we send out from ourselves will be of the kingdom.

Keep watch in all you do. Don't succumb to the emotions and the feelings of this world, but stand firm in the faith. Keep the commands of the scriptures and resist the temptation to go down roads that aren't good for you. We don't have to be on our own for this. The Holy Spirit is always there to help us discern the difference between those things that are good and bad. Allow Him to be the filter in your life.

> How can you trim all those bad things that
> may be trying to enter your heart?

NOVEMBER 15

Family Expansion

> Behold, children are a heritage from the Lord, the fruit of the womb a reward. Like arrows in the hand of a warrior are the children of one's youth. Blessed is the man who fills his quiver with them! He shall not be put to shame when he speaks with his enemies in the gate.
>
> —Psalm 127:3–5

Those precious little ones. What a gift they truly are from the Lord. In our faith, it's always one generation away from there being fewer believers in the world. We have a duty as parents to lead our children in the direction of the Lord. Those little ones need to grow up and have a faith of their own one day. Their faith cannot be dependent on their parents' faith. Everyone must have their own personal relationship with Christ which doesn't fly from the coattails of someone else's faith. We should be very grateful and honored to bear that responsibility of raising children as believers.

My wife and I have two beautiful daughters and another child on the way. We have agreed on both of us wanting a big family. It's always a little off-putting to me when I hear other believers say, "We only want one or two kids and no more." Why do people often put limits on that? I think big families are great and that Christian parents have more opportunities to lead more children to Christ with a bigger family. Personally, I am open to as many children as the Lord allows. We have also been open to the idea of adoption. I think we need to take that gift of procreation more seriously.

When we have more children to teach about Christ, the amount of believers here on earth will most likely increase. It does happen where children raised in a Christian home end up rejecting the faith later in life, which makes it even more important that point our children in God's direction. We need to raise these little ones in accordance with the scripture so that we may live pleasing lives to God and that one day, our children in their own faith will do the same.

How can you expand your family for the sake of the kingdom?

NOVEMBER 16

Getting Equipped

And He gave the apostles, the prophets, the evangelists, the shepherds and teachers, to equip the saints for the work of ministry, for building up the Body of Christ.

—Ephesians 4:11–12

When we think of being equipped, we might think of a battle. If you are not equipped with a weapon going into war, it's not going to end well. This is also true in our faith. Sundays are great for worship and for learning more about our Lord, but what really counts is how we apply those teachings to our daily lives. We need to be equipped to face our world throughout the week with a mission of living out our faith and sharing it to others. As the scriptures says, God gave the tools to many different kinds of people. Whatever your profession is, you are included in that list as a believer.

Another big reason in today's world to be equipped with the right knowledge of Christ is that some unbelievers will do anything they can to make you doubt your own faith. Sometimes we don't have all the answers when they ask questions, but we don't want to be dead in the water or spinning in circles contradicting ourselves when they come at us. Our message to those who don't believe takes work. We have to be diligent and careful with our words to present the Gospel in a loving way to those still in the dark.

I want to encourage all of you to start by working on your message to the world. The message of Christ to unbelievers in your own words. Follow scripture and pray for the courage and the words to speak. We all need the right tools in life no matter what we do. Don't miss an opportunity to share Christ with an unbeliever just because you are not ready to give a message. The time is now to get ready. You never know who God will put in your path that needs the reassurance of Jesus.

How can you be equipped to share the Gospel?

NOVEMBER 17

Only the Beginning

And He said to them, "What is this conversation that you are holding with each other as you walk?" And they stood still, looking sad. Then one of them, named Cleopas, answered Him, "Are you the only visitor to Jerusalem who does not know the things that have happened there in these days?" And He said to them, "What things?" And they said to Him, "Concerning Jesus of Nazareth, a man who was a prophet mighty in deed and word before God and all the people, and how our chief priests and rulers delivered Him up to be condemned to death, and crucified Him. But we had hoped that He was the one to redeem Israel. Yes, and besides all this, it is now the third day since these things happened."

—Luke 24:18–21

The road to Emmaus after the resurrection of Christ where He walked with these two travelers. Little did they know, they were talking to the one they were talking about! At that time in history, imagine how hopeless you would have felt if you followed Jesus all that time just to see Him die on a cross. All the things He taught and said and just like that, He's gone. They had His teachings to fall back on, but having the privilege to be in His presence back then and lose Him must have been devastating. Fortunately, though, they didn't lose Him at all.

This week was the last week for our five-member men's group going through the book *Experiencing God*. (I encourage all of you to inquire further about that book.) We have spent twelve weeks together going through this course. As it comes to a close tomorrow, now is the time to take action. Now is the time to take all that we learned and go out into the world and use it. Just like back then, when Jesus left the people at the ascension, they were left with the Holy Spirit to guide them in a new beginning to tell the world about Jesus.

Christ's resurrection proves one thing—sometimes, when we think it's the end, it's only the beginning. Christ led by example and gave us the teachings to live holier lives and also to trust in Him. It's our turn to go out into the world and take what we know to lead by His example. Jesus gave us everything. Let us give back what we can.

> How can you find a new beginning when
> something comes to a close?

NOVEMBER 18

Signing Off

> I Paul, write this greeting with my own hand. If anyone has no love for the Lord, let him be accursed. Our Lord, come! The grace of the Lord Jesus be with you. My love be with you all in Christ Jesus, Amen.
>
> —1 Corinthians 16:21–24

These are the last three verses of 1 Corinthians. This is how Paul finished his letter. I wanted us to look further into this because sometimes, the last thing we say or do to people is what will impact them the most. Our Sunday school teacher every week starts class with "The Lord be with you!" and ends class with "Grace and peace to you all." Whenever we encounter someone in public that we may only be meeting for the first and last time, we need the Holy Spirit's words to speak through us before we depart from them. We need them to see Jesus when we speak while we hide behind the cross.

In my life, I always try to remember to at least say, "God Bless" whenever I'm in public or delivering as I end conversations with people. I also have on my email signature one of my favorite verses. It just says, "Galatians 6:17" at the end of it. These are just little things, but they could always turn into bigger things when it comes to the Lord. You don't know what kind of impact you will have on others if we speak the truth of the Lord to them before ending conversation. It's not that we are doing or saying these things for recognition from the Lord. Rather, we do it to keep the focus on Him.

Wherever you go, people are watching. They are especially watching when they find out you are a believer. They may be watching to see if you make a mistake or that you live what you believe.

Either way, we need to be willing to put God first always, especially in our conversations with our close friends and complete strangers. In some ways, you may be the only picture of Jesus someone else may ever see, so don't screw it up! Give a laugh at that. There is always grace. So I say to you all, grace and peace to you and God bless. Tim signing off.

How can you have faith lead conversations that leave an impact?

NOVEMBER 19

The Karma Christian

> David said to Nathan, "I have sinned against the Lord." And Nathan said to David, "The Lord also has put away your sin; you shall not die. Nevertheless, because by this deed you have utterly scorned the Lord, the child who is born to you shall die."
>
> —2 Samuel 12:13–14

I'd encourage you to read a little more this time. Chapters 11 and 12 in 2 Samuel will give more context to the story. In our lives, it's often easy to think that God will punish us if we do something wrong. As believers, most of us subconsciously think that if we sin, God will always give us harsh consequences. We might wonder if He will bring harsh consequences on our loved ones as He allowed that to happen in David's story. Our sin needs to be dealt with. When we sin against God, we need to repent of our failures and accept His grace. Sometimes with sin, it might cost us our own lives. What are we to do, then, if we put sin first and God last?

Onto the title of this one. Don't be a karma Christian. In eastern religions, karma is the force of our own work and our own actions that has good and bad consequences no matter what someone does. Our belief in Jesus debunks that pretty quickly. There are people who sin against God constantly who seem like they have everything of this world, and on the other side, there are people who remain as faithful to the Lord as they can, and they face ailments or other tragedies for whatever reason. We need not look only at our own actions like we are in control of the outcomes and look to God's grace and His plans even though they may not make sense to us just yet.

The main thing we need to keep in mind is that we don't want to feel like we are just obeying God simply out of fear for what will happen to us if we don't. When we look at what God has done for us by sending His Son, Jesus, to us, what could ever be so bad in life that we can't handle if we all know Jesus? In turn, we should have a desire to obey in thankfulness, not fear. If our hearts truly belong to Jesus, then what shall we be afraid of? We all have our faults, and we all sin. Our lives need to come to a point where we make those conscious decisions to stay far away from the temptations of sin to give reverence to God, not to keep us free and clear of God's wrath.

How can you obey God out of thankfulness over fear?

NOVEMBER 20

Is It All Here?

Now Jesus did many other signs in the presence of the disciples, which are not written in this book; but these are written so that you may believe that Jesus is the Christ, the Son of God, and that by believing you may have life in His name.

—John 20:30–31

A lot of skeptics have a hard time believing that what's in the Bible is all that we need to know. A lot use that as reasons to doubt. Some would think that the Bible itself has too many loose ends or not enough depth about certain things. When it comes down to it, God gave us all we need to know. Faith must take over from there. I think even if we did know every last detail, some would still find reasons to doubt God's existence and His purposes for us. It's okay to wonder about some of the details that aren't in scripture, but we must not let that be the determining factor of whether we have faith in God or not.

There are many stories in the Bible that we don't know every last detail of. What was Ishmael's journey like as God made him into a great nation along with Isaac? Where was Jesus from age twelve to thirty? These are things that are never really explained. I think if we were meant to know these things and many others, they would be in scripture to teach us one thing or another.

So when you go through scripture, just remember that God's Word is exactly what it needs to be. It's okay to wonder or have questions, but don't obsess over these things to the point where your faith starts to crack. God's given us a great guidebook to get through life. For what we don't know or are unsure of, faith is there to take over. We all say that when we get to heaven, we will have a lot of questions to ask our Lord. If we get the opportunity, I know I will ask a lot!

> How can you allow faith to take over what
> you don't understand in scripture?

NOVEMBER 21

No Other Gods

You shall have no other gods before me.

—Exodus 20:3

This one is pretty cut and dry. The first commandment out of the ten is first for a reason. God is God. End of story. Now this verse is not just restricted to not believing in other deities. Another god could be anything. Anything in our lives that we are putting before God could be a breach of this commandment. It's easy to get caught up in the world where we are almost worshipping something else over God. We tend to find these lowercase *g* gods all around. There are many examples that all of us may succumb to. What's important is to get back to the one and only capital *G* God.

People in this world all lust over things that aren't good for us. It could be money, relationships, hobbies, things, and the list goes on. When we place something ahead of God, we are disobeying this commandment. I have stressed a lot in this book how church on Sunday mornings alone is not enough. If we are only giving God a couple of hours on Sunday mornings and that's it for the week, then what are we holding ahead of Him with the rest of our time? It's a hard question that we may have to ask ourselves over and over.

Wherever you are in your faith, if you are new or have been a believer for years, we all will fall short of this commandment. We must be on constant watch for things that can potentially take our time away from the Lord. While those things may not be inherently wrong, they can be wrongly prioritized. Let's prioritize our Lord first always.

How can you tell if you have a god in your life keeping you from God?

NOVEMBER 22

The Cornerstone

> For it stands in Scripture: "Behold I am laying in Zion a stone, a cornerstone chosen and precious, and whoever believes in Him will not be put to shame." So the honor is for you who believe, but for those who do not believe, "The stone that the builders rejected has become the cornerstone," and "A stone of stumbling and a rock of offense."
>
> —1 Peter 2:6–8

The cornerstone in these verses is referring to Jesus. In the metaphorical sense, this verse suggests Jesus was indeed the stone that the builders rejected, and they truly needed that stone in the end. Without Christ, we have no foundation. Life may be wonderful at times, but it's not the true wonder that a life with Christ has. On the flip side of things, life may be terrible at times, but how would you ever hope to get through whatever it may be without Christ? Our foundations need to grow even more sturdy and solid in our relationship with Christ.

Have you ever built something from the bottom up and realized after you went so far that you missed a piece at the bottom? No matter what it is, whether it's a skyscraper or Legos, it's not going to be right or even secure without that piece at the bottom. This brings you a choice to make. Do you continue, or do you tear it down and rebuild with that missing piece being put in its proper place? This is exactly what we need to do in our lives. Go for the missing piece and make haste before it's too late! When Christ becomes that missing piece in our life, we need to be broken down, and our spiritual lives need to be reevaluated. We will never be fully secure without Him.

Sometimes we don't always recognize when Christ becomes that missing piece in our lives. It's important that we are regularly in prayer and in His Word every day. Our weeks can get very long when we are only in church on Sundays and doing nothing else for our spiritual growth. Make Christ your cornerstone today, forever, and always.

How can you tell what your cornerstone is?

NOVEMBER 23

Give Thanks with a Grateful Heart

Therefore, as you received Christ Jesus the Lord, so walk in Him, rooted and built up in Him and established in the faith, just as you were taught, abounding in Thanksgiving.

—Colossians 2:6–7

A simple thank you can go a long way in someone's life. Showing gratitude is not just a form of respect, but it's also a way to show the love of Christ to others. We should also be coming to the Lord in Thanksgiving every day. Since we have received Christ, there is a magnitude to that which we will never fully comprehend. We need to truly be thankful for what our Lord did for us by dying on the cross and rising from the grave to defeat death so that we may also defeat death and be in eternity with Him. Being grateful is something we all need to work on.

Being Thanksgiving Day, for a lot of folks, this is the only day of the year they reflect on what they may be thankful for. Thanksgiving shouldn't be restricted to just one day out of the year, though. Every day, there are reasons to be thankful of God's blessings, especially the ultimate blessing of His Son, Jesus. There are little glimpses of God's blessings every day that we should be in Thanksgiving for. When we really break down just one day's events and our hearts are tuned to feel God's presence, we find that there are always more reasons to be thankful.

It's not always easy to be thanking the Lord every day. We oftentimes want to give ourselves the credit. We want to pat ourselves on the back and take all the glory for the good things in our life. The truth is, we can do nothing on our own. We are given what the Lord wills. We only accomplish things by His grace and what His plans are. Be thankful for His presence in your life every day.

How can you make Thanksgiving every day?

NOVEMBER 24

Black Friday

> But Godliness with contentment is great gain, for we brought nothing into the world, and we cannot take anything out of the world. But if we have food and clothing, with these we will be content. But those who desire to be rich will fall into temptation, into a snare, into many senseless and harmful desires that plunge people into ruin and destruction.
>
> —1 Timothy 6:6–9

Well, it's only the day after everyone talks about how thankful they are, and then the shopping begins! Black Friday is the biggest shopping day of the year, and some definitely take it far too seriously. I don't think the Lord has a problem with us using our money to buy things of enjoyment for our families, even if they are material things. The problem occurs with a greedy mindset. When we are not content, we are in a mindset that God cannot make us content alone and that we need things of this world along with it. If that's your mindset, then something needs to change.

We all find ourselves wanting things we don't have at times. Personally, I am a big model train collector. Let's face it, no matter how much I gain, there is always more. Sometimes it is frustrating when other priorities have to come first and I have to put my hobby last. I'm sure you can relate at times in your own life. What's important for us all to remember is no matter what our hobbies are or the things we would like to have, nothing can compare to the blessings God has given us.

We must be mindful every day to keep giving thanks to God for what we do have and don't be so covetous of what we don't have. Our whole state of mind needs to always be fixed on God to fulfill us, not the things of this world. While there are things out there that we do enjoy, God must continue to be first in our lives. Don't let personal greed get in the way of your faith. Material things and experiences of this world will come and go, but God is always and forever.

How can you tell if you are struggling with greed?

NOVEMBER 25

Mr. Brightside

For God has not destined us for wrath, but to obtain salvation through our Lord Jesus Christ, who died for us so that whether we are awake or asleep we might live with Him.

—1 Thessalonians 5:9–10

This is a big one, and let me preface by saying God does not destine anyone to go to face His wrath and end up in hell for eternity. That's something we can be certain of. Our destiny changed course when Christ conquered death and gave us the opportunity to rise from the grave with Him. We only have life if we are living in Him. God gave us the gift through Jesus for eternal life. We have two options at this fork in the road. Accept Christ and live forever or reject Him and die to an eternity in hell. Some might call this a doomsday message, but it's really that simple. God destined us to receive Christ.

Some people out there will go to the grave rejecting Christ. That is a choice many will make. Some of these same people think it's God who's sending them there or even just punishing them while they are still on earth. When you have Christ in your life, certain earthly situations may cause heartache, but our perspective changes when we have Him in our lives. Imagine not having Him in your life and being permanently separated from Him forever with no second chances. Some say that hell will be fun and all their friends will be there. Let me tell you folks, there is nothing fun about eternal separation from God. If we think this world is bad at times, this is pretty easy compared to what it would be like if we died not knowing Christ.

Today's message isn't to scare you into believing. It's just stating the obvious. It's one or the other in the end. No purgatory, no second chances, no praying your way out. This goes back to the love of Christ. His blood was poured out for us on the cross. We shouldn't just believe because we are scared of going to hell. We should believe because of the love that was shown to us that we could not even comprehend. Jesus paid the price so we don't have to. Don't let His sacrifice be in vain in your life.

How can you believe because of love over fear?

NOVEMBER 26

Rebuilding the Temple

> So the Jews said to Him, "What sign do you show us for doing these things?" Jesus answered them, "Destroy this temple and in three days I will raise it up."
>
> —John 2:18–19

The temple Jesus was really referring to was His own body. His death on the cross, burial, and resurrection was going to fulfill this statement He made to the Jewish elite. The Jews were so fixed on the temple itself that they were neglecting the fact that it's not about a building. It's about worshipping our Lord every day and everywhere. Jesus isn't just restricted to the temple or a modern church. He's with us all the time, everywhere we go.

While our churches may be very important to us, it's not about the building. Our church is a wonderful place that is constantly seeking God's direction for us and to be led by the Spirit in our decisions and worship. Even so, it's important to realize that this place that we do love is nothing more than just a building. Without the people kneeling in reverence to Jesus and following His commands, it can be nothing. Our faith needs to be lived out every day no matter where we go.

So in all you do, whether in church or out in the world, keep Jesus first. Allow Him to work in you and through you so that others may see Him when they see you. Be mindful of your church and know that it's not just about the church itself. It's about who's leading it. If Jesus is the head of your church, may we continue to get to know Him better and serve Him, not just in church but outside of church as well. We are to be the body of Christ in this dark world, not just attend a body of believers on Sundays.

How can you be the body of Christ wherever you go?

NOVEMBER 27

Representation

My little children, I am writing these things to you so that you may not sin. But if anyone does sin, we have an advocate with the Father, Jesus Christ the righteous.

—1 John 2:1

The most important part of our faith is Jesus. What He did on the cross sealed the deal for us. Death was conquered, and we may now have a relationship with the Father through Jesus. See, God cannot be in the presence of sin, and we lost that privilege from the beginning with Adam and Eve's sin. We were in deep trouble until Jesus paid the ultimate price. When we have Him in our lives, we have an opportunity to be in communion with the Father. Jesus truly is our representation. He is advocating for us to live in eternity when we truly don't deserve it.

Union employees have a lot of perks when it comes to representation. I cannot be disciplined without having my union representative present to stand in the gap and defend me for whatever the company is accusing me of. Under no circumstances am I ever going to be called into the office and written up alone. I will always have my representation there with me. Thinking of how our faith is, Jesus is that true representation, so we never have to go through anything alone. While the evil one may be lurking about in this world, Jesus is there to stand between him and us to hold him back and keep us closer to the Father.

There are a lot of people in this world who reject that representation. Far too many will struggle and suffer alone when they don't have to. If I were to go into the office alone at work and accept write-ups and admit to something I didn't do, then I may be out of a job. The same for our faith. We don't want to be out of an eternity with Christ by rejecting Him during our time on earth. He loves us so much that He represents us with His offering of Himself on the cross. We must not let that ever be in vain.

How can you be represented by Christ?

NOVEMBER 28

Dancin' in the Dark

> Therefore God has highly exalted Him and bestowed on Him the name that is above every name, so that at the name of Jesus every knee should bow, in Heaven and on Earth and under the Earth, and every tongue confess that Jesus Christ is Lord, to the glory of God the Father.
>
> —Philippians 2:9–11

It's pretty black and white from this point. Whether we believe now during our time on earth or when it becomes too late to enter the kingdom of heaven after death, everyone will admit that Jesus is Lord. So if this much is true, then why would anyone want to wait? Why wouldn't you want to be a part of this? Far too many people are so caught up in their own sin. As you've heard me say many times, sin is never unappealing. If sin was unappealing, then there would be no temptation to do it. Those out there dancing in the dark right now will be in for a rude awakening if they don't know Jesus.

So what makes our faith more appealing than sin when it comes to a worldly perspective? That's a question we all must ask ourselves and have the answer prepared when we are sharing the Gospel message with others. Living as a Christian as opposed to an unbeliever has a lot of challenges in today's world, but it's a cost well worth paying. Nothing this world has to offer could ever surpass what we have in Jesus. It's sad that a lot of people don't realize and don't want to realize what their life could be like following Jesus.

As the verse says, *every* knee will bow, and *every* tongue will confess. Bow and confess now while you are still on earth instead of going to the grave not knowing who Jesus is. This life will pass away sooner than you think. We are just a vapor in the wind if we look at the bigger perspective of time. If you haven't done so already, give your life to Jesus today. Be willing to share with others this news He's given us.

<blockquote>How can you use these verses in
your message to the world?</blockquote>

NOVEMBER 29

Slap in the Face

When Israel was a child, I loved him, and out of Egypt I called my son. The more they were called, the more they went away; they kept sacrificing to the Baals and burning offerings to idols.

—Hosea 11:1–2

If we read through the Old Testament on the history of the Israelites, this one pretty much sums it up. The Israelites were always brought out of whatever situation they were in by God but ended up rebelling against Him afterward. What a terrible way to show gratitude. If we look at the escape from Egypt, God brought them out and then down the line that wasn't good enough anymore to them. It's like they forgot all about their enslavement to the Egyptians when things weren't going how they planned.

How often do we do this? We beg God for something, and sometimes He does grant that to us, and then we go back to being miserable about something else. Sometimes our greed gets in the way, and being content and grateful goes to the wayside. When God brings us out of bad situations in life and then we run right back to those things, it's like a slap in the face to what He has done for us. When we are caught in repetitive sin, there may come a time that God does not deliver us from it and we must face even worse consequences.

When God delivers us from bad situations, our gratitude needs to be all that we can give. We can never repay God for what He's done for us, but we can make a conscious effort every day to live for Him. Don't let His deliverance be in vain. Stay away from those situations that He brings you out of. Don't go back to them and run toward Him.

How can you stay away from the things God delivered you from?

NOVEMBER 30

Skin of Your Teeth

> And if the righteous is scarcely saved, what will become of the ungodly and the sinner?
>
> —1 Peter 4:18

No one in this world is good or deserving of an eternity in heaven. By our own merit, we cannot earn our way back to God because of the sins we have committed. Consider some of the most wicked people you may have encountered or even the ones with the cleanest record. Neither person is deserving of paradise after death. If we really break it down, one sin dismisses us from the presence of God. We are forever separated from Him because of it. We are only saved through grace, the grace of God through Jesus.

One year on a family retreat through our church, each family was given a tube of toothpaste. We were all instructed to squeeze out the entire tube onto a paper plate. We were then told to put it all back in. At that point, no one could do it. (My dad actually cut the top off and let me put it all back in, but that didn't count!) This is what our sin is. It's a squeezed-out toothpaste tube, and no matter how hard we try, we can't take it back. Sin needs to be paid for, and because Jesus walked this earth and never sinned, He was able to take on the sins of this world to pay the price for our debt.

We truly are only saved by the skin of our teeth. If we are sinners like the rest of the world who have been forgiven and recognize the need for change and even we are not worthy of heaven, imagine what awaits the people who won't repent and follow Jesus. It's a scary thought of going through this world without Jesus. There is far too much uncertainty, but one thing that is for sure is where these folks without Him will go after the grave. Don't wait to ask Jesus into your life.

How can you give more thanks to the Lord for Jesus's life?

DECEMBER 1

O Come All Ye Faithful

And in the same region there were shepherds in the field, keeping watch over their flock by night. And an angel of the Lord appeared to them, and the glory of the Lord shone around them, and they were filled with great fear. And the angel said to them, "Fear not, for behold, I bring you good news of great joy that will be for all people."

—Luke 2:8–10

Today is December 1! The season of Advent is upon us at last as we prepare to celebrate the birth of our Savior. It's easy to get caught up in the presents and festivities that we may not be recognizing what this season is really about. When those shepherds met the angels long ago, I'm sure they never could have imagined what was in store for this world, and they got to be there firsthand. Being a shepherd wasn't really anything glamorous back then. It was a blue-collar job, and these guys weren't really anything special. Nevertheless, the Lord called them to be present at the Savior's birth. Jesus is for everyone.

When we look at the world today and how people celebrate Christmas, it's done in many different ways. For some, it's lavish parties and a lot of presents and going here and there, but for others, they may be just scraping by to give their families a small meaningful Christmas. Either way, when we are celebrating the main reason for Christmas, it doesn't really matter what we are doing. The Savior came not just for the ones of high status but of those that are far less fortunate as well. The Christmas story is for all to believe, no matter where we come from. I think God wanted these shepherds there to teach us that even the lowest standards or classes in the world can come and worship the King.

TIMOTHY A. MILLS

Wherever you are in life, celebrate this time of year by giving thanks to the Lord for sending His Son. This is only the beginning of the life of Jesus, but in the backdrop of the nativity, be reminded there is a dark cross there foreshadowing the future of Christ's life. This is where it all must start to fulfill the prophecies of the Old Testament prophets to achieve the greatest rescue mission in history. That little baby born of a virgin will grow up to be a man laying down His life for all.

How can you keep the cross in mind in this season of Advent?

DECEMBER 2

Who's Really Coming to Town?

> The true light, which gives light to everyone, was coming into the world. He was in the world, and the world was made through Him, yet the world did not know Him.
>
> —John 1:9–10

As Christmas draws near, many people are getting ready to celebrate. I often wonder how many people are really celebrating the birth of the Savior. It seems that far too many people are just celebrating Christmas for the fun. Most children are taught about Santa Claus coming to town, but a lot are never really told the greater story of who's really coming to town. In today's world, Jesus has already come and gone in the flesh, but He is still with us, and with us He will remain.

Today we were at an event at my union hall called Breakfast with Santa. It's always a wonderful time, especially for the kids. In the past couple of years we attended, the guy who dressed up as Santa took the focus off Santa and reminded the children who the real focus should be on. He reminded them of the birth of our Savior coming up. What a light in the darkness for an event that isn't really focused on our Lord. I truly hope and pray there were people there who really needed to hear that.

So as you get your house lit up with decorations, do your Christmas shopping, and wrap presents, remember the meaning behind it all. As nice as those material things may be, there is an even greater gift to celebrate. As the verse says, the world did not know Him. The world needs to know Him, and we need to lead by example in how we celebrate this wonderful time of year.

How can you show people Jesus through your Christmas celebration?

DECEMBER 3

Do Not Be Afraid

And he came to her and said, "Greetings, O favored one, the Lord is with you!" But she was greatly troubled at the saying, and tried to discern what sort of greeting this might be. And the angel said to her, "Do not be afraid, Mary, for you have found favor with God. And behold, you will conceive in your womb and bear a son, and you shall call His name Jesus."

—Luke 1:28–31

The phrase "Do not be afraid" is in the Bible 365 times. That's one for each day of the year. We don't often realize that with God, there is no real reason to be afraid. Our earthly desires and sinful nature give us reason to fear, but God is bigger than all of that. Take Mary, for example. She was young, unmarried, even a virgin, and now she was with child. How hard that must have been, but with God, all things are possible. It's far too easy to use those familiar excuses like "I'm not ready" or "I can't handle this," but the good news is, we don't have to worry. God will take care of all of that.

This world lives in fear today. Turn on the news on any given day and see for yourself what people are afraid of. It's pretty sad to know that the reason they fear so much is because they don't know Jesus. Take the COVID pandemic, for example. While there is nothing wrong with taking the proper precautions, living in fear of something to the point where you are not relying on God's mercy to get you through is keeping you in fear. On every occasion we feel the fear coming on, we need to feel God's comfort coming on even stronger.

No matter what the situation may be, God is bigger than it. The light may seem dim at times, but it's there nonetheless. God is always in control of those dark situations even when we feel hopeless. Keep your hope in Him and do not be afraid. May you be comforted by Him and His Word this Christmas season and always.

How can you not be afraid with God?

DECEMBER 4

Go Tell It on the Mountain

> And when they saw it, they made known the saying that had been told them concerning this child. And all who heard it wondered at what the shepherds told them. But Mary treasured up all these things, pondering them in her heart. And the shepherds returned, glorifying and praising God for all they had heard and seen, as it had been told them.
>
> —Luke 2:17–20

Go tell it on the mountain, over the hills and everywhere! What great news we have that Jesus Christ is born into this world. In this Christmas season, it's an even more important time to witness to others. This is the birth of our Savior. The beginning of His mission on earth to redeem us from our sins. Oftentimes, we find it difficult to start a conversation about faith with others, but what better a segue into the gospel message than talking about Christmas?

For some people, this is a hard time of year. Some folks are just far more vulnerable than the rest of the year. Some are dealing with grief from the loss of a loved one. Others may be dealing with an illness of their own. Whatever the case may be, there's no time like the present to be introduced to Jesus. As Christians, we have a responsibility all the time to tell others the good news. Christmas gives us an even better opportunity. Everyone in this world is searching for something to fulfill them. The problem is that only Jesus can do that, and He's not always what people are looking for, but He's definitely what we all need.

In your travels during this Christmas season, do not be afraid to share the message. Wherever you are, whether it be a long-lost family member, someone struggling with a mental or physical ailment, or even just some stranger you meet while shopping at the mall, tell everyone, and do it unashamedly so. The public eye will always notice something different about those going against the grain this time of year. When we are kind and polite to others during the busy shopping days and all the other activities Christmas brings, we may have an even better shot to tell the world about Jesus. Go tell it on the mountain that Jesus Christ is born.

> How can you be an even better witness
> during the Christmas season?

DECEMBER 5

Let It Snow

> Bring the full tithe into the storehouse, that there may be food in my house. And thereby put me to the test, says the Lord of hosts, if I will not open the windows of Heaven for you and pour down for you a blessing until there is no more need. I will rebuke the devourer for you, so that it will not destroy the fruits of your soil, and your vine in the field shall not fail to bear, says the Lord of hosts. Then all nations will call you blessed, for you will be a land of delight, says the Lord of hosts.
>
> —Malachi 3:10–12

For those of you who like snow, this isn't really about it! It's about other more important things coming down from heaven for you. God is ready and able to send down His blessings to you falling from the sky like snowflakes. We are to obey Him to be able to fulfill these promises He makes to us. We aren't just obeying to receive. We are obeying because we already have received. I believe every blessing from God is more of a bonus than a reward because we already have the true reward through Jesus and what He did for us on the cross.

It is the season of giving, after all. We need to freely give to others, but most of all, we need to freely give back to God. Even though we will never be able to fully give back to Him what He deserves, our desire needs to be fixed on giving what we can to Him. I'm sure for those of you on social media, you have come across a post that may go something like "If you like this post, God will send a blessing your way." That couldn't be further from the truth. God isn't a genie in a bottle who bows to our every demand. When we truly have Christ in our hearts, we are more thankful and more responsible to accept these blessings that He graciously gives us.

Friends, don't rely on just getting things from God. Rely on giving things to God. When we are humble and put the Lord first in obedience to Him, we are keeping His commands and being faithful to His Word. Don't be greedy and only follow God to "get stuff." Follow Him because you are thankful and already so blessed through Jesus.

> How can you follow God without expectations for blessings?

DECEMBER 6

God Rest Ye Merry Gentile Men

> For I tell you that Christ became a servant to the circumcised to show God's truthfulness, in order to confirm the promises given to the patriarchs, and in order that the Gentiles might glorify God for His mercy, as it is written, "Therefore I will praise you among the Gentiles, and sing to your name." And again it is said, "Rejoice, O Gentiles, with His people." And again, "Praise the Lord, all you Gentiles, and let all the peoples extol Him." And again Isaiah says, "The root of Jesse will come, even He who arises to rule the Gentiles; in Him will the Gentiles hope." May the hope of God fill you with all joy and peace in believing, so that by the power of the Holy Spirit you may abound in Hope.
>
> —Romans 15:8–13

When the Hebrews were anticipating the arrival of the Messiah, there was no way they were thinking He was going to save the gentiles as well. They predicted He was only going to rescue them being His chosen people. This was just one misconception they had about Jesus. Jesus is bringing hope to all who believe. Back in those days, He proved that His time on earth wasn't just for the Jews but for the gentiles alike that His promise was fulfilled in everyone's lives if they followed Him. We all need hope in our lives. There is no greater hope than what we receive through Jesus.

Fast-forward over two thousand years later, and that same hope still applies to us today. Being part of the church in America today or one particular denomination doesn't mean that we are the only ones going to receive the promises and the hope Christ gives us. There are far too many churches who think they are the only ones doing things the right way and that because other churches aren't doing it that way, they must be wrong. Jesus came to us in the most vulnerable way possible, lived a perfect life, died on a cross, and rose from the grave for all of us.

This Christmas season, a lot of people are hurting. Many different reasons make this time of year very hard and definitely not so joyful for some folks. This is all the more reason they need Jesus. Be kind to those struggling. Do not be so judgmental of someone's situation, but come alongside them in love as Christ would do and lead them to Him.

> How can you share the hope in Christ
> with someone this Christmas?

DECEMBER 7

Angels from the Realms of Glory

> And the angel answered him, "I am Gabriel. I stand in the presence of God, and I was sent to speak to you and to bring you this good news."
>
> —Luke 1:19

When Gabriel met with Zechariah and Elizabeth, he sure did have some good news for them. Before Mary was with child, Elizabeth was to be with child as well. She was the mother of John the Baptist. Now Elizabeth was up there in years and also barren. Hearing the news that she was to have a child was probably something she waited her whole life for, and it was finally here. Just imagine the excitement she had knowing what was about to take place. When God sends a clear message like that, He is sure to deliver it.

In our lives today, sometimes we need a clear message from God. He might not be audibly speaking to us, but His message will get to us one way or another. Whatever message or sign you might think you need from Him is nothing compared to the greatest gift He's ever given us, and that is His Son, Jesus. Jesus is our good news from God. This Christmas season, may we remember that He is why we celebrate and ultimately why we have what we have.

In this wonderful Christmas season, remember the sign from God and the message of good news has already been delivered. Jesus is here to stay. He may not be with us in the flesh, but He's always with us no matter where we are. God has blessed us and continues to bless us every day with Jesus.

How can you keep the good news all year round?

DECEMBER 8

O Holy Night

> Behold, the virgin shall conceive and bear a son, and they shall call His name Immanuel. (Which means, God with us).
>
> —Matthew 1:23

Imagine being around to see this prophecy fulfilled. Jesus had many different names, but Immanuel is a very good description of who He truly is. It's a concept that no human can completely understand, but Jesus was fully God and fully man at the same time. We could discuss that for days! What's important to remember is that even though Jesus is called the Son of God, He is also God Himself. The Father, the Son, and the Holy Spirit. One God, three parts.

Jesus coming into this world meant that God was walking among us. Only then could be done what needed to be done. As this prophecy explains that God will be with us in the form of Jesus, more prophecies will be fulfilled about how the world rejected Him. The Christmas story and celebration is beautiful, but there is an ugly cross coming down the line that reminds us what had to be done for the rescue mission to be fulfilled.

While it may have been a very holy night when Christ was born, it's still a holy time of year. When it comes down to it, God is still with us, even over two thousand years after Christ was born. Even when it seems like times are tough, there is always that light of Christ shining through the darkness for us. Keep Christ held high, not just during Christmas but all day every day.

How can you be reminded that God is still with us?

TIMOTHY A. MILLS

DECEMBER 9

Angels We Have Heard on High

> And suddenly there was with the angel a multitude of the heavenly host praising God and saying, "Glory to God in the highest, and on earth peace among those with whom He is pleased!"
>
> —Luke 2:13–14

That chorus of angels must have been an amazing sight! Seeing that heavenly host praising God and singing to the King. It's the time of year where churches are filled with people singing Christmas hymns to celebrate the birth of our Lord. Whether you feel you can sing or not, sing those praises anyway with your congregation as we prepare for the Christmas celebration. We may not have voices of angels, but we can certainly join in the chorus to our Lord.

In any case, whether it be singing or just being together, when we are all in fellowship this time of year celebrating Jesus, that is also praising God. Tonight we attended our pastor's open house gathering hosted by him and his wife at their home. It was a wonderful time of fellowship with our church family. As I looked around the room and conversed with others, I was reminded how we all came from different backgrounds and different pasts and struggles, but we shared that common goal of living together in Jesus.

We may not be as pure and beautiful as that heavenly host was singing the night Christ came into the world, but we do sing our praises to the Lord. This is a perfect time of year to be in fellowship with others celebrating Christ. We should be doing that all year, but this time of year should restore us and replenish our souls so that we may go into the new year in full force with our desires to grow closer to Christ.

How can you prioritize fellowship with other believers?

DECEMBER 10

Come Thou Long Expected Jesus

I will put enmity between you and the woman, and between your offspring and her offspring; He shall bruise your head, and you shall bruise His heel.

—Genesis 3:15

Throughout the Old Testament, it's all leading up to Jesus's arrival. The long-awaited Messiah is mentioned many times in the Old Testament even if not by name. From way back to the garden of Eden after Adam and Eve had disobeyed God and sinned, the plan was already in motion. The world needed a Savior, and God had to do it Himself in the form of Jesus. The more we get to know Jesus, the more we can see that it could only be done by Him. No one else could have been born into this world to live a perfect life, die, and rise from the dead.

This verse describes that in the end, Jesus will overcome it all. Even the serpent who deceived Adam and Eve will lose in the end. When Jesus came into the world, He was not thought of as the Messiah by a lot of people because He wasn't doing what they predicted. They thought He was coming to slay the Romans and free the Jews from their control. He came to save them from a whole lot more than that. No matter what we go through on earth, our own sin is something we have no way of coming to terms with. One sin separated us from God, and it needs to be paid for. Jesus came to settle that debt with the Father by taking our place on the cross.

As Jesus has already come and gone in human form, let us be reminded that one day, He is coming back. We may want Him here quicker, but His timing is perfect. He will return one day, and all those who believe will be spending an eternity with Him. This Christmas, I pray we can all take the time to keep in mind the ultimate plan. Christ had thirty-three very impactful years on this earth, but overall, He has a greater purpose than that. Are you prepared for His return?

How can you prepare for Jesus coming back?

DECEMBER 11

Do You Hear What I Hear?

There shall come forth a shoot from the stump of Jesse, and a branch from his roots shall bear fruit. And the Spirit of the Lord shall rest upon Him, the Spirit of wisdom and understanding, the Spirit of counsel and might, the Spirit of knowledge and the fear of the Lord. And His delight shall be in the fear of the Lord. He shall not judge by what His eyes see, or decide disputes by what His ears hear, but with righteousness He shall judge the poor, and decide with equity for the meek of the earth; and He shall strike the earth the rod of His mouth, and with the breath of His lips He shall kill the wicked. Righteousness shall be the belt of His waist, and faithfulness the belt of His loins.

—Isaiah 11:1–5

Throughout the Old Testament, there are signs and whispers of the coming of Christ into the world. These verses encompass only a fraction of what He came to do here. He came to save us all from the unseen enemy known as sin. This Christmas season, we should be encouraged to continue searching for signs of Christ in the world today. Even as dark as the world can be, His light is everywhere if we tune our hearts to notice it.

When the Spirit was upon Him on earth, He bore much fruit as the verses consider. He followed the commands of the Father even up until death as He hung on that cross. In our lives, we need to follow in His footsteps and bear the spiritual fruit as well. We will never be close to living the life Jesus did, but we can certainly obey and live our faith out in our actions every day.

As the day we are reminded of His birth draws near, I encourage you all to listen. Take time to stop in the midst of the busy season of Christmas and be reminded of what it's all about. I'm reminded of the movie *The Polar Express*, where those who didn't believe in Santa couldn't hear the sound of the silver bell at the end of the movie. In the same way, we don't often hear God because we aren't truly believing in His promises. It's okay to step back every now and then and take that time to hear God and His plans for us. Remember that as we prepare for the birth of the Savior and hear what He has done for us.

> How can you hear God through the busy Christmas season?

DECEMBER 12

God, Whose Giving Knows No Ending

But if anyone has the world's good and sees his brother in need, yet closes his heart against him, how does God's love abide in him?

—1 John 3:17

As Christmas draws closer, there are a lot of people shopping out there. Everyone is trying to "get stuff." Whether it be for themselves or others, greed can be a problem these days. We must be careful to not make this time of year too material based. While receiving the newest things and desires as gifts, we need to be thinking about giving as well. We have received the greatest gift of all from God sending His Son, Jesus, into this world.

I grew up in a Christian home, and I always remember watching *VeggieTales*, especially "The Toy That Saved Christmas." Even for a children's show, the message of that movie can speak to us all. Just like in the movie, the world tells us that "Christmas is when you get stuff." If we all lived by that philosophy, no one would be getting anything because there would be no giving. Without giving, no one receives. We must keep that in mind this Christmas and always. Also, we aren't giving just so we can receive. We are giving because that's what God commands us to do.

This Christmas season, I challenge all of you to look for ways you can give. Remember, this time of year is not always an easy time for everyone. I remember when I was younger, my sister had a friend in school whose mother confided in our mother that she was struggling financially and didn't know whether to get her kids new winter coats or toys for Christmas. She was faced with a choice over needs or wants. My mother used this as an opportunity to help her with this decision. She got coats for these kids and had me drop them off on their doorstep without being seen. That's the kind of giving we as Christians need to be doing this season. Give without expectation of a return.

> How can you look for ways to give to others
> this Christmas season and always?

DECEMBER 13

Tiny Tots with Their Eyes All Aglow

> All Your children shall be taught by the Lord, and
> great shall be the peace of your children.
>
> —Isaiah 54:13

There's no greater excitement for a child than waking up on Christmas morning to presents under the tree in a warm house surrounded by their families. All month long, they are getting their Christmas lists together with anticipation of getting those much-desired gifts. While these are all fun things for children and parents as well, the most real gift a child could ever receive on Christmas Day is the gift of knowing Jesus. That's the most important gift anyone could ever receive.

While this Christmas may be filled with joy and fun for some, others may not be having such an easy time. In any holiday, especially Christmas, it always seems to be a hard time of year for some. Whether it be loneliness, the loss of a loved one, or financial burden, there are real struggles out there that bring people down this time of year. This is all the more reason for those folks to know the true hope and receive the gift of Jesus for Christmas.

If you are a parent, talk to your kids about the true message of Christmas. If you are not a parent, there are other opportunities to minister to children who may not know Jesus yet. Starting kids off early in life with their foundation built on Jesus will go a long way in life. Sometimes, even if people stray, they end up back at their childhood roots eventually. If that is true for a lot of people, then that foundation in any kid's life needs to be on Jesus. Jesus is the only true peace we may have during Christmas and all year long.

How can you share the peace of Christ with children?

DECEMBER 14

We Three Kings

> When they saw the star they rejoiced exceedingly with great joy. And going into the house, they saw the child with Mary His mother, and they fell down and worshipped Him. Then, opening their treasures, they offered Him gifts, gold and frankincense and myrrh.
>
> —Matthew 2:10–11

This passage refers to the wise men. In some translations, they are also referred to as kings or magi. Either way, with all three titles, it's a beautiful thing to see men of high status and intellect be humble enough to come and worship a newborn baby. If only we could see leaders in today's world humbling themselves and bowing down to that same baby who became a man and redeemed us. Anyone of high status can easily lose humility and start giving themselves all the credit for their position, but it's truly the Lord's work that gets them where they are.

How often in our world today do we see people of high status bowing to Christ? It doesn't seem very often, but when it does happen, it happens with a bang, and everyone knows about it. Some publicity may be positive, while a lot may be negative, but the whole world then finds out where someone stands. I find it extremely amazing when one of these celebrities finds God and then the whole world knows about their relationship with Jesus. Two people's stories I encourage you to look up are of Brian Welch, the front man for the band Korn, and Kat Von D. Their stories could only have been accomplished by the work of the Holy Spirit.

On a much smaller scale, imagine how your relationship with Christ could impact others. When you have that true joy in your heart that only Christ can provide, people will notice. They will also want that kind of joy, whether they admit it or not. Our relationship with Christ can leave a mark on more people than we could imagine. Those in the dark are ultimately looking for the light. Live it out and share that light of Christ wherever you go, especially as we count down the days to celebrating Jesus's birthday.

> How can your faith in God
> leave an impact in others?

DECEMBER 15

Christmas over Time

> Remember not the former things, nor consider the things of old. Behold, I am doing a new thing; now it springs forth, do you not perceive it? I will make a way in the wilderness and rivers in the desert.
>
> —Isaiah 43:18–19

As we go through life, we store up memories. Some can be fantastic, while others can be very heartbreaking. Either way, we are to not focus too much on the past and look forward to God's new plans for our lives. Faith is always moving. It can never be just stagnant. It's going forward or backward. If we are not doing what it takes to keep our faith growing, then it's only going to slip, and we fall back to places we really don't need to be.

I can remember Christmastimes over the years that felt like dreams come true. Everything was wonderful, and being a child at the time, I got a lot of gifts I wanted. Other Christmastimes were not so memorable. There were years I was so lonely, or I was drinking heavily and just felt all around lost. These days, my wife and I have two beautiful little girls and a third child on the way. I get the joy of seeing them enjoy Christmas and get to be blessed by the Father with this family He gave me. While those good and bad memories may not be completely forgotten, the new things He's done in my life show me that His purposes for everything good and bad that happened over the years had Him leading me right where I am at.

Remember, friends, this isn't just restricted to Christmas memories. We need to focus on those new plans from the Lord every day.

There's no shame anymore as we are redeemed by Christ. Since we are heading toward Christmas specifically, I encourage you all to have the best one yet. No matter where you are in life, be joyful in the birth of the Savior and celebrate what God has done and is continuing to do every day.

> How can you be focused on the
> new things God brings?

DECEMBER 16

No Room at the Inn

> And she gave birth to her firstborn son and wrapped Him in swaddling cloths and laid Him in a manger, because there was no place for them in the inn.
>
> —Luke 2:7

We all know that Mary and Joseph had to go to the stable to spend the night because there was no room for them at the inn. Do we ever stop and think of the importance of this story? The birth of the Savior should have been in a palace surrounded by royalty, right? Lavish gifts and music playing while the entire world awaited in anticipation for His arrival? Not quite so. Jesus came into this world in such a humble way for a king. Mary and Joseph were nothing special and just ordinary people chosen by God for this mission. He could have picked anyone to be His earthly parents and any place for the Savior to be born, but He chose something more people can relate to. Jesus was born in a way that is appealing and paralleled to any common person.

While there was no room at the inn that night, we might think, *Did that innkeeper have any idea who he was turning away?* Probably not, like most people who turn away from Jesus. When people turn away and reject Jesus, they don't truly know who He is. Now anywhere in the world you go, people know the name of Jesus, but people don't know the man Jesus or His part in the Trinity, for that matter. Those of us who haven't had the mission of Christ taught to us in our upbringing to lay the foundation must then get to know Jesus. We don't just do that on our own. The Holy Spirit softens our hearts to allow us to recognize who Jesus is. That may come in many ways, even if you don't realize it just yet.

In your life today, is there room for Jesus? If not, well, it's time to consider why and what you should do from here. If there is, then how much? Are you giving Him all the room He deserves? He is to be the Lord over our lives, and we must be willing to give up everything to follow Him. It's a much narrow path, but it's a much greater eternity for following Him. Let Him have all the room in your life.

How can you tell if you are giving Jesus the room in your life?

DECEMBER 17

Joy to the World

> You have turned for me my mourning into dancing; you have loosed my sackcloth and clothed me with gladness, that my glory may sing your praise and not be silent. O Lord my God, I will give thanks to you forever!
>
> —Psalm 30:11–12

We've sung this hymn every year around this time, but do we ever stop and think about that joy? You see, joy is not something we find. It's something we are given from God. While we might think that earthly things give us joy, that ultimately comes from God. I believe that is what keeps us humble and keeps us fixed on Him. If we gained joy on our own, what good would God be in our lives? We wouldn't think we had much of a need for Him, and that's why any ounce of joy we ever receive will always come from Him.

Every Christmas season brings lots of joy to most. I think of the children receiving the gifts of their hearts' desire that they have longed for all year. While these things may seem to give us joy, no joy could ever be greater than the gift God gave us on Christmas and every day in His Son, Jesus. If you read this entire twelve-verse psalm, you will find there is a lot more that we have received from God than just material things in the forms of gifts at Christmas.

Suffering may come to us all in many forms, but the joy of our Lord comes with new mornings each day. This earthly life will pass away, and we are sealing our fate for a beautiful eternity when we put our trust in the Lord. Be humble and recognize the extent God took to give us the most joyful gift we could ever receive in His Son, Jesus. When we look at what the alternative is for eternity, we should be ever so grateful each and every day for what the Lord continues to do for us.

How can you receive true joy from God?

DECEMBER 18

Mary Definitely Knew

My soul magnifies the Lord, and my spirit rejoices in God my Savior, for He has looked on the humble estate of His servant. For behold, from now on all generations will call me blessed; for he who is mighty has done great things for me, and holy is His name.

—Luke 1:46–49

Mary, who has had her entire life flipped upside down, has a very thankful heart. Most women who are expecting a child out of wedlock are never this happy. Most anyone who is in the middle of experiencing any kind of curveball in life is never this happy. This joy and gratitude can only come from the Lord. When we live with a servant's heart in today's world, our perspective on life can change drastically. Whatever comes our way, no matter how terrible we think it may be, we have the hope in Jesus.

How many people do you know immediately say they can't do something right off the bat using some lame excuse as to why? Unfortunately, we all know someone like that. We might not like to admit it, but we may be that person at times. The Bible gives us many examples of those least likely heroes who He equipped to do something great. Look at Mary specifically. She got to be the earthly mother of the Savior. Do you think at times she was nervous or felt not worthy enough? I'm sure she did, but she had the faith to keep trusting in the Lord.

So wherever you go this Christmas season, always be an encourager. Lead people to the true hope in Jesus. When we get to know Jesus even more, those things we thought were a big deal really weren't so bad. Others may not see it that way, and that's why it's up to us to be willing to share. Be grateful for what Lord has done for you. Be willing to be led by Him to do His will. Be grateful and tell the world about His holy name!

> How can you be willing to go where God wants
> you, be thankful, and share the news?

DECEMBER 19

A Strange Way to Save the World

> And her husband Joseph, being a just man and unwilling to put her to shame, resolved to divorce her quietly. But as he considered these things, behold an angel of the Lord appeared to him in a dream, saying, "Joseph, son of David, do not fear to take Mary as your wife, for that which is conceived in her is from the Holy Spirit. She will bear a son, and you shall call His name Jesus, for He will save His people from their sins."
>
> —Matthew 1:18–21

Let's look at Joseph here. Joseph was just your run-of-the-mill blue-collar guy. He may have been a descendant of David, but it was the simple life for him. Just when he thought things were going fine, Mary, his wife-to-be, drops a big bomb on him when she tells him she is pregnant. He never knew her in a sexual way at that point and probably got really suspicious. As the verse reminds us, he was going to break things off and probably just start over with his life. The Lord had other plans for him.

When we look at how the Savior came into the world, He had two ordinary parents like the rest of us. God used them for a greater purpose. It was indeed a strange way to save the world. You see, the Hebrew people of that time were waiting on a Messiah to come in and slaughter all the Romans who kept them under their rule. Little did they know, there was a much bigger problem than the Romans—sin. Sin is something we could never absolve on our own. It had to be paid for. Jesus wasn't just coming into the world to announce forgiveness to everyone and depart. His mission was to pay for it himself, and that had to be done by going to the cross.

We all may have moments in life where we feel like Joseph. Just when things are going fine in our lives, we get a big ball dropped on us. In Joseph's case, that big problem turned out to be the greatest thing that ever happened to him. Sometimes we will go through things like that in our lives that will have us faced with a choice. Do we continue to try to do it on our own, or do we trust God's plan for us and let Him lead us? Joseph could have carried out his plans to leave Mary behind and keep his simple life. He could have stayed in his comfort zone and lived a quiet blue-collar life. Instead, he obeyed God and got the biggest blessing he could have ever asked for—the hope Christ brings to us all.

> How can you step outside your comfort zone to follow God?

DECEMBER 20

What Child Is This

For to us a child is born, to us a son is given; and the government shall be upon His shoulder, and His name shall be called Wonderful Counselor, Mighty God, Everlasting Father, Prince of Peace.

—Isaiah 9:6

Nothing could be greater in our faith than Jesus. We as Christians need to work to get to know Him better. Every day we need to strive to understand who He is, why He did what He did, and how we can obey His commands. No matter how much time you spend getting to know Jesus, there is always more to learn. Do not be discouraged by that. Be encouraged by this lifelong sanctification process of growing closer to the Son. We can't fully know everything because of our flaws and humanly limits, but that reaffirms why we need Jesus even more.

The world has such a huge misconception of who Christ is. There are unfortunately a lot of people in this world who hate Him because of misinformation. Anyone who truly knows Him knows His mission out of love for us. What could ever be a greater gift than that? The reality of all these folks that reject Jesus still doesn't change His love for them. At any point in their lives, they could turn to Him, and like all of us, all their sins would be washed away as well.

Consider the other names given to Christ in this passage. If that's what describes Jesus, then count me in! As you celebrate this Christmas season, be reminded of these names and Christ's mission while here on earth. That innocent baby, born of just an ordinary woman, came down for a much greater purpose. I encourage all of you this season as you pass by nativity scenes to be reminded of who that child really is.

How can you keep Christ's greater mission in mind?

DECEMBER 21

Silent Night

> The people who walked in darkness have seen a great light;
> those who dwelt in a land of deep darkness, on them has
> light shone. You have multiplied the nation; you have
> increased its joy; they rejoice before you as with joy at the
> harvest, as they are glad when they divide the spoil.
>
> —Isaiah 9:2–3

As Christmas is getting even closer, the reality is that some folks are struggling to hold it together. Some people are dealing with grief, others with financial burden, and the list goes on. Even for us within the church, people can still be hurting especially around this time of year. Sometimes we just need a silent night filled with reflection and prayer to remind us of the hope we have in Jesus. As the verse says, those who walked in darkness are now seeing the great light. Let us turn our eyes and our hearts toward Jesus to receive the true hope we have in Him.

Today marks the longest night of the year. The winter solstice, if you will. That means more physical darkness in an already dark season for some. At our church, we had our Longest Night Service. It's a very small and more reflective service offering prayer and communion for those who may be struggling. I had the privilege to attend it, and even though it was a very small group of people with all different stories, it was a wonderful reminder of Christ's hope for all of us. Christmas is not just about the baby Jesus. It is a reminder of the man Jesus who came to rescue us from sin and restore our hope for a greater eternity.

If you are struggling this time of year, I pray you will find your hope in Jesus. Jesus is the only true light in the darkness. Earthly things will come and go and never offer you the true hope and peace that could ever sustain you throughout life. As this long night goes on, be reminded of the light and His joy that comes with new mornings every day.

<blockquote>
How can you have hope in Jesus
through your trials of life?
</blockquote>

DECEMBER 22

Last Christmas

> Lord, now you are letting your servant depart in peace, according to your word; for my eyes have seen your salvation that you have prepared in the presence of all peoples, a light for revelation to the Gentiles, and for glory to your people Israel.
>
> —Luke 2:29–32

This passage refers to Simeon, a righteous man who God revealed that he would not go to the grave without meeting Jesus in the flesh. These older folks in our church we refer to as seasoned saints. Those ones who God still has a plan for even later in life. No matter what age you are, God's promises can still be fulfilled in your life. Simeon was one of those seasoned saints. He also obeyed God and followed His commands and was blessed with an old age where he could still be around to meet the baby Jesus.

While the holidays may be joyful for some, others are going through a time of grieving the loss of a loved one. Today, our family went to my wife's grandmother's house to say our goodbyes to her. She is on hospice at home, and for the nine hours we were there today, she just slept. This woman, who welcomed me into the family from day 1, is definitely someone who deserves that title of seasoned saint. In her lifetime, she lost two sons, two daughters-in-law, and her husband. When her second son passed away, someone at the funeral actually said to her, "God must be mad at you." Never once did that ever cross her mind, and never once did her faith falter. She got to see God's grace be more sufficient in her life than anything else. When the exact moment comes for her to go, I know she has already seen those promises of God all through her life.

So as our seasoned saints move onto glory with Christ, be reminded that they are exactly where they have been longing to be. I look around our church especially and see all those still here and the empty seats of those who have left us. There is peace in Christ and a promise of eternity for all those who truly believe in the miracle of Jesus. His life, His death, and most importantly, His resurrection that saved us all.

How can you be at peace when an older believer passes away?

DECEMBER 23

The Reason for the Season

And while they were there, the time came for her to give birth.

—Luke 2:6

Why even celebrate Christmas if it's not about Jesus? The material things can be fun like presents and decorating and all the get-togethers we attend, but if it's not about Jesus, then what else could it be about? Only ourselves. When we really get down to business with the true Christmas story, we can find that the only thing it's about is all the stuff we did wrong. Think about it. Had there been no sin in the world and no wrongdoings of any of us humans, Jesus would not have had to come down to earth. The mission began on the day of His birth.

Today was our Christmas celebration with my wife's side of the family. As my father-in-law led us in prayer, he made the statement that none of this would be possible without Jesus. It's like the old saying goes, "Keep Christ in Christmas." I think it's okay to give and receive gifts and also get together in fellowship, but those all need to be secondary things when it comes to the true meaning of Christmas.

In your Christmas travels this weekend, be reminded of the light Christ brought with His first coming into the world. This is one of the best times of the year when we can share this light with others. When we don't know how to start the conversation, we can start with Christmas and move in on it's true meaning. Many people are hurting and very vulnerable around this time of year, but they are also really looking for a hope and peace to come with it. They may not realize it, but they need Jesus too, and we as Christians have a responsibility to share the message with all who will hear.

How can you keep Christ in Christmas?

DECEMBER 24

Christ the Savior Is Born

And while they were there, the time came for her to give birth.

—Luke 2:6

Ready or not, baby on the way. At this point in our Christmas journey, the time has come for Jesus to enter this world in a very humble way. No more time for preparations. He's coming. No more last-minute decorating the stable or running out to the store. A good reminder of this day is when we can no longer make those last-minute shopping trips or it's too late to order a gift online. Like Mary back then, we need to keep our primary focus on Jesus.

How many people stress out so much over Christmas that they just want it to be over? There are a lot out there who do. When we're being caught up in the worldly aspect of Christmas, it's easy to get caught up in the gifts, wrapping them, going here and there, that by the end of it, you're just ready to be done. If our focus would be more on Jesus than just the holiday side of it, we would truly never want Christmas to end. Christmas is a reminder we need all year when it comes to its true meaning.

As you lay down to sleep tonight, children and adults alike, I pray you may be at peace. Be at peace with whatever is going on in your life, not just the Christmas hustle and bustle. Be reminded of the Savior who came into this world over two thousand years ago to give you that peace that passes understanding down in your heart today and every day. Christ the Savior is born.

How can you keep the message of Jesus higher than the holiday aspect?

TIMOTHY A. MILLS

DECEMBER 25

Yea, Lord, We Greet Thee

> For unto you is born this day in the city of David a Savior, who is Christ the Lord. And this will be a sign for you: you will find a baby wrapped in swaddling cloths and lying in a manger.
>
> —Luke 2:11–12

Yea, Lord, we greet thee, born this happy morning. Out of all the Christmas hymns I've used this month, this is my favorite lyric of them all. Jesus has arrived. It sure is a happy morning when we think of the Savior taking His first breaths of life on that day so long ago. We have built up to this moment all month, and now the time has come to reflect on what this day really means. Everything you have read so far this month is now coming together to celebrate the newborn King.

In our house, we have been counting down the days since December 1 with an Advent activity for our girls. My wife filled up toilet paper tubes with candy and stickers along with a Bible verse for each day of the month. As our two girls made their way downstairs this morning, they were in awe of all the presents under the tree. Before we got to that excitement, we had our last Advent activity to do. As I read the verses on the note, our two little ladies listened patiently to the finale of our ongoing Bible story. That's what it's all about.

Jesus came first today in many ways and how we started our day in our home. As Christmas comes to a close for another year, may you be reminded to keep Christ at the head of your life each and every day. Today may be just the day to celebrate His birthday, but we must continue to celebrate Him and what's He's done for us all year round. As we head into colder weather with the coming new year and the stillness of no holidays for a while, may you be warmed by the Spirit and take time every day to give back to our Lord. Merry Christmas!

How can you celebrate Christ all year?

DECEMBER 26

The Final Countdown

> Preserve me, O God, for in you I take refuge. I say to the Lord, "You are my Lord; I have no good apart from you."
>
> —Psalm 16:1–2

It's hard to believe we have been on this journey for almost a year, and now we are less than a week away from welcoming in the new year. A new year awaits, but that also brings more challenges. We often hear of the New Year's resolution, where we pledge to do better in certain areas of our lives. It's important to remember that without God in our lives, we can do nothing on our own. As the verse requests, we want God to preserve us as to not fall back from where we are and only move forward in our relationship with Him.

In years past, in my own life, I often had these crazy New Year's resolutions that weren't inherently bad on their own, but I wasn't seeking the strength I needed through God. I wanted to do these things on my own. Even if I didn't think that at the time, I was not relying on God for my strength and purpose in life. I wasn't seeking His guidance for what He wanted me to do. We all have dreams and plans that we would like to accomplish, but those might not necessarily be His plans for us. We often need to be reminded to take a step back and look at what God would want for us and not just what we want for ourselves.

As this year is coming to a close, I pray you can reflect on what this past year has brought. I know, for myself, there has been good and bad all the same. Like every year past and years to come, we will find good and bad. What's important is how God is affecting

TIMOTHY A. MILLS

our perspective of that. Are we humble in the good? Are we sinning more because of the bad? These are hard questions we need to ask ourselves every day. We may find that there are serious changes we must make in our lives. Keep hold to the Lord for your strength in all you do. Only through Him can we achieve the greatest life we could possibly live.

How can you assess the changes you need to make in your life?

DECEMBER 27

In the Bleak Midwinter

> Humble yourselves, therefore, under the mighty hand of God so that at the proper time He may exalt you, casting all your anxieties on Him, because He cares for you.
>
> —1 Peter 5:6–7

Being anxious about things is never good for us, but to some extent, we all get anxious. The Lord cares for us and never wants to see us suffer. Are we taking the right steps to cast our burdens on Him? Or are we trying to deal with these things on our own? It's hard going through a season of anxiety or depression. What's important to realize is that we can't fix those things on our own. Only God can do that. When we surrender our struggles to Him, He will always watch over us in His timing.

In high school, I was officially diagnosed with clinical depression. However, I've had it as long as I can remember. Even at a young age, I can remember feeling a sense of emptiness, almost like there was a piece missing that was never going to be there. My worst time of year growing up and into my adult years was always the fall. Those first three months of September, October, and November were always a struggle for me, especially when it got dark earlier. The older I get, the more that has shifted to January until the springtime. I've found, though, that it's a great opportunity to become closer to God. When there's nothing going on midwinter and it's quiet, it's a great time to hear God. I'm often reminded of His presence when I go for walks at night in the winter and the only thing you can hear is the snow coming down. The almighty healer isn't just restricted to physical healings. He can heal you mentally as well.

TIMOTHY A. MILLS

So as we head into this dormant time of winter, be mindful of God's presence. As you may have more idle time, take advantage of that to grow closer to Him. If you're like me and you struggle from anxiety and depression this time of year, it's okay. Remember, you are not defined by your mental illness. You are defined by your faith in Christ. We all have flaws, and that kind of mental illness can be one of them. Don't let it consume you by keeping your faith in the One who will pull you through it no matter what. I know when the light at the end of the depression tunnel can be dim, but the light of Christ is much greater than that.

How can you get through the depression season through Christ?

DECEMBER 28

End of an Era

> When the Spirit of Truth comes, He will guide you into all the truth, for He will not speak on His own authority, but whatever He hears He will speak, and He will declare to you the things that are to come.
>
> —John 16:13

When Jesus ascended into heaven, He didn't leave everyone empty-handed or, in a way, empty-hearted. The Holy Spirit descended to earth to live in the hearts of all who believe. As the early church moved forward, they had a Helper to guide them through. Christ Himself may have been gone from the flesh, but He is alive and well along with the Holy Spirit, who is still around today. The disciples and other believers of the time may have felt that it was the end of an era, but it was just the beginning of another. Christ paid the price for our sins. That mission was complete. The new mission was to share the message with everyone.

I was in a twelve-week men's group this year. It was a phenomenal experience for my own faith. The five of us got together every Saturday morning for the duration of the course and went through the workbook *Experiencing God*. When it was over, it was a little sad to see it go for all of us. That course, however, was only the beginning for our mission. For we have gained more knowledge of God and His message to us, and now we must apply that to our lives and share it with others. We even discussed how we could do this course again and even take a leadership role in leading a new class with different people.

Once you gain knowledge through a course, a Sunday School class, or even just reading a book like this one, tell those who are willing to hear it. Your small journey of getting to know the Lord better may come to an end when you close this book for the last time this year, but this next year could be the start of someone else's journey. Don't be afraid of an ending, because there is definitely going to be a new beginning in one way or another to follow. Ask yourself, what's next?

> How can you start a new beginning at this one's end?

DECEMBER 29

Whose Side Are You On?

If the world hates you, know that it has hated me before it hated you. If you were of the world, the world would love you as its own; but because you are not of the world, but I chose you out of the world, therefore the world hates you.

—John 15:18–19

When we want to share the message, that's a pretty hard sell putting it like that. The truth is, they hated Christ then, they hate Him now, and they hate us for following Him. What a life, huh? There's a whole lot more to it than that. When it comes to eternity, how short will our lifetime look in the bigger scheme of things? We're like a mist that fades away when it comes to this life. The world makes things look appealing that really shouldn't be. The rebellion against God, by the world, has gone on since the dawn of time. Knowing these scriptures, like this one, which still goes on today, what would you say is the best side to be on?

Out of all the scriptures, I believe this is one of the most relevant ones today. We see examples of this every day. There is deep hatred that gets revealed in some people when the name of Jesus is mentioned. People call it offensive. They say we are pushing our "religion" on them and that we are judgmental. These feelings are all derived from one's own sin. When a person is a slave to sin, they don't want to hear about the truth of Christ that could set them free. The accusations and poor assumptions they make about Christ are the furthest things from the truth. Little do they know, they could be freer than they have ever been if they would surrender and get on the right side of life.

When it comes down to it, there's two choices. Surrender to Christ and spend an eternity in heaven or deny Christ and spend an eternity in hell. This is not a threat or a scare tactic to get people to believe. This is the only reality—the ultimatum, if you will. We have that choice to make. God doesn't force us to believe, but He also does not send us to hell. We choose to go there. When I look at both options, I'll suffer through this life and live a life of restraint from the sinful pleasures this world has to offer and follow my Lord all the way to glory.

How can you figure out which side you are on?

DECEMBER 30

Edge of Glory

A voice says, "Cry!" And I said, "What shall I cry?" All flesh is grass, and all its beauty is like the flower of the field. The grass withers, the flower fades when the breath of the Lord blows on it; surely the people are grass. The grass withers, the flower fades, but the Word of our God will stand forever.

—Isaiah 40:6–8

One day, we will be on that edge between life and death. It's a reality that we must all come to terms with, whether we like it or not. When we know Christ, there is no fear in death. When a loved one passes on who knew Christ, there is comfort in the sadness knowing that they truly are in a better place. The world tells us to cry, as the verse says, and to fear death and do everything we can to prolong it. If we know Jesus, then whenever it may come to us, our soul is secure by the debt Christ paid with His precious blood for all of us.

Today was our grandmother's funeral on my wife's side. What a lady she was, a true servant of Christ and woman of faith. In her eighty-seventh year of life, she was ready to go home to the Lord. In her Bible, we found a little message that she wrote: "Death is simply putting out the candle because morning has come." How true is that? No matter what kind of heartache we may have in the darkness, the joy of the Lord comes to us in the morning. Even about death as she wrote, the new morning has come.

Glory could be many years away or just a breath away. Now is the time to take action in your own life. As these bodies of ours get older every day, we are one step closer to that day we will meet our

Maker. When we have Christ in our hearts, death can be greeted as an old friend and not an enemy just out to end our lives. Whenever that time comes for you, I pray it is well with your soul, and you can greet death with a smile knowing you will spend an eternity in paradise with Jesus.

How can you have a well ready soul when your day of death arrives?

DECEMBER 31

The Road Goes on Forever

The Spirit and the Bride say, "Come." And let the one who hears say, "Come." And let the one who is thirsty come; let the one who desires take the water of life without price.

—Revelation 21:17

If you think back to our first day of this year, I used 2 Corinthians 5:17 ("Therefore, if anyone is in Christ, he is a new creation. The old has passed away; behold, the new has come"). I hope as this year comes to a close, you can honestly say that you are a new creation in Christ. While you still may be struggling in certain areas of your life, if you have Jesus, then you are not defined by those struggles. He gives us our hope and our peace, no matter what we may be going through. As our last verse tells us, we as believers will one day drink that water of life and live forever because we have accepted Christ as our Savior and Lord. Not just every year but every day we get closer to that time.

A lot can happen in a year's time. In our family, we moved, said goodbye to some older folks passing on to glory, got to meet a new little relative born in late November, and we are patiently awaiting the arrival of our third child in the spring of this coming year. All of that aside, the primary focus has been our whole family fixing our eyes on Jesus and running that race to grow closer to Him every day. It's not always easy, but when you tear off that rearview mirror and see Jesus through your windshield, you know you are headed in the right direction. In our family, that's what we were missing for a few years. We were doing things our own way, and it clearly wasn't working. When Jesus was put first, things began to change drastically for us in the right direction.

Now some of you might be reading this and you are still right where you are at the beginning of the year. Don't be afraid. God is still working in your life. He is still speaking to you, and He still has a plan for your life. Maybe you start this book over and do it another year. Maybe you need to get more involved in a church to get on the right track. Whatever situation you may be in as you read this final entry tonight, God is right there with you. He wants you to get to know Him better. May God be with you today, every day, and forever as you journey down this road that will never end once we cross into eternity with Him. Grace and peace to you all each and every day. God bless you friends.

How can you evaluate your past year?

EPILOGUE

Dear Reader,

It is a privilege to be writing to you again. I hope this year has been the year you have been waiting for. The year that you have made that step up in your faith in God and have allowed Him to put your stumbling blocks behind you. If this year was still a struggle, then I encourage you to not only read this book for another year but also to consider spiritual help from a trusted church leader. Most of all, continue to pray wherever you are in life. You never know what God may be up to in your life or where He may be leading you. May you be comforted in knowing Him more and grow closer to Him. Grace and peace to you all.

ABOUT THE AUTHOR

Timothy A. Mills currently lives in Pittsburgh, Pennsylvania, with his wife of seven years and three children, ages five, three, and one born this year. Tim is a teamster in his local union working for a popular water company. In his free time, Tim enjoys writing, fishing, playing tennis, building model railroads, learning better ways to barbeque, and spending time with his wife and kids. He also serves as a deacon at his church, where he has attended since childhood. Nothing is more important than Tim's faith in God and relationship with Jesus Christ.